LEAVE ONLY FOOTPRINTS

LEAVE ONLY FOOTPRINTS

My Acadia-to-Zion Journey
Through Every National Park

CONOR KNIGHTON

CROWN
NEW YORK

This book is an account of the author's experience visiting the national parks.
Some events appear out of sequence, and some names and identifying
details of individuals mentioned have been changed.

Copyright © 2020 by Conor Knighton
Map copyright © by David Lindroth Inc.

Published in the United States by Crown, an imprint of Random House,
a division of Penguin Random House LLC, New York.

CROWN and the Crown colophon are registered trademarks
of Penguin Random House LLC.

LIBRARY OF CONGRESS CATALOGING-IN-PUBLICATION DATA
Names: Knighton, Conor, author.
Title: Leave only footprints / Conor Knighton.
Description: First edition. | New York: Crown, [2020] | Includes bibliographical references.
Identifiers: LCCN 2019038706 (print) | LCCN 2019038707 (ebook) |
ISBN 9781984823540 (hardcover) | ISBN 9781984823564 (ebook)
Subjects: LCSH: Knighton, Conor—Travel—United States. | National parks and reserves—
United States. | United States—Description and travel.
Classification: LCC E160 .K65 2020 (print) | LCC E160 (ebook) |
DDC 917.304/932092—dc23
LC record available at https://lccn.loc.gov/2019038706
LC ebook record available at https://lccn.loc.gov/2019038707

Printed in the United States of America on acid-free paper

randomhousebooks.com

9 8

Book design by Jo Anne Metsch

For my parents, who gave me the compass
I've always used to find my path

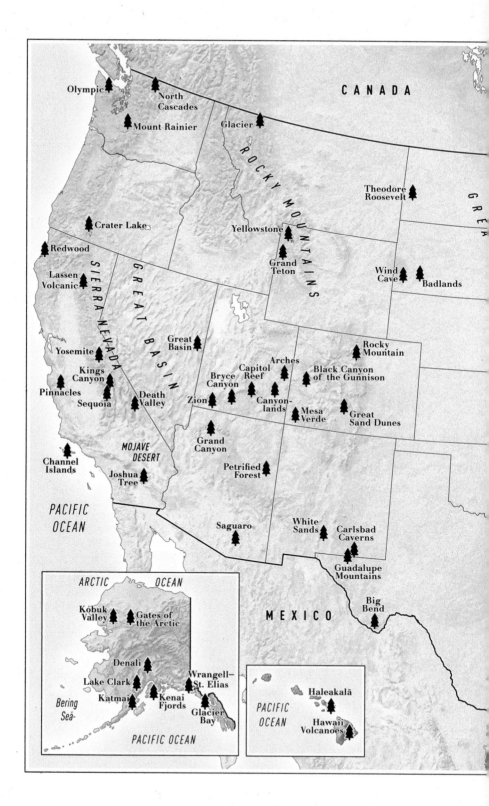

Olympic

North
Cascades

Mount Rainier

Glacier

CANADA

GREA

Theodore
Roosevelt

Crater Lake

Yellowstone

Redwood

Grand
Teton

Wind
Cave

Badlands

Lassen
Volcanic

GREA

Great
Basin

Rocky
Mountain

Yosemite

Arches

Kings
Canyon

Capitol
Reef

Black Canyon
of the Gunnison

Pinnacles

Bryce
Canyon

Sequoia

Death
Valley

Zion

Canyon-
lands

Mesa
Verde

Great
Sand Dunes

Channel
Islands

MOJAVE
DESERT

Grand
Canyon

Joshua
Tree

Petrified
Forest

PACIFIC
OCEAN

Saguaro

White
Sands

Carlsbad
Caverns

Guadalupe
Mountains

Big
Bend

MEXICO

ARCTIC   OCEAN

Kobuk
Valley

Gates of
the Arctic

Denali

Lake Clark

Wrangell–
St. Elias

Haleakalā

Katmai

Kenai
Fjords

PACIFIC
OCEAN

Bering
Sea

Glacier
Bay

Hawaii
Volcanoes

PACIFIC OCEAN

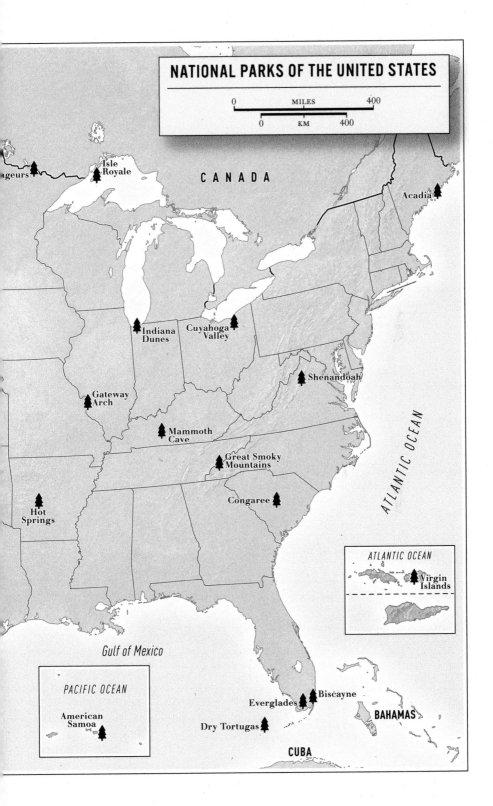

NATIONAL PARKS OF THE UNITED STATES

MILES
0   400

0   KM   400

CANADA

ageurs

Isle
Royale

Acadia

Indiana
Dunes

Cuyahoga
Valley

Shenandoah

Gateway
Arch

Mammoth
Cave

Great Smoky
Mountains

Congaree

Hot
Springs

ATLANTIC OCEAN

ATLANTIC OCEAN

Virgin
Islands

Gulf of Mexico

PACIFIC OCEAN

American
Samoa

Everglades

Biscayne

Dry Tortugas

BAHAMAS

CUBA

CONTENTS

LEAVE ONLY FOOTPRINTS

PROLOGUE

(Badlands)

It is a sunny Saturday in May, and I've been on the road for five hours. Or five months, depending on how you're counting. Ever since I left Los Angeles back in January, the days and weeks have started to blur together, like the South Dakota scenery now zipping past my window. I am deep in America's Great Plains—a vast ocean of green and brown, broken up only by the occasional bright billboard.

The Great Plains sounds like a name cooked up by a pioneer ad agency. A covered wagon full of Don Drapers, determined to market an expanse of seemingly unremarkable grassland. "The Spectacular Ordinary? The Magnificent Dullness? No wait, I've got it! We'll call it . . . *The Great Plains.*"

"Great Faces, Great Places" is the official state slogan printed on the license plate in front of me. The plate features a picture of Mount Rushmore—a man-made monument of men, designed to bring tourists to this part of the state. The plan worked. Today more than two million people a year come to see four dead presidents carved into granite.

Only one of those Great Faces had any claim to this place, though, a man who saw a certain kind of beauty in the desolate, wide-open spaces. Teddy Roosevelt first came to this region in 1883, back when it was all still just the Dakota Territory, six years before it was carved up into North and South.

Growing up in West Virginia, I always wished there was an *East* Virginia. Without one, I thought we sounded like a spin-off state. Tell someone you're from West Virginia, and they are bound to mention that they have friends in Roanoke, or that they've once been to Colonial Williamsburg. "No, no, West Virginia, not *western* Virginia," I'd try to explain. It wouldn't matter. We were forever the Diet Coke to Virginia's Coke, seen as a sequel instead of an equal.

West Virginia is rural, but it is full of mountains and valleys and streams, always disguising what treasure might be around the next bend. The prairie is different—out here, you can see what's coming from miles away.

But when the tears come, they surprise me. I'm instantly embarrassed, even though there is no one else in the car. *I thought I was done with this part.* My GPS is guiding me toward the gray, mysterious hoodoos of Badlands National Park, but they have not yet come into view, and so, with nothing to distract me, I've become lost in my own head. Alone with my loneliness.

Roosevelt once wrote that "nowhere, not even at sea, does a man feel more lonely than when riding over the far-reaching, seemingly never-ending plains." Here I am, 131 years later: a grown man, sobbing in a Subaru. As much as I'd like to just blame it on the plains, I know this breakdown is not the scenery's fault. I should have anticipated this. I should have scheduled something fun. Instead, I have foolishly routed myself through the middle of the loneliest damn place in the country on what was supposed to be my *wedding day.*

Great.

.　　.　　.

We had just ordered the "save the date" cards when she suddenly called everything off. Still plenty of time to cancel all of the arrangements, but too late to un-save the date in my memory. At the time, I actually tried to blame those announcements. I argued that there was probably just something about seeing our two names together in cursive, finally attached to a date, that was causing a temporary panic attack. It was normal, I said. It would pass, I promised. But it didn't.

She had returned from a work trip a few days earlier, and before I knew it she was packing her bags to leave again. I didn't know where to this time; she just said that she needed some space. She didn't want to talk about things, didn't want to try to see a counselor. It all seemed so extreme, so out of nowhere. Was this because I'd made fun of the idea of hiring trumpeters? Hire the trumpeters! I was so sorry. I couldn't understand.

My fiancée was the only daughter of a large, wealthy family, and we were gearing up for a fairy-tale destination wedding at a European castle. Anyone trying to crash would have to contend with a *moat.*

Her parents were happily footing the bill, but the opulence made me anxious. I was worried none of what was planned felt like "us." Was this really who we wanted to be? The lord and lady of Downton Abbey? The suggested reception menu featured line items like "frites et mayonnaise: 615 euros." For generations, Knighton blood has always run ketchup red.

Mostly, I felt guilty about how much everything was costing because I knew I would have happily married her *anywhere,* just as long as we got to be together. My brother was going to be my best man, but she was my best friend. She was funny and smart and kind, and whether we were hiking up into the San Gabriel Mountains or strolling around the neighborhood, it always felt like we were the only two people in the world.

But suddenly I was on the receiving end of a series of businesslike emails, arranging the final move-out day and time. I wrote back to each request with a simple "as you wish," the phrase farm boy Westley said to the beautiful Buttercup in *The Princess Bride*—a last, coded "I love you." Which, *yeesh*, looking back on it . . . sounds pretty pitiful.

When the day finally came, I couldn't bear to be in our apartment. I found the earliest movie showing nearby—a screening of *Ant-Man* at 10 A.M. in IMAX—and sat in the theater until everyone else had left, long after the credits, long after the obligatory Marvel after-the-credits scene. I couldn't make myself get up—I was still in shock. By the time I got back home, half of my furniture was gone, and with it what felt like all of my future.

Working in television, my professional future has always been difficult to visualize. It's an unpredictability I signed up for, but a nerve-racking one. I've gotten some great gigs, and I've also been unemployed for months on end. People either thrive on those ups and downs or they quit because they can't take them, and I long ago made my peace with the fact that I probably wouldn't be able to plan too far ahead in life.

But for a brief moment, I had known exactly what my future held. Or the most important part of it, I thought. I knew who I would be sitting on the porch with decades from now, holding hands, celebrating our fortieth anniversary by eating fries with mayonnaise, laughing about how I ended up developing a taste for them over the years.

But there will be no anniversary, because today, instead of walking down an aisle, I will be hiking down a trail.

An anniversary is actually what inspired this journey—the one hundredth anniversary of the National Park Service. In late 2015, nursing my wounds, I had seen a news article about the upcoming centennial. The Park Service, established via the Organic Act of 1916, was gearing up for a yearlong celebration.

It was also around this same time I received another bit of news: My ex-fiancée was a fiancée again. Four months after she had moved out, she had gotten engaged to a coworker. I went from feeling very sad to feeling very stupid.

I desperately tried to busy myself with work, but work wasn't very busy. It had been a slow year, and I was getting nervous about my dwindling bank balance. I wrote an email to the producers at *CBS Sunday Morning*, suggesting I could do a segment on the centennial for them. For the last four years, I'd been doing occasional freelance reports for the show, the rare program on which a story about the national parks wouldn't feel at all out of place. Or even a few stories. Or . . .

My mind started racing. Wait . . . What if . . . What if I somehow did a *year's* worth of stories? There had to be enough material, right? I'd only been to a handful of parks, but they seemed full of history and culture and art and . . .

And these parks were *everywhere*. Alaska, American Samoa. Seventy miles off the coast of Florida. The National Park Service, I learned, manages well over four hundred "units," ranging from national seashores to national battlefields to national monuments to national preserves and national recreation areas. It's a bit of a branding disaster—there are more types of parks than there are models of the Fitbit—but the ones I'd heard the most about, like Yellowstone, Yosemite, and Everglades, *those* were listed simply as "national parks."

National parks can only be created by an act of Congress, and while the Park Service claims it doesn't play favorites, the national parks are typically the marquee kinds of locations, spots you might plan an entire vacation around. You could spend two weeks exploring the sandstone formations at Arches National Park in Utah and barely scratch the surface. But Thaddeus Kosciuszko National *Memorial* in Philadelphia? It's a couple of rooms in a house—less than nine hundred square feet. If you're super into Polish American history, I'm sure it's heaven, but otherwise probably not a must-visit.

So I decided to focus on the "official" national parks. I knew I'd be excluding some amazing places, but it seemed like a more manageable list. There were only fifty-nine, I'd learned. Theoretically, you could hit them all in a year.

You could hit them all in a year. I actually said that out loud. Shouted it, almost. In the aftermath of my breakup, I'd gotten into the habit of giving myself occasional muttered pep talks ("Get it together, Conor," "It'll be okay, Conor," "Stop watching so much Netflix and go the gym, Conor"), but this was a full-volume "aha" moment. Fifty-nine parks, fifty-two weeks. I could do that. Maybe I *should* do that.

My friends had been encouraging me to get back out there again. What if I really got *out* there? Out of this apartment—filled with memories—that I couldn't really afford on my own, out of Los Angeles, out into some of the most beautiful places in the world. It sure seemed like it could do a world of good.

I quickly rewrote the email to my bosses, outlining all the types of tales I might tell. No need to send a field producer—I'll produce them all myself! I'll stay in budget motels! I'll help you find a sponsor! I was actively negotiating against myself before anyone had even expressed interest, but I didn't care. I knew I was going to find a way to do this no matter what.

While the brass debated in New York, I gave thirty days' notice to my landlord and started packing up my stuff and selling what I could. Each night, I would invite a new batch of potential murderers from Craigslist to come check out the TV, the table, the Ikea Hopen dresser my fiancée and I had built together. I wanted it all gone.

Eventually, *Sunday Morning* suggested it might actually be interested in doing some pieces on the parks. Not *every* park—not by a long shot—but the money I'd make on my work stories would help me cover the cost of going to the rest on my own. Taking a year off from the sky-high rents of California would help as well. My "plan" was to live on the road for a year, camping and crashing with friends along the way.

Some of my high school pals had been homeowners since their early twenties. Here I was, headed toward my mid-thirties, still renting, and I was about to stop doing even that. It definitely sounded a little insane. I'd occasionally pause while packing, wondering what on earth I was doing. Was this all a giant mistake? The national parks are frequently touted as "America's Best Idea." I worried that this could easily end up being my *worst*.

I also worried that I was just running away from something. It certainly looked like I was. But when I'd flip through the books I'd checked out from the library, marveling at photos of one natural wonder after another, the parks felt more like something I wanted to run *toward*. I felt drawn to these places: peaks and streams and fields and valleys that had existed for millions of years but had waited until this specific year to turn their siren song on me. Or, in the words of naturalist John Muir, whom I'd started reading voraciously: "The mountains are calling and I must go."

So I went. Which is how I found myself in hiking pants in South Dakota on what was supposed to be my wedding day, barreling toward my twenty-fifth national park of the year.

Teddy Roosevelt got engaged on Valentine's Day. Or at least that was the day when his fiancée, Alice Hathaway Lee, publicly announced that she had *accepted* his proposal. Roosevelt had popped the question on some random day back in June, and he had been working for months to win Alice's favor. Based on his diaries and love letters from that period, it appears as if the "Rough Rider" was really a big ol' softy.

Roosevelt wrote of Alice in 1880:

She is so marvelously sweet, and pure and lovable and pretty that I seem to love her more and more every time I see her, though I love her so much now that I really <u>can</u> <u>not</u> love her more. I do not think ever a man loved a woman more than I love her; for a year and a quarter now I have <u>never</u> (even when hunting) gone to sleep or waked up without thinking of her; and I doubt if an hour has passed that I have not thought of her.

Even when hunting! Coming from Roosevelt, that's quite an endorsement. In other entries, he writes of "a real case of love at first sight." He writes the name "Alice" over and over again, like a lovesick schoolboy.

Three and a half years after they were wed, Roosevelt received a telegram while on the floor of the New York State Assembly. Alice had just given birth to their first daughter. It was fantastic news, and Roosevelt began making plans to head back from Albany to New York City to see his family.

But a second telegram arrived soon after. His young wife had fallen mysteriously ill. Her pregnancy had been hiding what historians now assume was kidney failure. Roosevelt rushed home at once.

He arrived to a house his brother, Elliott, described as "cursed." Elliott was home caring for their mother, who had been ill for some time, but who had just taken a drastic turn for the worse. Roosevelt shuffled back and forth between the two beds, checking in on the two women he loved most in the world as they both simultaneously slipped away from him. His mother died in the early-morning hours of February 14, 1884. His wife died that same afternoon.

That Valentine's Day, Roosevelt's entry was just a giant "X" across the middle of the page. An X, and one sentence, eight words long:

"The light has gone out of my life."

After her funeral, he never wrote in his diary about Alice again.

A few months after burying his wife and mother, Roosevelt set out for the Dakota Territory. On a prior hunting trip, the lifelong New Yorker had made an impulsive investment in a cattle ranch there, but now he wanted to actually live the life of a rancher, to work the land himself. Desperately in need of a distraction, Roosevelt went looking for a change in scenery.

It ended up changing his life. The Teddy Roosevelt we all remember—the conservationist, the environmentalist—that guy was forged out on the plains. The city boy quickly took to the "perfect freedom" of a life in the wild, writing that "there are few sensations I prefer to that of galloping over these rolling limitless prairies, with rifle in hand, or winding my way among the barren, fantastic and grimly picturesque deserts of the so-called Bad Lands."

Roosevelt had immersed himself in nature to heal a broken heart, to recover from his life's greatest setback. As president, he went on to protect more than 230 million acres of land, spread out all across the country. He saw the value in preserving wilderness so that it might affect others in the way it had affected him. On a return visit to North Dakota, Roosevelt told the crowd, "here the romance of my life began."

When I pull into the Pinnacles Overlook at Badlands National Park, I realize I've been had. I've fallen for the greatest trick of the Great Plains—its ability to lull you into *thinking* you know what might happen next. Absolutely nothing in the miles and miles of grassland I just traversed came close to preparing me for the ragged, sharp buttes that now stretch out in front of me. Nature craftily served up a palate cleanser to make my first taste of this park even more startling.

The Badlands is a landscape as vast as the prairie, but much more difficult to process. Each formation demands its own form of attention, dramatically different from whatever bizarrely shaped hill might be sitting right next to it. While the predominant hue is a washed-out gray, little racing stripes of red and white and orange and tan cut through the hills. The conical deposits of rock were once described by Roosevelt as being "so fantastically broken in form and so bizarre in color as to seem hardly properly to belong to this earth."

Not to *this* earth, but to Middle-earth, perhaps. If Mordor and the Shire had a baby, it might look something like the Badlands. In between the imposing, gray spiky mounds, I see improbable patches of lush, bright-green grass—reminders of kinder, gentler land. Even after five months of hopping from one stunning vista to the next, I'm still shocked by the scenery—how can this exist in the same country as the Everglades?

I've only just barely passed the entrance station—there's still more than 240,000 acres of park waiting for me out there. I pull out my map to figure out where to head next. A scenic two-lane highway travels the length of Badlands, but I'm surprised to see how few designated hiking trails there are. Adding them up, there appears to be only twenty miles or so *total* in the park. That can't be right. I remember similarly sized Rocky Mountain National Park has more than 350 miles of trail.

"Ah . . . see, that's the beauty of this place," a ranger tells me at the visitor center when I stop in to ask for some advice. "Here, you get to make your *own* trails."

"So . . . just pick a direction that looks good and start walking?"

"That's right," he says. "And, you know, take lots of water and watch out for rattlesnakes. All that good stuff. But if you've already done a lot of the shorter walks, and you're itching for more of an adventure, then that's what I'd recommend. Have fun!"

I thank the ranger, then drive back down the road toward a promising-looking pullout. I park my car, put on my backpack, and start walking out into the twisted, rippled stone hills.

The beauty of Badlands comes courtesy of a twofold process. First the land was built up. Prehistoric seas and rivers deposited silt and sand and clay. Over tens of millions of years, the sediments stacked higher and higher.

Then the land was torn down. In geological terms, it was a fairly sudden shift. Starting just five hundred thousand or so years ago, erosion began to rip the soil apart. Not all of it at once—just certain sections—carving the fantastic shapes we see today. Without that destruction, the Badlands would just be flat. Because of it, they're stunning. It made them what they are.

I remind myself of that as I wander farther into the park. I know there's a lesson there, even if I'm not quite ready to receive it. For now it seems enough to focus on my surroundings, to dial into where I am instead of thinking about where I might have been. Once, today would have been choreographed down to the minute. Now it's completely uncharted territory—it's up to me to choose my own path forward.

After an hour, I stop to reapply my sunscreen. Badlands doesn't offer much in the way of shade, and the South Dakota sun has been beating down hard on my face. With my backpack open, I see my wallet down at the bottom of the bag. I can't resist pulling it out so I can look again at the scrap of paper I've slipped inside it.

While my fiancée and I never did get around to planning our rehearsal dinner menu, I'm pretty sure it wouldn't have involved P. F. Chang's Spicy Chicken and Lettuce Wraps. That's what was spread out across my desk at the Hampton Inn last night when I'd suddenly realized what weekend it was.

When I cracked open my fortune cookie, I was feeling so low that I was ready to imbue whatever might have been inside its tiny crunchy shell with outsized meaning. But what I saw was *so* on the nose, all I could do was burst out laughing. Damn you, Chang. How'd you know?

"As a chapter ends, you will find yourself on a road to discovery."

1

SUNRISE

(Acadia)

Yellowstone was the world's first national park. The first sentence on the park's website makes sure you are aware of that bit of trivia. To be first is to be remembered.

Every journalist wants to be the first to publish a story. Every company wants to be the first to market with their product. Every kid in my first-grade class in West Virginia knew local hero Chuck Yeager was the first pilot to break the sound barrier. Who was the second? They didn't teach that in school.

But first does not always mean best (although in Yellowstone's case, it just might). Still, a first kiss, a first love, a first date—these are the moments that we memorialize, even if they end up not being all that great. First equals special.

That may be why there are so many spots that claim to offer the first view of the sunrise in the United States. The sunrise marks the first light of a new day, and town tourism bureaus across the country claim that they alone are where you can see that light before anyone else. Of course, with the sunrise, being first is just a matter of seconds.

Guam bills itself as "Where America's Day Begins." Out in the middle of the Pacific, closer to Japan than to Hawaii, Guam is fourteen hours ahead of the East Coast, since it lies just west of the International Date Line. But to count Guam as the first sunrise almost seems like cheating, especially since, fifteen hundred miles farther east, there's Wake Island, an air force base where the sign on the runway once read WHERE AMERICA'S DAY *REALLY* BEGINS. Dang, Wake Island. Way to throw a little sunrise shade.

After passing over Asia and Europe, the sun eventually shines on Cadillac Mountain at Acadia National Park in Maine. From mid-September through mid-March, this is where the first rays of sun are said to hit the *contiguous* United States. Even that honor is true only during the winter months, since the tilt of the earth affects the sun's position on the horizon. In the summer, Mars Hill, Maine, sees the first light. (And since both spots are pretty remote, Eastport, Maine, advertises itself as the first *city* to see the sun rise.) Perhaps there's a reason an asterisk looks just like a sun.

Anyway, as far as I can tell, on January 1, the highest peak of Acadia National Park is the first place in the contiguous United States to see the sun rise. The first sunrise on the first day of the year. And so that's where I decided to kick off my quest to see every national park in the country. I knew it was going to be a busy year—I wanted to get a head start.

In the summer, tour buses can drive to the top of Cadillac Mountain in a matter of minutes. But in the winter, the road shuts down. *Everything* shuts down. In the nearby town of Bar Harbor, even big chain hotels put up SEE YOU NEXT SPRING signs. Only a few restaurants stay open, feeding the locals who have decided to brave the winter.

Those who stay have a national park to themselves. Acadia gets 80 percent of its visitors in just four months of the year, but it's gorgeous in the winter—crystal blue lakes become bright-white ice-fishing destinations, hillsides become ski runs, and the road that leads to the top of Cadillac Mountain, covered in snow, becomes a dangerous, slippery hike.

. . .

My headlamp shone on the first part of the road, illuminating the snow in the distance and my breath in front of my face. I could see sets of fresh bootprints up ahead, both reassuring and unsettling. There were other people out here in the dark, other people who had gotten up even earlier than I had to climb this mountain. Wherever they were, I couldn't hear them—the only sound came from my brand-new boots, crunching down into the snow.

On my drive to the park, I had passed people who were still coming home from their drunken celebrations. The night before was the first time since I was seven that I didn't count down to the New Year. It was the first time—ever—that I spent New Year's Eve by myself. The desk clerk at the Hampton Inn back in Ellsworth thought I was joking when I asked for a 3 A.M. wake-up call. I was in bed by ten. I slept with the lights on so that, when the early-morning call came, I'd be less tempted to go back to sleep.

I was wide awake now—the freezing air made sure of that. I took a swig from my thermos, full of mid-tier chain-hotel lobby coffee. I could feel it more than I could taste it, the hot liquid sliding down my throat and warming my entire body. It felt amazing. I wanted to keep drinking, but I was nervous: I know what happens if I drink too much coffee. I didn't fly all the way to Maine to begin the year by taking a shit in the snow.

Acadia is on Mount Desert Island—pronounced by the locals more like *de-ZERT*. Which, sadly, makes it sound way more delicious than it really is. In the 1600s, French explorer Samuel de Champlain named the area l'Isle des Monts-déserts, because the mountain summits were so bare and rocky. "Deserted."

Of course, Native Americans were here thousands of years before Champlain. This will be a common theme at almost every park I visit. A "discovery" of land that was already inhabited by someone else, a history written by white settlers. The Wabanaki, "the people of the Dawnland," greeted the dawn on this island long before the first wave of French Jesuits arrived.

Maine seems so quintessentially New England that it's hard to remember it was once New France. It might have stayed that way too had an English ship not attacked the Jesuits just as they were starting to do some baptizing. For the next 150 years, Mount Desert Island was plunged into a series of small skirmishes, but neither side really cared that much. Nobody saw much value in Acadia.

Nobody except for Antoine Laumet. Laumet immigrated to New France in 1683 and decided to reinvent himself, a process that began with making up a hilarious fake name and title: "Antoine Laumet de la Mothe, sieur de Cadillac." He allegedly made up all sorts of stories about his nobility and military conquests and eventually talked his way into a land grant of one hundred thousand acres—all of Mount Desert Island.

While the "sieur de Cadillac" didn't last long in Maine—the farming life wasn't for him—the chilly mountain I was walking up still bears his invented name. As does an eighty-thousand-dollar Escalade, by the way. It's the same damn Cadillac. This Talented Monsieur Ripley went on to found Detroit.

Plodding uphill in the snow was making me sweat, and I stripped off another layer. Most of what I was wearing was purchased two days earlier at Gander Mountain Sports in West Virginia, or "Redneck REI," as my pal from high school lovingly described it. As a matter of policy, REI doesn't sell guns, bows, or even fishing rods, but the entire back half of Gander Mountain is an arsenal. REI goes after hippie hikers; Gander Mountain is more for hardcore hunters. But there's overlap in that Venn diagram—both groups need synthetic long underwear to stay warm. I had picked up a pair before I left my family's weeklong Christmas celebration to head north by myself.

There was no camera crew coming today. Despite my best efforts, I still hadn't totally convinced the bosses at *CBS Sunday Morning* that a series of stories on the national parks would be worth airing. There was some understandable concern back in New York that the whole thing "might just end up being a lot of trees." I'm sure they were also worried that I might be the wrong guy for the job. I was just an occasional freelancer, a pinch hitter infrequently called upon when other, more established correspondents weren't available.

But they had said they were intrigued, and that was all the encouragement I needed to book my ticket to Maine. I brought along a cheap video camera so I could capture some of my own footage. *No trees*, I reminded myself. *Just people.* A few shots of people who—like me—felt compelled to begin their year with an uphill climb in the dark.

Approaching the top, the pavement started to become visible again. I'd forgotten I'd been walking up a road this whole time, but, sure enough, there was a double yellow line, peeking out for the first time underneath the blanket of snow. It didn't make sense at first; I was much higher up than when I'd started. Shouldn't there be way *more* snow up here? But then I figured out what was happening. I *felt* what was happening.

Powerful gusts of wind whipped at the mountaintop, blowing the snow away and exposing patches of slick ice underneath. The black ice was almost impossible to see in the dark, leading to several stumbles but no outright falls. The traction on my new boots had passed its first test.

When I finally reached the summit, there was no triumphant view to take in. Not yet, anyway—I'd arrived too early. As I jumped up and down to stay warm, I could hear muffled voices coming from somewhere nearby, and I scanned for the source. Eventually, my headlamp reflected off a bright-green parka, and I walked toward a father and son huddling under some rocks to shield themselves from the wind. I asked if I could film them. I knew this was a moment I would want to include—proof that other people started their year this way. That I wasn't the only crazy one.

Maybe not crazy, but definitely stupid. Taking off my gloves to fiddle with my camera settings turned out to be a terrible idea. Within moments, my fingers had gone almost completely numb. I clumsily fumbled through my backpack to find the hand warmers I had brought, those weird white baggies that magically heat up when exposed to air. One day, I'm sure there will be a study that proves they cause knuckle cancer, but there was no time to think about that—my hands were turning blue.

The sky was turning orange—the sun was about to make its debut. In the time it had taken to save my fingers from amputation, a surprising number of people had shown up. They must have been close behind me—there were now easily fifty hikers standing in clusters around the summit. Two weeks later, after finally receiving the green light from CBS, I would come back to this very same spot with a camera crew and an escort from the Park Service. On that morning, we would be the only shivering idiots up here. But there's apparently something about the promise of a new year that makes people do things they would never do otherwise. Something that had convinced a squad of optimistic, bundled-up strangers to stand together in silence on a mountaintop.

I thought somebody might attempt a countdown, but you never quite know when the sun is going to crest over the horizon. As we waited together, the seemingly drab boulders around us started to reveal themselves as canvases for colonies of bright-green and yellow lichens. Frenchman Bay, spread out below, began to glisten. And then, with very little fanfare, the sun peeked through the low clouds. I shouted back at it.

"Happy New Year!"

From the moment I'd woken up, I'd focused only on getting to the top of this mountain so that I could witness the first few seconds of the year. But now that I had, the enormity of what I'd planned for the *rest* of the year started to sink in.

Or, more accurately, the enormity of what I *hadn't* planned. I didn't know where I would be sleeping the next week. I'd barely looked at a highway map, and I hadn't thought about how to get to the parks that weren't accessible by car. I hadn't so much as spoken to a single park ranger. I definitely wasn't sure how much any of this would cost, or if I could afford it.

The year before, my New Year's resolution was to go to the gym each morning, and that lasted for *thirteen days*. For some reason, this year I was convinced I might somehow make it to every national park in the country.

I should have been freaking out. Later, I definitely would be. Planning such a massive undertaking on the fly meant that plenty of things would go wrong. I would get lost, I would get stressed, I would get sick. But basking in the first light of the first day of the year, I was perfectly calm. I had a good feeling about this, and I was filled with gratitude for an adventure that hadn't even started yet.

As I walked back down the mountain, eating a pepperoni roll I'd brought with me from West Virginia, I passed a few hikers still on their way to the top, late sleepers who'd missed the sunrise. One couple moved especially slowly—they had clearly underestimated how steep the mountain was. But everyone was still in good spirits. It was a beautiful day. We waved to one another. "Happy New Year!"

By 9 A.M., I had already hiked ten miles. I warmed up inside my rental car and ate my second pepperoni roll while trying to figure out how Instagram worked. After years of protest, I had reluctantly joined; my friends had told me it was the perfect way to share my park journey. I figured life was about to start getting pretty scenic, so I might as well. I uploaded the photo I'd just taken of the sun's first rays.

"This morning, I got a sneak peek at 2016. It looks beautiful."

Only a few hours in, and I had already made the understatement of the year.

The national parks are America's Greatest Hits Collection, and Acadia was just the first track on my playlist. But before I go any further, I'd like to pause for a moment and press shuffle.

Unlike, say, the *Star Wars* prequels or the P90X workouts, there's not really much debate about the "correct" order in which one should experience the national parks. That's mostly because the idea of approaching fifty million acres of land as a "completist" activity is a little insane to begin with. Most park fanatics who have attempted such a quest end up tackling it as a lifetime goal, a mission they slowly grow into. What might begin with a few childhood visits to places like Yosemite and the Grand Canyon gradually morphs into a piecemeal pastime.

Since my goal was to see everything in a calendar year, I could be a bit more deliberate in my approach. All of that research I had done into the sunrise debate had convinced me that wherever I went *first* needed to be significant. But . . . tenth? Twenty-seventh? That didn't seem quite as important.

I briefly considered attacking the parks alphabetically, until I realized that would have meant hitting *American Samoa* next— geographically, the *farthest* possible park from Acadia. Search online for flights from Bar Harbor to Pago Pago and the only result you're likely to get is a recommendation for a therapist.

At least American Samoa would have been warm, though. The closest park to Acadia was snowed-in Shenandoah, high up in Virginia's Blue Ridge Mountains. Its legendary Skyline Drive sporadically closes throughout the winter, making much of the park inaccessible. I ultimately wouldn't end up making it there until much later in the year, when I circled back to conduct interviews at a few of the eastern parks.

From the moment I left Acadia, I was chasing more than weather—I was chasing stories. Death Valley might be lovely in January, but the scientist I wanted to chat with there wouldn't be available for at least a month. Cuyahoga Valley might have been close by, but Ohio isn't particularly telegenic in the winter. CBS had given me the go-ahead, but I was serving as my own producer and travel agent. I started making calls and sketching out a ridiculously confusing series of constantly evolving cross-country zigzags, keeping an eye out for how I might work in side trips to the dozens of parks I wanted to see that would never end up on the broadcast.

I'm sure the literal logistics of my eventual routing would frustrate even the most dedicated cartographers. That's why I won't be focusing as much on the chronology or geography that separates the parks I visited. Far more interesting, I discovered, are the threads that tie them together—and that tie us to nature. Some of those connections are literal—there are three different parks where volcanoes play a starring role—while others are more abstract: searching for God, finding forgiveness, and the importance of disconnecting.

For now, I'll fast-forward a bit to mid-February, when I visited two national parks that were created not to preserve the land, but to preserve the *water*. At one, the water is hidden deep underground. At the other, it's all you can see—that is, until you dive below the surface to discover a world of submerged treasures. At both, I met rangers who told me that—while their park may not look like your "average national park"—it was just as important as the rest.

It was a good lesson for me to learn early on. As I quickly realized, there's no such thing as an *average* national park.

2

WATER

(Hot Springs, Biscayne)

In the late 1800s, if you lived in Maine and had a nasty case of syphilis, your doctor might write you a prescription for a bath in Arkansas. An actual prescription, something like "bathe twice a day for three weeks at ninety degrees, followed by periods of rest and moderate exercise." To fill it, you'd pack your bags, hop on a train, and make the journey south to stay at one of the many fine establishments on Hot Springs' "Bathhouse Row." There you would soak in the geothermic water, your every move carefully monitored by a team of bathing attendants. The water was thought to have miraculous healing powers, capable of curing everything from rheumatism to polio.

The Native Americans called it the "Valley of the Vapors." Deep in the Ouachita Mountains, they had discovered steaming streams, fed by springs of hot water, well over 140 degrees Fahrenheit. Legend says feuding tribes put aside their weapons and grievances to enjoy the water together. Later, New York and Chicago mobsters did the same. Al Capone and his gang would frequently head south to gamble and take a dip. Hot Springs was neutral ground.

The actual ground was first protected in 1832, when Congress passed legislation preserving "four sections of land including said springs, reserved for the future disposal of the United States." It marked the first time the federal government had protected land for recreational use. Hot Springs Reservation, as it was called back then, was established forty years before Yellowstone became a national park. The Department of the Interior didn't even *exist* yet. Hot Springs was later redesignated a national park in 1921, a fact that lends itself to some fun "stump the ranger" trivia—Yellowstone was our *first* national park, but Hot Springs is actually our *oldest.*

"Most people were coming here as their *last* resort, not because it was *a* resort," ranger Tom Hill told me during the first interview I had ever conducted in a men's room. We were sitting in the Fordyce Bathhouse, built by Colonel Samuel Fordyce in 1914. Fordyce had moved to Hot Springs after the Civil War because he believed the healing waters he'd sampled here had saved his life.

Back then, there wasn't an ailment a good soak *couldn't* cure. Baseball teams came to Hot Springs for spring training "to boil out the alcoholic microbes that they would accumulate in the wintertime, during the season of excess," Tom explained.

But there was no water flowing through the Fordyce today. While the town of Hot Springs once provided more than a million baths a year, advances in science in the decade after World War II started to make the idea of a "medicinal soak" sound like quackery. Advances in travel allowed leisure travelers to explore other, more remote destinations. Hot Springs lost its allure.

One by one, the palaces on Bathhouse Row turned off their pipes. In 1962, the Fordyce—by far the most opulent—was the first to shut down, but they all eventually met the same fate. All but one. The Buckstaff Bathhouse never closed its doors. I had an appointment there the next day at 7 A.M.

.   .   .

A seventy-year-old man was vigorously scrubbing my naked body, and I hadn't even had breakfast yet. His name was Walter, and he was tall, bald, and wearing socks with sandals that he never seemed to lift off the tile floor. His walk was more of a slow shuffle, which was why I was so surprised by the strength with which he was rubbing my thighs.

I had paid four dollars extra for the "loofah mitt" treatment, which is what I assumed this was. Walter hadn't been great about explaining things. "Sit here, lie there, walk over here, get in this tub." It was all very matter-of-fact and routine, and, as he removed all traces of my epidermis, I could hear him humming. This was just another day at the office for him.

When I'd walked into the Buckstaff and purchased my bath regimen, they had given me a thin white sheet to cover myself. Walter had pulled it right off as he'd nudged me toward my bath. There was no modesty in here. All of the other patrons of the Buckstaff were wandering around buck naked.

The vibe was more "YMCA locker room" than "high-end spa." The lights were harsh and bright, and the century-old marble walls echoed with the sounds of the bath attendants at work—creaking faucets on and off, pouring and mixing the baths. It felt like the employees could just as easily be servicing cars at Jiffy Lube or loading lumber onto a truck. They were tough, no-nonsense, and hardworking, ensuring the bath regimens ran on time.

I started wishing I'd paid more attention to the description out front, because when Walter motioned for me to get out of the tub, I had no idea where we were headed next. I could see the "needle shower" in the corner, a horrifying birdcage-like contraption, resembling an iron maiden, that squirted water out of a series of tiny holes in the pipes. But that wouldn't be turned on until later. Instead, Walter pointed to a piece of porcelain straight ahead. It looked like a shorter, fatter bidet. Was I supposed to wash my feet in this?

Oh God, no. *I was supposed to sit in this.* The name, I guess, should have given that away—it's called a sitz bath. Walter muttered something about it being good for hemorrhoids and directed me to squat. With my first bath, in the normal tub, I had been facing the wall. Now I sat naked facing the entire room, knees up to my nose as hot water trickled up my butt. It was by far the least dignified I'd ever looked, and I had once appeared as an unpaid commentator on the Oxygen network's *25iest Celeb-U-Tots* countdown special.

Perhaps this was relaxing a hundred years ago, but the sitz bath couldn't finish quickly enough as far as I was concerned. The next stop was "the vapor cabinet," a tiny enclosed room filled with steam. It was more like a fourth of a room, and it reminded me of the little cupboard under the stairs where that family made Harry Potter live. Walter closed the door and the steam enveloped me.

After a cocoonlike wrap in hot towels, a turn in the needle shower, and a trip to the "cooling room," it was time to leave. I was glad to be done, but also glad I had done this. It's one thing to read the displays in the museum, but it's another to actually experience a historic bath firsthand. As I walked back out onto the streets of Hot Springs, the modern cars seemed out of place. I felt like I'd just emerged from a time machine.

Really, everything about the busy road felt out of place in a national park. There were honking horns and revving engines. Hot Springs National Park is in the middle of a *city*.

"I have had people stop me on the sidewalk out front, and say, 'How do I get to the national park?' I'm like, 'Well, you're *here*,'" ranger Tom told me. He's used to disappointing hikers.

"They're expecting the Yellowstone experience," he said, "where you drive through the little shack, and the ranger leans out and hands you a map, saying, 'Don't get run over by a bear!' That doesn't happen here."

At this urban park, you're more likely to get run over by a Ford Taurus. Technically, there are a few trails back in the hills to hike, but they're not much different from anything else you might find in rural Arkansas. The nature isn't really the draw. Tom pointed out that there was another distinction that made this park unique.

"We are the only national park that is mandated by federal law to give away its primary resource. We are to preserve the geothermal springwater, but to make it available to everyone. So that's why people line up at the jug fountains."

Locals must laugh at anyone gullible enough to buy bottled water in this town. Unlike most geothermal water, the Hot Springs water is potable and delicious—there's no sulfur smell. Families will pull up to the fountains scattered around town and fill a dozen or so bottles at a time, free of charge.

Drinking a cup was once known as "quaffing the elixir," an expression I can only imagine being said in Pauly Shore's stoner chuckle. The various springs around town were once thought to have different medicinal properties based on their mineral content. One in particular, according to an 1878 *Harper's Magazine* profile of Hot Springs, was preferred by the "fair sex, who fancy that it improves their complexions." For all visitors to Hot Springs, a visit was said to "have a very rejuvenating effect, and the faded beauty blooms again after a short residence."

There's also some speculation that Hot Springs was the mythical "fountain of youth" that Ponce de León was said to be seeking when he sailed north from Puerto Rico. He never made it to Arkansas to quaff the elixir, though. Instead, he landed in a place he named La Florida.

I was helping video journalist Efrain Robles carry his camera equipment out to Biscayne National Park's dock in Homestead, Florida, when he casually mentioned, more to himself than to me, "This is going to be my first time on a boat."

"Your first time *filming* on a boat, you mean," I said.

He shook his head. "No. It's my first time *on* a boat."

Wait. What?

"Like, on *this* kind of boat?" I asked. I'd arranged for us to hitch a ride with the Park Service on one of their small white speedboats.

"Any kind of boat, dude."

I was sure this was not true. I ran down a list of boats.

"A pontoon boat. Have you ever been fishing?"

"No."

"A rowboat?"

He shook his head.

"What about, like, a kayak or a canoe . . . You've never paddled around a lake? At summer camp or something?"

"Nope."

"You must have at least been on a ferry or something. You've been to New York. What about the Staten Island Ferry?"

"No, dude. Zero boats."

He paused for a second, then reconsidered. *Aha.* I knew it wasn't possible that a thirty-two-year-old guy had never been on a boat.

"When my mom brought me over from Mexico when I was five, she floated me across the Rio Grande on an old piece of plywood. Do you count that as a boat?" he asked.

Ever since we'd linked up in Miami a few days earlier, I'd been realizing how little I actually knew about Efrain. We'd worked together years ago, but we were more acquaintances than friends. He came highly recommended, though, so when it came time to bring on a consistent video journalist for my parks project, I passed his name to CBS as a possible candidate. The plan was for Efrain to meet up with me whenever I needed him for a shoot. I would hit the rest of the parks on my own.

Efrain grew up in Phoenix, which at least sort of explained the lack of aquatic experience. We'd met back in 2012, when the E. W. Scripps Company—a broadcasting group that owns a handful of local stations across the country—moved me to Arizona to co-host *The List*, an ultra-low-budget national newsmagazine show that shot in a small studio near the Phoenix airport.

I'd say hi to Efrain whenever I saw him in the editing room, but outside of work he already had a network of pals to hang out with—guys he'd known since childhood.

I, on the other hand, didn't know a soul in Arizona, so after a couple of lonely months I decided to give online dating a try. I ended up only going out with one woman—the same one I would propose to two and a half years later.

She didn't really live in Phoenix, either. Like me, she had come to town on an extended work assignment. We got to know each other while getting to know Maricopa County.

For our first date, on an eighty-degree evening in mid-October, I foolishly wore a blazer in an attempt to look classy. I ended up just looking sweaty. But as I walked her back to her car, I was in no hurry to get back to air-conditioning. I didn't want the night to be over.

The lot was covered in desert-wildlife-themed signs, like GILA MONSTER and QUAIL, to help you remember where you'd parked. She was on the JAVELINA level. Neither of us had ever seen a javelina before, but we thought the drawing looked hilarious. For the next two days, we texted each other pictures we found online of javelinas making weird, scary faces. It was a strange way to flirt, but it worked.

I wonder what ever happened to "José Javelina," the plush toy I bought her in Sedona. When I last saw him, he was sitting in between the pillows on our bed in Pasadena—his usual spot—the day her movers came to take the bed away. I can't imagine she kept him—it seems weird to hold on to an ugly stuffed animal your ex-fiancé once gave you to remind you of your first date. But it made me sad to imagine José off in a dump somewhere.

When I accepted that gig in Phoenix, I never thought I would end up in a relationship. And then, later, I never thought that relationship would end.

I certainly never would have guessed, years down the line, I'd have Phoenix to thank for providing me with another significant relationship—a budding bromance with a guy who'd never been on a boat.

"Are you going to be okay?" I whispered to Efrain as we boarded. "Maybe you get seasick."

He shrugged and hoisted his tripod onto the boat.

"I guess we'll find out," he said.

And with that, we were off.

Almost as soon as we headed out onto Biscayne Bay, a pod of dolphins started following us. They stayed right behind the boat, frolicking in the wake we were creating, popping in and out of the water in perfect little arcs. I counted at least five of them, and just when I thought we'd lost them, up they came again—jumping higher, coming even closer. It was amazing.

Efrain filmed them for a few miles, grinning nonstop. Even the park rangers with us were taking pictures. They'd never seen anything like it. I leaned closer and shouted to Efrain over the motor.

"Hey! Just so you know . . . this is *not* a typical boat ride!"

The Staten Island Ferry was going to be a big letdown after this.

The dolphins weren't even what we had come here to see. It was as if they'd heard CBS was in town and wanted to put on a show.

"Greetings, you inferior beings! Welcome! Just so you know, there's more to this park than meets the eye."

Ninety-five percent of Biscayne National Park is water, encompassing the bulk of Florida's Biscayne Bay. From the visitor center, you can look across and see the skyline of Miami in the distance. The protected salt water that separates the two places does not, at first glance, appear particularly remarkable. It just looks like . . . the ocean.

"Well, when people think of a national park, they often think of places like the Grand Canyon or Yosemite. Places with dramatic and beautiful natural topographic landscapes that stretch off into the horizons, with tall mountains and deep canyons," ranger Chuck Lawson had told me before we got on the boat. He could tell I was underwhelmed.

"What *you* see is the ocean. A flat horizon. But we have topography that is comparable to those grand vistas," he said. "They're just hidden down there, beneath the water a little bit . . . Biscayne is a park that is best appreciated with just a little bit of extra effort."

The extra effort he was talking about was the three days' worth of scuba certification I had just completed back in Miami.

Scuba training consists of practicing everything that could possibly go wrong. And as I quickly learned, there is a *lot* that could go wrong. But even when everything was going *right*, I was terrified. I almost quit after my second day of lessons. My body kept telling me, *Stop. This isn't right. Humans aren't supposed to do this.*

I realize that flying thirty thousand feet above the surface is just as unnatural as swimming sixty feet below it, but it never feels that way. On a plane, there are drinks and snacks and screens playing *We Bought a Zoo* to distract us from the fact that we're hurtling through the atmosphere at five hundred miles an hour in a metal tube.

There is no room for any of that underwater. You're constantly focused on your surroundings, just three millimeters of neoprene separating you from the great, vast ocean. You're in control of your own destiny, the captain on your own underwater cruise.

Ranger Chuck had promised me the lessons would all be worth it. He's an underwater archaeologist, which is easily one of the coolest titles I can imagine ever printing on a business card. He's not paid to study the fish or the coral. He's paid to interpret the *human* story of this park. That's what he wanted to take me out into the ocean to see.

While our boat had GPS and a depth gauge, the first ships to sail through these waters had, at best, a woefully inaccurate map. Florida's landmasses were well charted, but the coral reef a few miles off the coast was unmarked. The shallow waters—home to a dizzying array of aquatic life—became a watery grave for *dozens* of ships.

By 1875, enough ships had wrecked in Biscayne Bay that Floridians finally had the bright idea to light it up. Construction began on the Fowey Rocks Lighthouse, a 130-foot-tall multilevel cast-iron tower that still stands today, miles out into the ocean.

During construction, lighthouse workers would sleep out on the platform—it didn't make much sense to sail back and forth to the shore each day. The process was slow going, and by the winter of 1878, only the first level had been completed. On the night of February 17, relaxing out under the stars, the workers saw the distant lights of a steamship. It was heading straight for them.

The *Arratoon Apcar* was bound for Havana, its 250-horsepower engine propelling its cargo of coal. The men on the lighthouse platform jumped up, waving torches and flags—whatever they could find—frantically trying to signal to the boat. *Stop! Turn around!*

But the *Arratoon Apcar* was a 262-foot-long ship. Even if it *had* managed to notice the signaling, it would have been difficult to change direction. As it got closer, the workers started shouting. Screaming. The *Apcar* was set on its collision course. At the last minute, with just a couple of hundred yards to go until it reached the platform, the ship ground to a halt on the rocks. The exact rocks the Fowey Lighthouse was being constructed to warn against.

As Chuck put it, "An unbuilt lighthouse is not *nearly* as effective as a completed one."

Long after the lighthouse was finished, though, ships *kept* smashing into the reef. Mariners constantly underestimated its dangers.

We passed by the wreck of the *Mandalay*, a luxury yacht that sank on New Year's Day, 1966. That seemed surprisingly recent, and I started to worry that my chat with Chuck might be distracting him from navigating. It was obviously still very possible to crash.

Eventually, we slowed our boat and pulled up to a mooring buoy—a small white ball with the National Park Service logo on it—floating in the middle of the bay. We had arrived, although where, I wasn't sure. Again, all I could see was water.

Chuck told me it was finally time to strap on my gear. As I collected my fins and checked the air in my tank, he told me the story of the *Lugano,* a 350-foot steamer that sank here in 1913.

"At the time the *Lugano* sank," he said, "it was the largest vessel that had ever come to grief on the Florida Reef Tract."

I loved that phrasing. *Come to grief.* I'd never heard it before, although it's apparently a common way to describe shipwrecks. It makes *crashed* seem so inelegant.

I'm sure there was plenty of grief when the *Lugano* hit the coral. Not for any loss of life—all 116 passengers survived—but for the loss of the million dollars' worth of rice, silk, and wine on board, a bounty destined for Havana before it was rerouted to the ocean floor.

Chuck said we might actually see some of the old cargo still in the water: a part of a glass bottle, a fragment of a dinner plate. I was listening, but I was mostly focusing on not losing my lunch. The boat was rocking now that we'd stopped, and the listing motion combined with the heat of my wet suit and the Florida sun overhead was making me nauseous. Efrain, it should be noted, was doing perfectly fine.

He'd been filming me putting my gear on, and I'm sure part of the reason my stomach was queasy was that I was sucking it in like crazy. I'd done plenty of interviews in a business suit, but this was the first one I'd ever done in a wet suit.

Josh—another park diver who had joined us—did a final safety check with me. I'd been honest about my inexperience, but I hadn't mentioned how terrifying I'd found my scuba lessons. Moments away from entering the water, I struggled to remember *any* of that training. I was, for lack of a better word, a wreck.

"You good?" Josh asked.

The camera was rolling. I had to be.

"Mmm-hmmm . . ." I muttered through my mouthpiece. My jaw was locked so hard onto that piece of rubber that nothing could have pried it from my mouth. I stuck my leg comically far out in front of me—what divers call a giant-stride entry—and silly-walked into the water.

Here goes nothing.

I was bracing for a freak-out, but the waters were calmer than in my training, and somehow I managed to relax. We slowly descended to the ocean floor, where waiting for us was a giant rock with a metal placard affixed to it, inscribed with a version of the story Chuck had been telling me about the *Lugano*. It was the same kind of paragraph-long park sign you might see explaining the significance of a battlefield or listing off the names of the peaks of a far-off mountain range. Except it was on the bottom of the frigging ocean.

The *Lugano* is part of the park's Maritime Heritage Trail, a collection of wrecks that includes the *Mandalay*, the *Arratoon Apcar*, and three others. It's a "trail" in the loosest sense of the word— you have to boat from site to site, not swim. At each dive location, the park has signs near the wrecks so divers can understand what they're looking at.

Chuck swam up beside me and tapped me on the arm. He was pointing out the heel of a shoe. Cargo, most likely, or perhaps something one of the guests was wearing on the day the *Lugano* sank.

On land, when you're exploring the ruins of an ancient civilization, there are layers to peel back—hundreds of years of habitation in the same spot. That makes it difficult to date the artifacts you find—everything has been lumped together in the same place. Even Hot Springs' Bathhouse Row had been built and rebuilt over the years. But with a shipwreck, you know exactly when everything you're seeing arrived. In this case, it was March 9, 1913.

On our way out to the wreck, Chuck had told me about why he thought this was so amazing.

"Think about it. A shipwreck is a unique viewpoint into not even just one *day*, but a *moment* in time where a group of people who had everything they needed to survive at that point in history took all of that material and deposited it, at one moment, onto the seafloor."

It made me think about the boxes I'd packed up when I left Pasadena, a collection of everything I'd hurriedly decided was too important to throw away. I could only imagine how puzzling those boxes might be to future archaeologists.

"Okay, so I get why he kept the harmonica. But the install disk for iLife '03? What did he possibly think he was going to do with that? And who saves a generic Christmas card his *insurance agent* sent him? Like, this says 'Conor Knighton or *Current Resident.*' That's so sad."

I was determined to survive my dive so that the future Chucks of the world would not be picking the wreckage of my life apart. Surprisingly, when he eventually signaled that it was time to head back up to the surface, I didn't want to leave. Once I got over my initial jitters, I found I really *enjoyed* being underwater.

The *Lugano* had been covered with coral and colonized by all sorts of critters. Gliding through its rusty bones, I saw lobsters and eels and fish I could only identify by their colors—yellow ones and blue ones and green ones and purple ones. I finally got it. *This* was why people go through all the trouble of scuba training. The view out an airplane window isn't this good.

The hardest skill for a beginning diver to master is buoyancy. The goal is to "get neutral," to figure out the right balance of air in your vest and weights on your belt that will keep you from skyrocketing up to the surface or scraping the sandy bottom. When you finally do, you become weightless.

I'd struggled with this during training but at Biscayne I finally achieved equilibrium. When I did, it felt amazing. With just a kick or two, I was able to glide through an entire underwater world.

Once I had my buoyancy locked in, I could lock into my surroundings. I'd been looking at the fish, but now I *listened* to them. When I got up close to the *Lugano,* I could hear them nibbling at the coral, schools of them swimming past my mask through the body of a ship that had sunk a century earlier.

Sliding away from the wreck, I could only hear the sound of my own breathing. Every inhale and exhale was magnified, meted out in tiny bubbles. I focused on my breath in the way someone might during meditation. The water that was once so frightening became calming. Healing, even. I hadn't expected the bottom of the ocean to be more relaxing than the inside of a Hot Springs bathhouse, but it was.

The wild scientific claims that once drew the infirm to places like Hot Springs have long since been debunked. Penicillin turned out to be a much better cure for syphilis than a warm bath. But water *does* have healing properties, and now there's plenty of research to back it up. As Wallace J. Nichols chronicles in his bestselling book *Blue Mind,* we're *wired* for water—spending time immersed in everything from tubs to oceans has been shown to decrease stress and anxiety, improve physical performance, and boost brain function. After all, our brains are mostly made up of water.

But the proven benefits of water go beyond just being in or under it; Nichols points to studies that have documented the positive impacts of simply spending time *near* water. To fully appreciate a park like Biscayne might take some extra effort, but it's possible to appreciate the beauty of an unspoiled ocean view from its miles of protected shoreline.

There were once plans to build roads and bridges out to the islands—to fill them with fancy resorts and condos. Someone suggested a forty-foot-deep channel that would cut through the middle of the coral reef. But proponents of Biscayne National Park argued that the most beneficial use of these waters would be to leave them undisturbed. South Florida would continue to expand, but this section would forever remain a retreat—an ocean of calm to escape to when seeking a cure for the chaos of city life.

3

ANIMALS

(Everglades, Channel Islands, Pinnacles, Death Valley)

In the 2011 Sci Fi Channel original movie *Mega Python vs. Gatoroid*, Dr. Nikki Riley (played by '80s pop icon Debbie Gibson) sets a bunch of exotic pythons loose in Everglades National Park. The pythons feast on everything in sight, including the native alligator population. To fight back, park ranger Terry O'Hara (played by '80s pop icon Tiffany) gets steroids from a fellow ranger's grandson, stuffs the steroids in some dead chickens, feeds those chickens to the *gators*, and creates *Gatoroids*. The movie only gets crazier from there, and it isn't long before the CGI mutant reptile fights begin.

The film also features one of the best fights between two *humans* in cinematic history. The chance to hear Debbie Gibson yell, "You are gonna get it, *you gator-baiting bitch*!" at Tiffany, then slap her, and then dump a giant bowl of salad on her head is why I pay for cable.

Shockingly, though, there is a shred of truth in the film. Miami is an exotic pet hub, and irresponsible pet owners in South Florida *do* occasionally dump their pythons into the Everglades when they

tire of them. Once there, the pythons thrive—they're apex predators, biting and squeezing everything in sight, disrupting the food
chain and the delicate, diverse ecosystem.

The importance of that ecosystem was why ranger Alan Scott
and I were standing in murky water, and not in a concrete plaza of
condos.

"This was the first national park that was set aside by the National Park Service, by the people of the United States, for what is
alive," Alan explained. I was only half listening. I was pretty sure
something alive had just slipped past my foot.

Alan was leading me on a "slough slog," and we were knee-deep
in the Everglades' famous "River of Grass," a freshwater slough
(pronounced *slew*—a swamp, basically) that slowly channels water
through the park and toward the ocean. We were moving far
faster than the current, which inches along almost imperceptibly.
On a typical day, the near-stagnant water only advances one hundred feet.

Alan had insisted that this was the only true way to see the Everglades. That it was worth drenching a pair of boots to be surrounded by the marsh—to literally soak it all in. I splashed and
squished along behind him in the mud, using my walking stick for
balance and to scare off whatever creatures might be lurking ahead
of me.

The Everglades is the only place in the world where alligators
and crocodiles coexist in the wild. South Florida happens to be just
warm enough for crocodiles, which generally prefer the hotter climate of Central and South America, and just cool enough for alligators, which rarely travel south of Florida. Crocodiles tend to like
salt water, alligators tend to like fresh water. Everglades has a mix
of the two.

Both animals are also success stories of the park. Before Everglades was protected, hunting and habitat loss had made significant dents in the populations of Florida's two most famous reptiles.
At the park's dedication ceremony, President Harry Truman promised the crowd that "in this park we shall preserve tarpon and trout,

pompano, bear, deer, crocodiles and alligators—and rare birds of great beauty. We shall protect hundreds of all kinds of wildlife which might otherwise soon be extinct."

Twenty years later, when the United States published its first list of federally protected endangered species, the American alligator was part of the inaugural group. Just a few years later, the American crocodile was added to the Endangered Species List. At the time, there were only twenty or so crocs left in the country.

Today there are closer to twenty-five hundred of them. And alligators, well—they're now so common they've started roaming around Disney World. Neither species is considered endangered anymore, and while Alan assured me we weren't likely to encounter either animal on our walk, they're easy to spot elsewhere in the park. Neither would have recovered so quickly if not for the critical habitat protected within Everglades' boundaries.

All across the country, the national parks have been crucial in the rehabilitation of all sorts of species on the brink of extinction. But stories of *full* recovery are still pretty uncommon. In the history of the Endangered Species Act, less than 2 percent of all species that have ever been listed have been *delisted*.

A delisting is a major event. That's why, as soon as I started hearing rumors that one *might* be about to happen at a national park twenty-four hundred miles away from the Everglades, I headed back across the country to the state I'd left behind—California.

Despite living in the Los Angeles area for over a decade, I had never once ventured an hour and a half up the coast to Ventura Harbor. There, each day, boat trips depart for Channel Islands National Park—a collection of five islands twenty miles or so off the California coast.

It seemed crazy that it had taken a quest to see *every* national park to finally visit the one that had been closest to my apartment for all those years. I was excited to finally check it out, and Efrain was excited when I told him we'd be taking another boat ride. I asked him to meet me in Ventura, and I booked us a 9 A.M. ferry ride to Santa Cruz, the largest of the Channel Islands.

Biologist Tim Coonan was already waiting for us on the dock when we arrived, hanging out on a bench by the water. After nearly three decades with the Park Service, Tim had recently traded in his ranger uniform for good. On this beautiful Tuesday morning, he was wearing a light-blue T-shirt and shorts.

Tim was a dead ringer for John Slattery, the actor who played Roger Sterling in *Mad Men* and Tony Stark's dad in the Marvel movies—a handsome rogue with bright-white hair and a twinkle in his eye that made you think he knew an especially juicy secret. And Tim *did* know a secret: The Channel Island fox was about to be taken off the Endangered Species List.

The Channel Island fox is everything a crocodile is not. Instead of spiky, scaly skin, it sports a soft coat of fur—gray on top and a bright orange-red on its belly. Whereas a male crocodile can weigh over a thousand pounds, an island fox rarely weighs more than four. It's smaller than a house cat, and it's painfully, undeniably *cute*.

Tim used to run the national park's Channel Island fox recovery program. Back in the 1990s, he and other park staffers had noticed that the fox population on all the islands was dropping dramatically. Puzzled at first, the researchers eventually discovered the foxes were being killed by golden eagles.

The golden eagles had only just arrived—for centuries, the islands had been the exclusive turf of their cousin, the bald eagle. But when the bald eagles disappeared—the chemical DDT had largely wiped them out—the golden eagles saw an opportunity and moved in. While bald eagles mostly eat fish, golden eagles mostly eat small mammals. For the golden eagles, the Channel Islands were an all-you-can-eat fox buffet.

"We knew we were in a world of hurt," Tim told me as we cruised across the Pacific. Off in the distance, Santa Rosa Island— once home to an estimated 1,780 foxes—had just 15 left in 2000.

The fox situation on the other islands was nearly as bad. "They had one foot in the grave," Tim said. "There was pretty much no hope."

The national park staff quickly rounded up the few foxes that were left and put them in a protected captive breeding program. They trapped the golden eagles on the islands and relocated them to northeast California. They brought *back* the bald eagles. Eventually, they released the foxes, crossed their fingers, and hoped for the best.

When Tim and I got off the boat at Santa Cruz Island, it took us all of ten minutes to spot our first island fox. Out of the corner of my eye, I saw a little patch of fur slinking around under a bench at the campsite. Then another popped up, peeking around a tree. They were adorable—curious about what we were doing there, but skittish enough to run away whenever we approached. Back when the foxes were declared endangered, it was estimated that they had a fifty–fifty chance of going extinct in the next decade. Today there are twenty times as many foxes on Santa Cruz as there were when scientists went into panic mode.

"You don't get too many wins in conservation biology these days, but we're gonna take this one," Tim said as we walked around the island. The recovery of the foxes marked the fastest delisting of a mammal in the history of the Endangered Species Act.

Long before there was such a thing as the Endangered Species Act, birders noticed that California condors were disappearing from the skies. In ornithologist William Dawson's 1923 edition of *The Birds of California*, he worried that the "wanton destruction of these noble birds" would lead to their extinction within a decade.

The California condor is the largest flying bird in North America. It is also one of the least attractive. While there is something regal about the bright-white plumage of a bald eagle's head, the wrinkled pink face of a condor most closely resembles an old scrotum with a beak. But to Dawson, they were *sublime*. "I am not ashamed to have fallen in love with so gentle a ghoul," he wrote.

Dawson lamented the condor's decline, but he was not perplexed by it. The birds are large and easy to kill—hunters had already wiped out much of the population. California's surging population of humans was rapidly building cities in areas the condors once called home. Egg collectors, Dawson wrote, "not content with one or two specimens, set out to get all they might while the getting was good. The getting, we are told, is no longer good."

Condors are obligate scavengers, which means their entire diet consists of scavenged food—the carcasses of everything from elk to deer to sea lions. Condors start circling overhead as an animal is on its last legs.

That's why, when I saw a condor circling above me as I hiked the High Peaks Trail at Pinnacles National Park in Central California, I was simultaneously elated and offended. I knew I was dripping sweat after making my way up the steep mountain, but I resented the implication that I might be near death. Did I really look *that* out of shape? Ouch.

Mostly, though, I couldn't believe my luck. There are around three hundred California condors flying in the wild today, and I'd managed to find one accidentally on a hike I was just doing for fun. Pinnacles is famous for being a condor-spotting location, but a sighting is far from guaranteed. I got out my camera and started snapping away.

The giant birds have ended up surviving much longer than William Dawson predicted, but only thanks to large-scale human efforts over the last several decades. The California condors were part of what's become known as the Class of '67, the very first list of endangered species given federal protection. The bald eagle and the American alligator were part of the same batch.

Today the critically endangered birds are raised in captive breeding programs and occasionally put back into the wild at places like Pinnacles. There they take to the skies, flying over the spiky rock formations that give the park its name, then heading off to roam wherever they please. Nobody is trying to shoot them down—it's highly illegal to hunt a condor—yet bullets are still their biggest enemy.

The California condors have been dying of lead poisoning. Lead is a dangerous neurotoxin, banned in paint since before I was born. But it's still the most popular metal for making ammunition.

When hunters shoot and field dress an animal, they often leave behind a gut pile. The meat and skin and antlers all get carted away, and the innards are left behind for nature's garbage collectors. The condors swing by for a free meal and end up ingesting small scraps of lethal lead.

That's why, as of July 1, 2019, it's no longer legal to hunt with lead ammunition in California. Not surprisingly, the new law has encountered some resistance. Copper ammunition—the most popular alternative to lead—is more expensive. But at least there *is* an alternative. If the condors were to go extinct, as they so nearly have in the past, there would be no replacing them. A few extra dollars for bullets seems a small price to pay to ensure the "gentle ghouls" survive. As Dawson wrote, "The heart of mystery, of wonder, and of desire lies with the California Condor."

Unfortunately, the birds remain a mystery to me. As I was training my camera on the black spot flying above me at Pinnacles, snapping photo after photo, trying to use my zoom to push in closer, a jogger zipped past me on the trail.

"You know that's a raven, right?"

He didn't even break his stride as he crushed my dreams, rounding the bend before I could even stammer out an embarrassed reply. Whoops. I had *thought* it had looked a little small. At least I'd just been saved from posting a bunch of pictures of my sweet raven sighting.

I went the rest of the afternoon without ever seeing a condor. The birds can fly over 150 miles a day in search of food. While condors are frequently seen at Pinnacles, they could be *anywhere*.

It's far easier to track down the California animal that's the runt of the inaugural Class of '67 endangered species litter. Over the course of its brief little life, it never manages to travel more than twenty yards from where it was born. It can't—it's trapped.

To see it, I'd have to travel to a national park less than three hundred miles away from Pinnacles, to a place so inhospitable to life they called it Death Valley.

Death Valley is the largest national park in the contiguous United States. Its massive boundary encompasses more than 3.3 *million* acres, stretching across the California/Nevada border.

Only after the most careful examination of the park map would one ever even notice the tiny speck on the far right side of the page. A little green dot, representing forty additional acres of the park, sixty miles away from everything else. Devils Hole.

A visit to Devils Hole feels like you've stumbled upon a super-villain's lair. After an hour's drive from Pahrump, Nevada, down a lonely, dusty road, deep into what seems to be the middle of nowhere, an imposing black barbed-wire fence suddenly appears. Get out of the car and you'll notice security cameras scanning the perimeter, and various bits of mysterious technology—could that be a wind speed monitor?—whirring in the background. Something seems a little fishy. That's because . . . it is.

Behind the fence is the only known habitat of the Devils Hole pupfish, one of the rarest fish in the world. Against all odds, this one-inch-long, bright-blue fish has managed to eke out an existence in a puddle in the middle of the desert.

Death Valley is the driest place in North America, but long ago, water covered the entire area. When it dried up, the pupfish ended up trapped in a pond—just ten feet wide and sixty feet long.

"It's actually considered the smallest habitat known for a vertebrate species in the world," Kevin Wilson told me. Kevin is an aquatic ecologist for the Park Service, and he knows this hole better than anyone else.

He unlocked the fence so I could take a look inside. What appeared to just be a puddle was actually an aquifer—a deep cave full of water coming from an underground source.

"We know that divers have been down to 436 feet," he said. "They . . . did not see a bottom."

The water stays a consistent ninety-two degrees Fahrenheit, a little Jacuzzi in the desert. A Jacuzzi that contains a handful of rare fish, and at least two dead bodies.

In the 1960s, two locals died while exploring Devils Hole. Rescuers eventually found a mask, a flashlight, and a snorkel, but their bodies were never recovered—the young men sank deeper than anyone has even been.

Kevin was explaining the history of Devils Hole while strapping on his own scuba gear. He and a small crew of researchers were preparing to dive into the cave. I definitely wouldn't be using my newly acquired certification to join him. Cave diving is extremely dangerous, and they had no time to show an inexperienced journalist the ropes. The stakes were too high—it was fish-counting day.

"We reached an all-time low of thirty-five observable fish in the spring of 2013," Kevin said. That's thirty-five pupfish—*total*—left in the wild in the entire world. Kevin was hoping this day's number would be three times higher. Still small, but a sign of improvement.

The alarm bells were first sounded in the early 1970s, back when there were a few hundred or so pupfish swimming in the hole. Nearby cattle and alfalfa ranch owners had correctly theorized that, if there was water flowing under Devils Hole, then there was likely water under *their* land as well. They drilled a well, struck water, and, according to Kevin, "As soon as they turned on the well, the water in Devils Hole started to decline and so did the pupfish population."

Scientists started freaking out, but the farmers claimed it wasn't their problem. They needed water to irrigate their land. Environmentalists started a "save the pupfish" campaign, which locals responded to with KILL THE PUPFISH bumper stickers. The federal government was going to come in and tell them what they could and couldn't do with their water? No siree. Not in Nevada, they weren't.

It got ugly. Tempers flared on both sides as the water continued to drop and the pupfish continued to die. There was talk that someone might want to drop a bit of insecticide into the hole to finally end this nonsense once and for all. That's why the area looks like a maximum-security prison today—a couple of drops of bleach, and it's bye-bye pupfish.

It was a case that went all the way to the Supreme Court. In *Cappaert v. United States* (1976), the court unanimously sided with the federal government, upholding its right to protect the pupfish by regulating water use. It was a landmark case, paving the way for a number of environmental protections. The little Devils Hole pupfish was punching far above its weight.

Yet despite the legal victory, the fish are even more endangered today. The pupfish initially thrived after the well was turned off, but then, unexpectedly, their numbers started dropping again. Scientists couldn't figure out what was happening, and still aren't exactly sure. There's a theory that climate change may be playing a role—higher temperatures can lead to shorter spawning periods. To make the pupfish healthier, the team at Death Valley have been feeding them since 2007, an intervention Kevin justified by reminding me that "humans have played a role in impacting this ecosystem." The Park Service was just righting a past wrong.

As Kevin and his team descended into the hole to do their counting, Efrain and I filmed from the surface. We'd been given special access. Tourists generally can only peer down at the hole from a platform high above, which is why Devils Hole doesn't get many tourists. You can't make out anything from up top, but from our vantage point, squatting by the edge of the water, we could see the little guys scurrying back and forth. They were a bright, electric-blue color, with big bug eyes on the sides of their heads. Not quite Nemo, but more charismatic than I'd guessed. None were more than a year or so old—even healthy pupfish don't live for long.

As Efrain leaned in close to get the shot, I steadied his shoulders from behind. I was terrified we were somehow going to be responsible for some tragic accident. I thought of that scene in *Dumb and Dumber*, when Jim Carrey accidentally kills the endangered Icelandic snow owl with a champagne cork. That could easily be us. "CBS Crew Drops Camera Lens in Water, Kills World's Pupfish Population."

We managed not to fall in the hole, and when Kevin finally emerged from the water, he was grinning. I assumed that meant the news was good. There are multiple dives throughout the day— the overall count is an estimate, with different sets of divers assigned to look in different sections, and their results averaged. After a few hours, they had a set of numbers they were confident in. Kevin got out of his wet suit and jogged a couple hundred yards away in search of a spot on the hill where there was allegedly cellphone service. When a single bar finally appeared on his phone, he texted Washington, D.C., his preliminary count: 115 pupfish left in the entire world.

Just a mile away from the pupfish's natural habitat, scientists have been breeding them in captivity inside of a new four-and-a-half-million-dollar lab—the Ash Meadows Fish Conservation Facility, opened in 2013. The government built a *second* Devils Hole, a backup in case the fish go extinct in the wild.

Inside, there's a 110,000-gallon tank—an exact replica of Devils Hole, minus the freakishly deep bottom. The rock shelf close to the surface where the fish typically lay their eggs has been re-created—via a 3-D scan—in fiberglass. A water treatment room—full of pipes and gauges and computers—makes sure the water in the tank has the exact pH, oxygen content, and temperature as Devils Hole.

It certainly seemed like a lot of money to spend on a tiny little fish. But I reminded myself that the Endangered Species Act isn't just for foxes and eagles. You don't just get to save the cool animals. For all we know, pupfish DNA might contain the cure to some disease we've yet to discover. And even if it doesn't, I think there's something in *our* DNA that inspires us to root for the little guy. We're not protecting the pupfish because it makes economic sense—it's because it's the right thing to do.

There's a well-known John Muir quote—"When we try to pick out anything by itself, we find it hitched to everything else in the Universe." In the Channel Islands, a group of foxes nearly went extinct because some bald eagles were eating fish that had been infected with a chemical humans had created to kill insects. At Pinnacles, minuscule shards of lead left behind in the belly of a deer continue to endanger the country's largest bird. In Death Valley, farmers irrigating a faraway alfalfa ranch nearly wiped out one of the world's rarest fish. Everything is hitched to everything else in the universe, and we're finally realizing how all of those invisible threads inevitably trace back to us.

Humans are by far the planet's most destructive species, but we're also the only species that has ever worked together to ensure other forms of life don't go extinct. The concept of protecting species that don't offer us an obvious, tangible benefit is a fairly recent addition to our collective history, but it's an important one. Our ability to see a value in preserving life that extends beyond our immediate self-interest may be what makes us *most* human.

When Harry Truman dedicated Everglades National Park in 1947, he acknowledged that it might not look like much. "Here are no lofty peaks seeking the sky, no mighty glaciers or rushing streams wearing away the uplifted land," he told the crowd gathered in Everglades City. But Truman made the case that national parks were about more than just protecting the land. Parks were also about protecting the creatures who call the land home.

"We need places such as Everglades National Park where we may be more keenly aware of our Creator's infinitely varied, infinitely beautiful, and infinitely bountiful handiwork," Truman said. Places where we can see cute foxes, giant alligators, minuscule fish, and ghoulish birds. Places where our grandchildren can see them as well. The conservation of all that lives within the park, Truman argued, was necessary "for the conservation of the human spirit."

4

———

GOD

(Yosemite, Capitol Reef, Lake Clark)

When I was ten years old, I signed up for a week at Spring Heights, a Methodist church camp in the hills of Roane County, West Virginia. The camp was only an hour-and-a-half drive from Charleston, but I might as well have been going to a cabin on Mars. For the first time in my life, I was going to spend a week without talking to my family. I was excited—it seemed like a *big-kid* thing to do—but I was also terrified.

Right after my parents dropped me off at my cabin, they dropped a letter in the mailbox in the nearby town of Spencer. It was addressed to the nervous camper they'd just waved goodbye to. They wanted me to be one of the first kids to get a piece of mail the next night at dinner, a note full of encouragement about the wonderful week I had ahead of me.

But when it arrived Monday evening, it just made me terribly homesick. I'd been doing okay, but reading my mom's familiar handwriting in a dining hall full of unfamiliar faces made things worse. I almost burst into tears right there at dinner.

I knew I had to hold it together. Kids can be cruel—even the ones at church camp—and I didn't want anyone to see me cry. I steeled myself and sipped my "bug juice," a gross Kool-Aid concoction I hated, wishing it were the Ocean Spray Ruby Red I knew was back in our fridge at home.

From the moment we arrived, the counselors had been telling us about the "night hike." One evening, midweek, the entire camp wanders along a wide trail in the woods in the darkness. No flashlights, no talking. Just the occasional flicker of fireflies lighting the trail. Everyone stands twenty feet apart—just close enough to make out the T-shirt in front of you so you don't get lost, but far enough away that nobody can really see your face. It's a time to turn your thoughts inward. A time to listen, to breathe, to pray.

When the night finally came, I cried. I'd been waiting for those thirty minutes since our Oldsmobile station wagon had pulled away at the beginning of the week. I knew it would be my chance to get everything out. I'm surprised I had that kind of foresight as a kid, that I could hear the description of this supposedly magical night hike back in the dining hall and think, *Yes, Conor—that sounds like the perfect place to cry. Just hold out until then, and you can do it without anyone seeing.* Back in the bunkhouse, the beds were too close together. An improperly muffled sniffle could have given me away. But out under the stars, my tears were free to flow.

I don't know what I was even sad about. I was having a good time; everybody had been nice to me. I'd even told a joke that had made some of the older kids laugh. But I used every step of that hike to squeeze out the tears.

I went back to Spring Heights five or six more summers— I *liked* going—but I cried on that walk every time. That very first trip somehow linked the two experiences for me: A quiet hike in the dark is when you cry. In later years, I wasn't missing home or thinking about my parents anymore. I was mostly thinking about that scared little kid, the younger version of myself, carefully plotting his sobs. That image made me sad. It still does.

Camp was everything church was not—we swam and hiked and played outside. We prayed, more than I ever had back home, but somehow, with just the sky overhead, I felt that God might actually be listening. Moses didn't go to a building in the middle of a city when he wanted to talk to God—he went to the top of a mountain.

The week in the woods always went by quickly, and before I knew it the family I missed so much had returned to drag me away from all of my cool new friends, back to a home where we didn't even have bug juice, which I had now decided was delicious.

The campers would always put on a little performance for the parents. The camp director would make a speech, we'd watch a slide show of our week, and then all of us would come up to the front and sing hymns while making weird interpretive gestures that only sort of synced up with the lyrics. The songs would change from year to year (one particularly hip summer featured "Jesus Is the Rock and He Rolls My Blues Away"), but there was always one constant: "Here I Am, Lord."

The hymn, written by Dan Schutte in 1981, features a melody that's easy and sweet, and a bunch of elementary schoolkids singing it is catnip for camcorders. But it's also a song with a heavy emphasis on nature.

In each verse, Schutte has God describe Himself in the context of His achievements in nature. "I the Lord of sea and sky," "I the Lord of snow and rain," "I the Lord of wind and flame," and so on. Basically, "You know all of that awesome stuff you see outside? Guess what? I'm the guy who made it!"

It continues:

> I who made the stars of night,
> I will make their darkness bright.
> Who will bear My light to them?
> Whom shall I send?

Then the song (and everyone singing it) answers:

> Here I am, Lord. Is it I, Lord? I have heard you calling in
>   the night.

On the night hikes, I heard crickets and katydids, creaking branches and a light breeze whistling through the leaves. The chorus of a West Virginia summer night, calling out to me, letting me know everything was going to be okay. Or, as John Muir might call it: God.

John Muir grew up in a strict Protestant household in Scotland. His father was a fire-and-brimstone, sin-preaching taskmaster who made his son memorize the Bible.

"I could recite the New Testament from the beginning of Matthew to the end of Revelation without a single stop," Muir later wrote in his memoirs. He claimed to have memorized 75 percent of the Old Testament as well.

The Muir family moved to the United States in 1849, when John was just eleven years old. While Muir's father had only brought a few religious texts with him to their Wisconsin farm, Muir secretly borrowed everything from Shakespeare to science books from his new neighbors. He would rise early each morning to read and tinker in his cellar workshop.

Muir eventually left the farm to study at the University of Wisconsin, where he was exposed to subjects like botany and geology. While he was a talented inventor, Muir loved the natural world more than anything. After a factory accident nearly blinded him, he decided to wander America to "study the inventions of God." Muir wrote that he wanted "to store my mind with the Lord's beauty" lest his eyes ever be plunged into darkness again. He set off for Florida first, then found his way to the Sierras of California.

While sitting in a "little shanty made of sugar pine shingles" one Sunday night in Yosemite, John Muir wrote to his younger brother David. "I have not been at church a single time since leaving home," he confessed. "Yet this glorious valley might well be called a church, for every lover of the great Creator who comes within the broad overwhelming influences of the place fails not to worship as he never did before."

Like Muir, I stopped going to church on a regular basis when I left home. I used to go every Sunday. I sang in the choir, I went to Sunday school, I shot pool at youth group. For a few years, I even played on the Methodist basketball team, which might have been when I prayed the hardest. *Please, God, please don't let them pass the ball to me.*

Over the past decade, most of the churches I've visited have been as a tourist. The Hallgrímskirkja in Reykjavik, the National Cathedral in Washington, the Mosque-Cathedral of Córdoba. Whispering and wandering in those structures, my mind would not turn to God. I was always thinking about the people who had designed the impressive columns and Gothic spires, the artisans behind the stained glass and the intricate gargoyles. I would think about the time and care it must have taken to create each place.

As I traveled through the parks, I was finding that I did the same thing. I was always thinking about what created the forests and canyons and mountains. I would dutifully read the scientific explanations crediting everything from erosion to earthquakes, but they always seemed incomplete. I couldn't shake the feeling that some other unseen, unexplained force had also had a hand in things.

British journalist J. B. Priestley may have described that feeling best when writing about the Grand Canyon in his 1937 *Midnight on the Desert.* "The Colorado River made it," he wrote. "But you feel when you are there that God gave the Colorado River its instructions."

As federal land, national parks do not endorse a particular theology, but they frequently share the stories and beliefs of those who do. Perhaps nowhere are church and state more intertwined than at Capitol Reef National Park in Utah. The park, named after the resemblance that its white, pointy domes of sandstone have to the U.S. Capitol Building, also features a heavy helping of religion.

In the 1880s, a small group of Mormon homesteaders arrived at

Capitol Reef. They settled along the banks of the Fremont River in an area that, according to the national park, eventually became known as the Eden of Wayne County. The Mormons established farms and orchards there and gave their town a name to reflect its lushness: Fruita.

Less than ten families homesteaded in the valley at any given time. The settlers didn't have their own church, so they gathered for church meetings in the one-room schoolhouse—Fruita's only public structure—which still stands today. The sign out front credits the Mormons' success in such an isolated environment to "their cooperative spirit, determination, and spiritual bond."

Of course, the Mormons weren't the first to live and worship here. More than a thousand years earlier, the Fremont people occupied Capitol Reef. While the Fremont culture remains mysterious, the canyon walls offer clues to what they might have believed. Their stories have been etched in stone.

The park's petroglyphs are some of its most famous attractions, found all throughout the area. Anthropologists are reluctant to speculate about what, exactly, they mean, but they're clearly more than just graffiti. When I found my first batch—a series of animals, suns, and large figures with round heads and sharply triangular bodies that might have been people or might have been gods—it definitely didn't feel like I had stumbled upon someone's old grocery list. The etchings *must* have had some sort of spiritual significance. Whatever afterlife the Fremont may have believed in, in that moment they came back to life for me.

Charles Kelly, the first superintendent of Capitol Reef, was famously secular. Like Muir, he was the son of an itinerant preacher, a father he grew to resent and whose religion he rejected. And yet even Kelly, responsible for naming some of Capitol Reef's more remote features, decided to call the park's eastern collection of towering rocks Cathedral Valley. They were apparently just too majestic to be called anything else.

As Muir wrote, "The hills and groves were God's first temples, and the more they are cut down and hewn into cathedrals and

churches, the farther off and dimmer seems the Lord himself."
From Red Cathedral at Death Valley to Cathedral Domes in Mammoth Cave to the Cathedral Group—the tallest mountains in Grand Teton—it feels like the national parks have more cathedrals than Italy.

"Everybody needs beauty as well as bread, places to play in and pray in, where Nature may heal and cheer and give strength to body and soul alike," Muir wrote in *The Yosemite*. In his writings, Muir capitalizes Nature in the same way he capitalizes God. Nature, God, Creator, Beauty—they're all used to describe an entity greater than ourselves.

That healing, strengthening power of nature is why one organization—Operation Heal Our Patriots—spends hundreds of thousands of dollars each year to fly veterans to a church camp on the edge of Lake Clark National Park in Alaska.

Much like the church camp I went to in rural West Virginia, the church camp at Lake Clark isn't much more than a small collection of wooden cabins and a dining hall. The main difference is, in rural Alaska, the bug juice has to be *flown* in.

Lake Clark National Park is only accessible by plane or boat—all four million acres are entirely disconnected from Alaska's road system. Port Alsworth—founded in 1950 by a bush pilot who was looking for a home base—is a tiny settlement of fewer than two hundred people located along the lake's edge. There are a few private lodges, an air taxi hangar, the park headquarters, and . . . not much else. No restaurant, no grocery store. A large gravel runway splits the "town" in two.

When I visited the park, I came across the sign for Samaritan Lodge—the white letters were next to a picture of a cross surrounded by a circle. I was camping nearby, but I couldn't remember seeing that name on the list of possible park accommodations. As I later learned, that's because Samaritan Lodge wasn't meant for guys like me.

"What we're looking for are veterans—from 9/11 on—who have some kind of injury," Chaplain Jim Fisher told me later on the phone. "And when we say 'injured,' we don't necessarily mean a visible injury. There are a lot of *invisible* injuries such as PTSD, and everybody, I'm telling you *everybody* that comes through, struggles with some level of PTSD."

Jim had served as a military chaplain for over three decades before he retired from the navy. Today he serves on the staff of Operation Heal Our Patriots, a program that flies wounded veterans and their spouses to the wilderness of Alaska for six days of emotional and spiritual counseling, all expenses paid. Each week of the summer, a new group of ten couples arrives at Lake Clark. The actual facilities are on private land, but the view beyond the boat dock is of a national park.

"At first, a lot of people came thinking, *It's going to be a scam, it's gonna be a time-share thing.* That we were going to shave their heads and deprive them of sleep and protein and shove Christianity down their throats," Jim said. "And we *do* talk about Jesus. We make no apologies for the fact that we're a Christian, nondenominational organization. But it's not like we're gonna lock somebody in a room and beat 'em up with the Bible until they give up. It's not that."

Robbie Doman had grown up Christian but wasn't necessarily a church-every-Sunday kind of guy. When a buddy from his unit in Afghanistan had called to tell him about the free trip he and his wife had just taken to Alaska, Robbie thought it sounded too good to be true. But it also sounded like it could be just what he needed— a chance to disconnect from the stresses of everyday life, reconnect with his wife, and surround himself with other vets who had gone through similar experiences.

Robbie had served as an army staff sergeant in Iraq. In February 2008, he was severely injured when the Humvee he was riding in flipped while swerving to avoid an attempted improvised explosive attack.

Robbie's memories of that day—and the days that followed—

are hazy. He kept fading in and out of consciousness. He remembers struggling to grab his shotgun, not understanding why he couldn't get up. He remembers being loaded into a Black Hawk helicopter, then waking up in a series of different hospitals. Eventually, he found himself back at Walter Reed hospital in Washington, D.C., where he stayed for the next six months. All told, Robbie underwent over a dozen surgeries on his legs and back.

Eventually, he returned home to Colorado. With enough rehabilitation, his physical injuries started to heal, but reintroduction into civilian life was harder for him to manage. He felt adrift. The army had given Robbie a purpose.

At home, he realized that he hadn't entirely left the battlefield behind. Crowded places were sometimes difficult to deal with. His dreams were confusing and intense.

"Nighttime is when you can't really control much at all," he told me. "You don't know *what* you're doing."

Robbie began to drink to cope with the stress. It wasn't much, he told himself, just a few beers with friends, but it started to get out of control. After he got a DUI, he realized that something needed to change.

"A lot of these folks come, they're looking for hope, they're looking for a second chance," Chaplain Fisher said. "They want to be part of something bigger than themselves. And if you're looking to feel like you're part of something *bigger*, you can't get any bigger than being part of God's Kingdom. I mean, when you get here and you see Alaska, you see the mountains, you see the sky, you see the lake, you see all of that, you can't help but say, 'Man . . . This is *God* that created all of this.' "

That's exactly what Robbie thought when he saw Lake Clark for the first time, peering out the window of the small aircraft. But he'd also had a similar thought years ago, flying over a war zone. While you hardly ever see it on the news, parts of Afghanistan are *beautiful.*

"I mean, sometimes it's just super ugly," Robbie said. "And for a lot of guys, that's all they *can* see—their minds are in a certain place, and they've got a job to do. But there were moments for me when, all a sudden, I'd get to a point and . . . *wow*. I just thought, *somebody* had to put this here for a reason. To make these people have some kind of hope."

Jim uses Lake Clark's setting as part of his ministry. Psalm 23, the one about how "He makes me lie down in green pastures; He leads me beside still waters," features heavily in the week's teachings. A group walk through the woods, home to thousand-pound bears, leads to a lesson on the importance of sticking together. On the first day, Jim sends the couples out on the park's still waters in two-person kayaks.

"It's a bit of a setup, honestly," he admitted. "Kayaking makes you cooperate, and sometimes you'll see these couples come out of the water fuming and fussing with each other. We use that as a way to talk about communication."

You can't come to Samaritan Lodge solo; it's meant for married couples. There are daily seminars on love languages and communication strategies, and the couples spend time learning about their Myers-Briggs personality types.

For Robbie and his wife, Jackie, the seminars helped them work through some difficulties they'd been having. When I spoke with him by phone, he was already back home with Jackie in Colorado—we nearly overlapped in Lake Clark, but he'd left the park a week or so before I'd arrived. Jim had put us in touch.

"I know I'm not the most emotional guy," Robbie told me. "And sometimes my wife and I struggle to communicate. I guess we never talked much because of that. But that week really helped us. It gave us *time*. Time to focus on each other."

During free time, Robbie and Jackie would break off from the group and go on hikes together. They went bear-watching. There were no distractions to deal with. No crowds. They had *fun*.

Since Lake Clark doesn't get swamped with visitors (just twenty thousand or so a year), a ranger is generally available to come over each week and give a talk at the lodge. The presentation is purely secular NPS stuff—a talk on the park's history, answering questions about the wildlife—but it concludes with the ranger handing out lifetime Access Passes to the veterans, which get them into every national park for free. The passes—available to *any* American with a permanent disability—can be ordered by mail, but since almost all of the veterans who come to Samaritan Lodge qualify, the Park Service has decided to make it simple and just bring over a stack. For many of the vets, Lake Clark may be their first national park, but the message from the Park Service is, *We hope it won't be your last.*

Robbie and Jackie decided to get baptized in Alaska. They'd both been baptized before, when they were much younger, but this time they wanted to do it *together.* Surrounded by what Robbie described as "so much insane, secluded, untouched beauty," Lake Clark just seemed like the right place to do it.

So, on their second to last night at Samaritan Lodge, the couple walked out into the freezing-cold lake with Chaplain Jim. Waist-deep in the water of a national park, they looked up at the mountains and committed their lives to God.

John Muir wrote often of the metaphorical baptisms he experienced at Yosemite. Some days, the baptism arrived via waterfall, like the day he was "baptized in the irised foam" of towering Vernal Fall. Sometimes it arrived via light, like his baptism "in balmy sunshine that penetrated to my very soul." He dedicated his life to encouraging his fellow sinners to "come to the mountain baptisms" that he believed every trip to Yosemite provided.

In 1878, a group known as the Sunday School Union requested permission to build a chapel in Yosemite Valley. At the time of its construction, Galen Clark, one of the early "guardians" of Yosemite and a friend of Muir's, wrote that "it seems to me almost like a sacrilege to build a church within the portals of this grandest of all God's temples. It is like building a toy church within the walls of St. Peter's cathedral at Rome. But it will clearly show the contrast between the frail and puny works of man, as compared with the mighty grandeur and magnificence of the works of God, and I hope it will do good."

Over the years, the chapel has been relocated and restored, but its frame is still standing. It's the oldest structure in Yosemite Valley. Its bright-red wooden walls, light-yellow window trim, and prominent steeple pop out against the grove of trees surrounding it.

But on my visit, when I walked over to peek inside those windows, the church looked musty and depressing—just a few rows of pews leading up to a dark wooden altar and a cross. It was hard to understand why anyone would come to Yosemite to waste even a moment under those rafters. Just outside, Muir's beloved Sierra Nevada loomed, mountains "in whose light everything seems equally divine, opening a thousand windows to show us God." These days, I feel like *those* windows are where I'm more likely to catch a glimpse of a higher power.

I have fond memories of my formative years spent inside of churches, and I'm grateful for the community I met and the values I learned there. I've occasionally tried to recapture some of that as an adult—sporadically attending services in Los Angeles—but nothing has ever clicked. It was only now, during this year spent outside, that I found myself thinking more about God than I had in years.

Like Muir, I still mostly envision God through the lens of my Protestant upbringing. In its most basic sense, I'm drawn to spirituality for the same reason Chaplain Jim thinks that veterans need it in their lives: I want to feel connected to something greater than myself, and I do feel that. But I no longer think there's one specific path that leads to enlightenment or salvation.

I don't think Muir did, either. Except, perhaps, for the path of the trail itself. "The clearest way into the Universe is through a forest wilderness," he once wrote.

I don't know what, if anything, comes after this life. But I can tell you this: If there *is* a Heaven, I bet it looks a lot like Yosemite.

5

SOUND

(Great Sand Dunes, Katmai)

When the Great Sand Dunes first come into view, you're sure they're an illusion. A mistake, as if somehow two slides got stuck in the projector at the same time. The top half of the frame is filled with the snowcapped Sangre de Cristo Mountains, the southernmost range of the Rockies, dotted with clusters of spruce and pine. This is the Colorado you expect. But just below the mountains, it looks like the Sahara has been transposed onto the landscape. Rolling dune fields stretch out for miles and miles, whipped by the wind into new golden formations each day. It's a mash-up that doesn't compute, like a glacier suddenly appearing in the middle of the Everglades.

The visitor center had a display detailing how this miracle was made. I read it, and then, as I always do, I promptly forgot everything I had just learned. It's hard for the mind to comprehend complex processes that take place over millions of years. Or at least it's hard for my mind. My default explanation for any marvel of Mother Nature is generally "volcanoes and erosion and stuff," which tends to be right 90 percent of the time. Always bet on volcanoes.

A volcanic eruption in Colorado set all of this in motion thirty-five million years ago. Then some rare combination of wind and weather and streams and sediment created the dunes. The specifics beyond that are best left for those with a strong interest in geology. The little kids sledding down the sand in the distance didn't seem particularly concerned with *how* the dunes got here; they were just happy they'd found something soft and slippery to play on.

I could hear their screams of delight from the parking lot, which surprised me. The kids were hundreds of yards away, and yet I could make out most of their conversations. It was my first taste of how far sound travels in the dunes, and it was why I had traveled four hours south of Denver to experience them for myself. I'd been told this was the quietest place in the country.

Quiet can be difficult to quantify—it's easier to think of loud in relative terms. A rock concert is louder than a string quartet; a jet engine is louder than a car engine; the couple having sex on the other side of the hotel wall last night was louder than my TV, so I made my TV louder. Hope you like *Family Feud* reruns, lovebirds.

Loud is something we notice, whether it's a baby on a flight or an annoying laugh at a café. We plug our ears when we walk past the jackhammer on a New York City street. Loud *hurts*.

Quiet is subtler. It's relaxing. It can sneak up on us, but we also go looking for it. When we think of vacation, we think of getting a little peace and quiet.

But quiet isn't always peaceful, and too much silence can be unsettling. The park rangers here tell stories of city folk who freak out when they experience the extreme quiet of the dunes for the first time. The constant background noise they've grown accustomed to disappears, and it's terrifying. It's so quiet you can hear your heart beat.

Like most parks, Great Sand Dunes is positioned far away from the hustle and bustle of city life, but it's the sand that makes this park especially quiet. It absorbs the noise and deadens the sound.

The only two spots in the country where similar levels of silence have been measured are at Yellowstone in winter (the thick snow behaves much like the sand) and in the sound-sucking volcanic craters of Haleakalā National Park in Maui.

Scientist Kurt Fristrup is the man who does the measuring. As the chief of the Park Service Natural Sounds and Night Skies Division, he and his team set out audio equipment for thirty days. I was shocked to learn such a division even exists—I had never, no pun intended, heard of them. His small squad makes recordings of the parks, including Great Sand Dunes, which Kurt says is "noticeably quieter than the quietest recording studio you've ever been in."

He had come to show me how he collects his data, and we hiked together with a backpack full of gear to the top of a nearby dune. It was a more challenging climb than I had expected, made even harder by the thin Colorado air. With every step forward, we seemed to fall two steps back, the grains constantly sliding under our boots. There were no trails to follow—just sand—but Kurt seemed to have a destination in mind. He sped ahead while I awkwardly waddled after him, feeling like I was C-3PO chasing R2-D2 across Tatooine.

Eventually, he found a spot to place his microphones. As he set up, he told me about some of his "Greatest Hits."

While Kurt's gear is intended to record "typical" conditions—a general sense of the decibel level of a place—when his staff later scrubs through the monthlong recording in the lab, they occasionally stumble upon some pretty shocking sounds.

"I think it was a young black bear being weaned from its mother. It was a protest call," he told me wistfully, describing one of his favorite tracks as if it were the first Led Zeppelin chord he'd ever heard. A wolf pack hunting, elk bugling, lightning striking—Kurt has the most memorable sounds carefully categorized in a "best of" folder on his hard drive.

Occasionally, a curious creature will try to *eat* his equipment—those recordings are especially dramatic—but the microphone mostly goes unnoticed. Kurt has even collected and archived recordings of now *extinct* animals. It's one thing to look at a picture of a bird that no longer exists. It's another to hear the song it sang when it was alive.

Sometimes, the microphones will pick up humans—curious groups of hikers who have stumbled upon the odd-looking setup. A month later, Kurt will listen in on their conversations as they look at the equipment and marvel at why someone is recording what appears to be, well, *nothing*. From Kurt's perspective, it's weird that the hikers don't bring microphones of their own.

"Almost every visitor to a national park carries a camera and goes home with an image of the park," he said. "And I've often wondered why more people don't come to parks to make a recording of the park. Because, in some respects, sound evokes memory more powerfully than photos do."

I knew what Kurt meant. From the screech of a dial-up modem connecting to the opening chords of Pearl Jam's *Ten*, there are certain sounds that can instantly transport me back to a very specific place and time in my life. Talking with him, I was reminded of one of my favorite memories from childhood—a night when my parents attempted to re-create a magical memory of their own.

When I was seven years old, my favorite bedtime stories were tales of my parents' youth, of their courtship—dates to pep rallies and double features. It was fun to imagine their lives before we kids came along, full of adventure and root beer floats.

They were high school sweethearts, and whenever we'd drive around town, they would often point out locations from that chapter of their lives. There was the old store downtown where they once shopped for bell-bottoms, the bowling alley where the cool kids used to hang out after school. On one car trip, farther out of town, we passed an overgrown field. This, they said, was where they went to their first drive-in movie.

Whoa whoa *whoa*. A movie . . . in your *car*? How was this possible? I loved riding around in our station wagon, sitting up front and "helping" my dad shift gears, then sitting in the way back and making silly faces at the drivers behind us. Our family had only recently started going to movies in the theater—it was a special treat—but now I desperately wanted to see a movie in our car.

Sadly, by the late 1980s, drive-ins were in decline. The only one still open anywhere close to my home was showing R-rated horror movies—not exactly a night out for a family with three small kids. And that's really where my drive-in dream should have died.

But I kept asking about it—*tell me again about how you used to watch movies in a car.* It sounded so cool to me. And so, on one of the last nights of that summer, my parents decided to re-create a drive-in movie in our driveway.

I ran squealing outside to find a white bedsheet strung up across our garage. My dad had rented a sixteen-millimeter projector from the local library, along with some reels of old cartoons. Our Oldsmobile Cutlass was sitting down on the street. It's a *drive*-in, after all, not a park-in. To do the experience justice, it was determined that we actually needed to get in the car and pull up the driveway.

Our driveway was made of concrete but, on this night, it was covered in gravel. Earlier that day, my dad had gone to Lowe's to pick up a bag, and as the sun set he sprinkled the little rocks down our small hill. The sound—the little dings and pops—of gravel crunching under tires had stuck in my parents' brains for decades, ever since those date nights back in high school. For them, that noise was as much a part of the drive-in experience as were the buckets of popcorn my mom was filling upstairs. When it came time to pass on that memory to us, they wanted to pass on the sound.

I think about that night a lot—all of us laughing in the Oldsmobile, our neighbors wondering what on earth the crazy Knightons were up to this time. It's one of my favorite childhood memories, given new significance in adulthood as I've realized how hard my parents were trying to make summer special for us. I have no idea what cartoons we watched, but I'll never forget the sound of the gravel.

. . .

Sound does much more than trigger memories of the past. Our hearing is fine-tuned to alert us to potential dangers in the present. It is, as Fristrup told me, the "universal alerting sense."

While the world has gotten much safer for humans since we were hiding from lions in our caves, our prehistoric ears spring back into action when we lie awake at night, convinced a burglar or a ghost is traipsing around our kitchen. We're not afraid because we've seen something—we're afraid because we've heard it. Our ears put us on high alert.

The range of what our ears can detect—from the loudest loud to the quietest quiet—is remarkable. It's so vast that the decibel scale has to be logarithmic, just like the Richter scale, to even make sense of it. Just as a 6.0 earthquake is *ten* times stronger than a 5.0 quake, a lawn mower (ninety decibels) isn't one and a half times as loud as normal conversation (sixty decibels), it's 10^3, or a thousand times, louder. The loudest sound we can process—something like a jet plane taking off at close range—is one *trillion* times louder than the silence you might experience out here in the dunes.

Denver is home to the sixth busiest airport in the country, but wandering around the city a few days earlier, I was never aware of the aircraft that must have been flying above me. In the dunes, though—four hours from the city—I could hear small planes a hundred miles in the distance. I could hear cars ten minutes before I could see them driving down the road. They seemed louder than I was used to, but that was just a trick of the dunes. Everything else was so still and quiet, the new, disruptive sounds stood out.

That's what Kurt was worried about.

"The world is a much noisier place today than when I was a boy," he said. "I mean, to put a number on it, there are more than three times as many aircraft in the air today as there were in 1970. There's no place in the Lower 48 where you can go and not hear an aircraft every day."

Let that sink in for a second. A plane, every day, heard anywhere in the country. But the skies are actually the least of Kurt's concerns. Overall, air traffic isn't *that* disruptive to noise levels in a park. Automobile traffic is.

When John Muir first explored Yosemite, he did so on horseback. A few cars arrived in the early 1900s, but they weren't officially allowed in the park until 1913, when ranger Forest Townsley was issued the first automobile permit. Muir was none too pleased. "These useful, progressive, blunt-nosed mechanical beetles will hereafter be allowed to puff their way into all the parks and mingle their gas-breath with the breath of the pines and waterfalls," he wrote at the time. Muir died the next year. He didn't live to see the automobile explosion in the parks. Or perhaps more apt, he didn't live to *hear* it.

The revving of engines, the occasional honking of horns, a radio turned up a bit too loud—not only are these sounds annoying, they're harmful to wildlife. Imagine a bird in a tree, attempting to whistle its song. If the sound can't travel as far because of all of the cars traveling below, that bird isn't going to be able to find and seduce its mate. Animals that feed close to roadways may be scared away from their food source by all the noise, or perhaps they will be distracted from the threats that other animals present. Kurt told me about a study that had discovered that elk near the roadway at Grand Teton were less likely to exhibit defensive predator-detecting behavior due to the increased noise pollution there. For so many creatures, quiet can be the difference between life and death.

But at one park, I would learn, staying quiet might be what kills you.

As soon as my seaplane flight landed at Alaska's Katmai National Park, my fellow passengers and I were directed toward a small cabin near the dock for a mandatory "Bear School" orientation. There, a park ranger walked us through the bear basics: Always stay fifty yards away (even farther if you see a mother with her cubs), keep your food in lockers, don't run, and make a lot of noise while you hike. Bears have extremely sensitive hearing—twice as sensitive as ours—and given the chance, they'll generally scurry away if they hear us coming. The ranger recommended we hike in groups. I'd traveled to Katmai alone, so I'd just have to make extra noise.

In the cheesy welcome film, hikers with dated haircuts are seen meandering through the woods, periodically chanting "heeeeey bear." The video got a laugh, but as soon as we graduated from Bear School twenty minutes later, we were all out on the trail, doing the same damn thing. For days, that's all I'd hear: distant voices saying "hey bear, hey bear." It was more of a warning than a greeting, an alert to any of the thousands of bears that might be lurking in the woods.

Since bears do not speak English, literally any noise or sound would serve the same purpose. Singing a song, perhaps, or chanting the names of lesser-known U.S. vice presidents. *"Hannibal Hamlin!" "Schuyler Colfax!"* But everyone is so afraid of getting mauled that nobody wants to deviate even slightly from the protocol shown in the video. As a result, Katmai ends up resembling a summer camp for crazy people, its trails full of nervous adults clapping their hands while periodically talking to themselves.

Hey bear. Hey bear.

At Bear School, we also learned the difference between grizzly bears and brown bears. Grizzlies are considered a subspecies of browns and live in interior areas like Yellowstone. Brown bears, like the ones at Katmai, have access to coastal food sources and are typically bigger than grizzlies. Katmai's browns are *enormous.*

I stood with my fellow graduates on an elevated wooden platform next to a river as we stared, transfixed, at the thousand-pound creatures we had all come to see. Occasionally we would whisper to one another, but the hushed tones were unnecessary. As good as bears' ears might be, they couldn't hear us over the thundering rush of Brooks Falls.

The bears were clustered in the middle of the river, right up against the edge of the six-foot-high waterfall. They could definitely *see* us, peering at them through long camera lenses, but they hardly ever looked in our direction. They had more important things to worry about. It was lunchtime.

Every year, Katmai experiences what the rangers call a "predictable eruption." A million or more sockeye salmon swim from the Pacific Ocean into the rivers and lakes of the park, bound for the spawning ground of their birth. For over a month, it's a nonstop salmon flow, briefly turning the river into the bear equivalent of one of those sushi conveyor-belt restaurants.

Brooks Falls has appeared in countless televised nature documentaries and streams online twenty-four hours a day as the star of Katmai's summertime "Bear Cam." A couple dozen giant brown bears have been known to gather here at a time, mouths open wide, spending their midsummer days gnashing down on acrobatic salmon trying to fling themselves upstream.

The salmon are clearly the underdogs. Seemingly violating every law of nature and physics, the fish convulse in a way that sends them *flying through the air* while avoiding a gauntlet of razor-sharp teeth attached to creatures seventy times their size— all just to make it back to a home they haven't seen in years so they can give birth to their children. And yet, despite this admirable, incredible determination, everyone roots for the bears.

Pouncing on a salmon is like waiting for a pitch. A bear must swing and bite at just the right time, ignoring distractions that are too low or too fast or too high and outside. Salmon are slippery little fish and, even when caught, frequently wriggle free from claws and jaws. Whenever a bear nabbed a sockeye, the crowd erupted in cheers.

The two ladies in front of me, who had been on the platform for hours, told me they had nicknamed the largest bear "Scar Butt," thanks to a prominent scrape on his hindquarters. Scar Butt and two others were the only ones at the falls this afternoon. We were a few weeks past peak season, and most of the rest of the bears had already moved on to other feeding spots deeper in the park.

Watching Scar Butt on his endless quest for omega-3s, I realized he was my kind of bear—the kind of bear that knows it's best to shop for groceries late on a Tuesday night, not on a Saturday afternoon. His buddies had all left to check out a hip new restaurant on opening day, but he had hung back to keep fishing these falls, stuffing his face without having to worry about jostling for position. After a couple of hours of watching Scar Butt scarf down salmon, I started to get hungry myself and wandered back toward the dock.

There are two ways to stay at Katmai if you want to watch the bears. For over six hundred dollars a night, you can sleep at Brooks Lodge, a rustic collection of little cabins that's basically an expensive run-down 1950s fishing camp. You're paying for the location, and for the luxury of having wooden walls that separate you from the bears.

The other option is to camp for twelve dollars a night. That seemed more my speed.

I popped into the lodge for dinner, then decided to take a stroll before settling into my tent for the evening. The sun doesn't set until 10 P.M. at Katmai, so it was still plenty light as I walked down a trail toward what the brochure described as the "Cultural Site"— the foundation of a prehistoric home that proved humans lived on this island more than four thousand years ago.

On this night, though, I was the only human out wandering in the woods. But I was definitely not alone. As I rounded a blind corner, I almost slammed straight into two bear cubs.

As I gasped, I realized it was the first noise I had made in minutes. *Why hadn't I been chanting? Had I learned nothing at Bear School?*

I had been enjoying my peaceful after-dinner walk, but now, thanks to my stupidity and my silence, I was in danger of becoming dinner myself.

The cubs were sitting at the base of the sign marking the ruins, as if they were busy reading it. I instantly walked backward around the corner, not entirely sure if they had seen me or not. I didn't see a mother, but I knew she must be around somewhere. I crept backward, but I didn't run. Maybe she was watching me.

I had retreated fifty feet when she appeared. She was enormous, bursting at the seams after a summer of feeding on salmon. She slowly waddled toward me, but bears are deceptively quick—I knew that, in a second, she could easily close the gap between us if she wanted to. We locked eyes. *Wait, is that bad? I think that's bad.* I cast my eyes downward and spoke what I was convinced might be the last words I ever uttered.

"Hey bear. Hey bear."

She continued to advance as I backed away. I increased my volume.

"Heeeey bear. Heeeeyyyyy bear. Not looking for any trouble, bear."

I was stern but not shouting. I knew she was just protecting her children, and I needed her to know I had no interest in her or them. That I was just a dumb tourist, out for a stroll. I stepped back, stepped back again, and rounded another bend.

The second I was out of her sight, I quickened my pace. Still moving backward, but now at twice the speed, doing my best to put some distance between me and the bear. Although, for all I knew, I could have been speed-walking right back into *another* bear. Scar Butt could be waiting right behind me, ready to scar my butt beyond all recognition. I was frantically swiveling my head, stumbling backward, and clapping. I looked nothing less than insane.

I eventually made it back to my campground unharmed. The entire area was surrounded by an electric fence, the only one I'd ever seen in a national park. At Katmai, there are just too many bears in too concentrated of an area, so the fence is necessary as a deterrent.

And that's really all it is—a deterrent. The fence is far from bear *proof.* A determined, hungry thousand-pound mammal could easily force its way inside. Earlier that day, when I'd registered for my camping permit, the ranger had mentioned that I'd basically have the place to myself. I remembered how excited I'd been about the privacy, as I set up my new tent as far away from the other three occupied sites as I could. Now I was wishing I'd pitched it right next to them, surrounding myself with folks who were hopefully more delicious.

I tried to remind myself that, in reality, a bear attack is *extremely* unlikely. There has only been one fatal mauling incident in the park's entire history. You may have heard about it. The Los Angeles Film Critics Association proclaimed it the best documentary of 2005.

Werner Herzog's documentary *Grizzly Man* tells the story of Timothy Treadwell, a self-described eco-warrior who left Malibu to go live with the bears of Alaska. For thirteen summers, Treadwell camped deep in Katmai National Park. He did not hide from the bears. He sought them out.

Treadwell would camp right in the middle of bear country, way farther in than any tourist would typically go. He saw the bears as perfect creatures, giving them silly names like Cupcake, Booble, and Rowdy. He would spend his days filming them obsessively with his camcorder, occasionally interspersing straight-to-camera monologues about his days in the wild. Despite receiving multiple warnings from the Park Service to leave the bears alone, many of Treadwell's self-shot clips show him sleeping near the animals, kissing their mouths, and roughhousing with them.

In October 2003, when pilot Willy Fulton came to pick up Treadwell and his girlfriend, Amie Huguenard, from their Katmai campsite, he saw that it was deserted, save for one bear roaming around. Fulton called the Park Service, who ventured out to the location and quickly discovered that their long-held fears had finally come true. Treadwell and Huguenard were dead—dismembered and eaten by a bear.

Officers discovered Treadwell's camera at the gruesome scene. It had been recording during the attack, but there was no video on the tape. The image was dark, the lens cap likely left on. All that remained was the sound.

"They're both screaming, she's telling him to play dead, then it changes to fighting back. He asks her to hit the bear," Alaska State Trooper Chris Hill told reporters after listening to the tape. To this day, it has never been released to the public.

"There's so much noise going on. I don't know what's him and what might be an animal," Hill went on. "It's pretty disturbing. I keep hearing it in my mind."

Jewel Palovak has never listened to the tape, but, as the executor of Treadwell's estate, she has the original copy. In *Grizzly Man*, she agrees to let Herzog hear it through headphones. This listening session is captured on camera, but the audience only sees the back of Herzog's head and can only hear his stunned reaction as he presses play on what may be the most chilling bit of audio ever recorded in a national park.

"I hear rain and I hear, 'Amie, get away . . . go away.'" Then Herzog suddenly stops narrating. He listens a bit longer, appears to tremble, and asks Palovak to turn off the tape. He takes off the headphones and looks straight into her eyes. Whatever she sees in Herzog's face makes her start to sob.

"Jewel," he says. "You must *never* listen to this."

"I know, Werner. I'm never going to."

Lying inside my tent in the Katmai campground, I noticed my ears had gone into overdrive. With just a thin layer of nylon separating me from whatever might be outside, I studied the creak of every branch and the snap of every twig. Kurt was right—hearing *is* the universal alerting sense, but I hadn't fully relied on mine for so long that it was hard to make out what were just normal nature sounds and what might be a signal of danger.

When the first drop of rain hit my tent's roof, I nearly jumped up right through it. But as more and more arrived, I sat back as I recognized the familiar sound of a sudden shower. Their pitter-patter on my rooftop was comforting—just the noise I needed to quiet my mind.

As the drops bounced off the tent's taut domed ceiling, then drizzled down to thud softly on the leaves below, I listened to the storm in stereo, completely tuned in to its constantly improvising melody. There were no sirens, no cars, no hum of an air conditioner to distract me. When I think back to that night, the sound is what I remember most: the rhythm of a thousand tiny raindrops as I drifted off to sleep.

6

TREES

(Joshua Tree, Sequoia,
Kings Canyon, Redwood)

The Joshua tree is not really a tree. Which is a "fun fact" that's not really fun.

It's like when someone points out that raspberries aren't actually berries, or that peanuts aren't actually nuts. It's just . . . *annoying*. For the briefest of moments, the scientific technicalities are interesting—raspberries are disqualified because they're the fruit of a flower with more than one ovary; peanuts, because they're legumes that grow underground—but it's not like you're going to start excluding them from bowls of mixed berries or mixed nuts anytime soon. So for all practical purposes, the Joshua tree—technically the Joshua monocot, a *Yucca brevifolia*—is a tree. It's just a really, really weird-looking one.

"Their stiff and ungraceful form makes them, to the traveler, the most repulsive tree in the vegetable kingdom." That's how explorer John C. Frémont described his first encounter with a Joshua tree in 1844. Turns out not every traveler agreed with him. Nearly three million visitors a year flock to Joshua Tree National Park to gawk at these monstrosities.

The tree's name is said to have been bestowed by early Mormon settlers, who thought that its writhing arms, stretched to the heavens, resembled Joshua from the Bible. I didn't quite see it, but I could see why modern visitors frequently assume they're looking at the inspiration for the bushy, bending "Truffula Trees" chopped down in Dr. Seuss's *The Lorax*.

"Unfortunately, we have no evidence Dr. Seuss ever used the Joshua tree as a model," explained ranger George Land as we drove through the park's 790,000 acres together. With his wide, smiling face and thick, white mustache, George kind of looked like *he* could have been the inspiration for the Lorax. They certainly had similar job descriptions: George was the public information officer for the park. Or, as the Lorax might say, "I speak for the trees! I speak for the trees because the trees have no tongues!"

There are thousands of trees at the park, but according to George, visitors always ask about one in particular. It was a question I'd asked as well—I'd wondered if we might be able to see the Joshua tree from *The Joshua Tree*, the 1987 U2 album. Unfortunately, George told me "I Still Haven't Found What I'm Looking For." The legendary album photo was actually taken two hundred miles away, closer to Death Valley. That Joshua tree died years ago.

Still, sunny California is home to plenty of other *celebritrees*. But unless you somehow bribe a botanist, you're not likely to get anywhere close to most of the megastars. To protect them from paparazzi, their locations are carefully guarded secrets.

Deep inside of Redwood National Park's 139,000 acres, midway between San Francisco and Portland, hides magnificent Hyperion. Named after the Greek Titan god of heavenly light, Hyperion literally means "the high one." Of the more than three trillion trees on earth, it is the absolute *highest* one. Towering more than 379 feet tall, Hyperion was discovered and measured in 2006. It's still growing. When biologists realized what a beast it was, they decided not to publicize its whereabouts. A massive influx of tourists might damage the surrounding soil.

California is also home to the world's oldest tree—another

scientist-kept secret. Somewhere in the White Mountains, there's Methuselah, a twisted bristlecone pine confirmed by a core sample to be nearly five thousand years old. It started growing before the Pyramids were built. It had already turned two thousand by the time Christ walked the earth.

There are rumors of a tree in the White Mountains that's even older than Methuselah, although its location has been kept secret as well. There are *lots* of old trees in the mountains—even if you were standing right beside the oldest, you'd have no idea it was the one. Age on the inside isn't always apparent on the outside. Just ask Keanu Reeves.

So while I have never laid eyes on the world's oldest tree or the world's tallest—and likely never will—I have seen the world's *largest*. That tree is impossible to miss—there's a path leading right to its base.

As I started down Big Trees Trail, I wondered if Sequoia National Park had ever considered naming their well-known hike something else. Something a little more poetic or majestic, like "Path of the Titans" or "Wooden Walkway" or "Sentinel Lane." But I quickly realized they were right to keep it simple. A few steps in, and literally all I could think was, *Holy mother of Groot, these are some big trees.*

Sequoias are the biggest trees in the entire world when measured by volume. All around me, enormous orange-brown trunks poked out of the California soil like some experiment gone wrong. They were supersized plants, blown up to proportions that didn't seem possible. Even their scientific name doesn't beat around the bush: *Sequoiadendron giganteum.* Giant sequoia.

In 1852, a man named Augustus T. Dowd had stumbled across a similar grove of giant sequoias in Northern California. He had a difficult time getting anyone to believe his story—none of the prospectors in the nearby mining town had ever heard of trees so massive. Dowd eventually dragged his friends back into the forest, thus kicking off what would become a wave of big-tree tourism and subsequent destruction—it only took a year before the largest sequoia was chopped down. It was known as the Discovery Tree, and five men spent twenty-two days sawing away at its trunk. Afterward, its massive stump was turned into a dance floor—weddings and fancy cotillion balls were held on top of what remained. People literally danced on its grave.

"Any fool can destroy trees," John Muir wrote in *Our National Parks*. "They cannot run away; and if they could, they would still be destroyed—chased and hunted down as long as fun or a dollar could be got out of their bark hides, branching horns, or magnificent bole backbones."

It wasn't long before California settlers found groves of even more impressive sequoias. Logging operations set up shop in their midst, and the giants came thundering down. While most sequoias were cut for lumber, a few of the trees were felled to serve as traveling attractions, reassembled for tourists across the country. The bark of a sequoia called the Mother of the Forest was stripped and shipped off to London in 1856 so that we could brag to the British. The Brits thought it was a scam.

"The English who saw it declared it to be a Yankee invention, made from beginning to end; that it was an utter untruth that such trees grew in the country," California senator John Conness said in a speech on the Senate floor in 1864. "Although the section of the tree was transported there at an expense of several thousand dollars, we were not able to convince them that it was a specimen of American growth."

The skepticism was understandable. Here I was, *surrounded* by such giant trees, and I still couldn't believe they existed.

Conness instead suggested that perhaps the mightiest thing America could do with our newfound giants, our "magnificent monarchs of the forest," would be to *save* them. He had identified a sequoia grove on the land that would eventually become Yosemite National Park. "The necessity of taking early possession and care of these great wonders can easily be seen and understood,"

Conness argued. His colleagues agreed. In the midst of the Civil War, Abraham Lincoln signed the Yosemite Grant Act.

Not surprisingly, Sequoia National Park—created in 1890 to combat "the rapid destruction of timber" still occurring in California—contains an *especially* impressive collection of its namesake tree. The act establishing the park proclaimed the sequoias "wonders of the world," and after a half-mile walk down Big Trees Trail, I finally found myself at the base of the world's largest tree: the General Sherman.

Named after Civil War general William Tecumseh Sherman, the General Sherman is the largest living *thing* in the world. It's massively thick—52,508 cubic feet, with a width of over 36 feet at its base. It's 274.9 feet high. I eventually gave up on trying to get a picture of the top and bottom in the same frame—it was impossible.

At its base, a sign attempted to put Sherman's size in perspective. "Looking up at the General Sherman Tree for a six-foot-tall human is about the equivalent of a mouse looking up at the six-foot-tall human," it said.

The night before, I'd encountered a mouse scurrying around the musty mountain cabin I'd rented for the weekend. If only I had thought of myself as a mighty sequoia, I might not have jumped so high or screamed so loudly.

I was staying sixteen miles away from the General Sherman, near a tree once *thought* to be the world's largest—the General Grant. One week after Sequoia National Park was established, General Grant National Park was created to protect another grove of giants. Expanded and renamed King's Canyon in the 1940s, today the park is comanaged alongside Sequoia.

At forty feet in diameter, the General Grant tree remains the world's *widest* known sequoia. As I took a lap around its trunk, I noticed its battle scars. A large swath of the backside of the tree had been blackened by fire.

Fortunately, sequoias' tough bark contains a natural flame retardant. I'd seen similar markings on trees throughout the grove—it appeared as if most had survived multiple blazes. In fact, fire is *necessary* for their survival—the heat dries and opens sequoia cones so that seeds can fall out onto the freshly cleared underbrush. There, after the fire has passed through, they have a fresh chance to grow.

Not a very good chance, mind you. Any given sequoia seed has around a one in a *billion* shot at turning into a mature tree. General Grant himself never fought a battle with such miserable odds.

But for the rare trees that *do* take root and soar skyward, the hardest part of their lives is behind them. Mature sequoias are hard to kill—they live for thousands of years, largely immune to usual suspects like insects, fungi, and fire. The only real threat the trees lack a natural defense for is *us*.

Just down the road from General Grant Grove is a place known as "Big Stump Grove," the former site of the Smith Comstock Mill. There, massive stumps line a two-mile trail, remnants of the giants that once towered over the meadow. While few tourists ever visit this part of the park, it should be a requirement. Walking past the stumps felt like walking through a cemetery—seeing what had been lost helped me appreciate what had been saved.

In a 1966 speech before the Western Wood Products Association, gubernatorial candidate Ronald Reagan famously mocked the majesty of California's redwoods.

"You know, a tree is a tree—how many more do you need to look at?"

He was playing to his base. Or rather, his stump. The lumber industry was vehemently opposed to the creation of Redwood National Park.

By the 1960s, logging had already wiped out 90 percent of California's original redwoods—the thinner, taller cousins of the sequoias. Fortunately, some of most impressive groves had been safeguarded years earlier in a series of state parks by the Save the

Redwoods League, an organization formed in 1918 after scientists noticed how quickly the ancient giants were disappearing.

But World War II, and the construction boom that followed, had increased the demand for lumber. The Sierra Club and the National Geographic Society started campaigning heavily for the federal government to step in and set aside even *more* land. Finally, in 1968, Redwood National Park was established.

As I walked down one of the park's trails, it felt like I'd entered a cathedral nave. More densely packed than the sequoias, the giant redwood pillars stretched heavenward on each side of me, effectively blocking most sun and sound from penetrating deep into the forest. If the sequoias were generals, then the redwoods were the army—a massive brigade that seemed to function as one. That's what was most awe-inspiring about them. There weren't just a few giant trees—they were *everywhere*.

"How many more do you need to look at?" All of them. That's the point.

Walking underneath the towering redwoods, I felt I was being watched. Not by another person—it was a deserted, foggy weekday morning—but by the ancient trees themselves. Of all the sights I've seen at national parks—stalactites and geysers and waterfalls and arches—trees are the only ones I've ever felt see me back.

Trees that were present for significant historical events are known as "witness trees." There are oaks in Pennsylvania that saw the Battle of Gettysburg. Magnolia trees on the south side of the White House have watched more than thirty-nine presidential administrations. The Park Service has identified a series of historic trees around D.C. as part of its Witness Tree Protection Program.

From the fighting apple trees of *The Wonderful Wizard of Oz* to Treebeard from *The Lord of the Rings*, we imagine trees as having not just sight and memory, but personalities. We name them after our heroes, from generals to Joshua. We speak of our own lives on their terms—we put down *roots*, we chart our *family tree*. We see faces in their trunks and arms in their branches. My body is 60

percent water, yet I do not feel any kinship with a lake. For whatever reason, I feel that connection with a *tree*.

I wonder if it's all just wishful thinking. Who *wouldn't* want to
be like a tree? Stately and generous, strong and unshakable. The
hero of *The Giving Tree* is the tree, after all. That's who we all
want to be. Even if, deep down, we know we're the boy.

Lately, there's been lots of scientific interest in how trees might
"talk" to each other. Studies have demonstrated how certain trees
can communicate via electrical impulses in their roots. In his bestselling book *The Hidden Life of Trees*, German forester Peter
Wohlleben calls this a "wood wide web."

As I walked through the redwood grove, eyes to the sky, I was
passing over a vast, unseen root network buried just a few feet
below the surface. For such tall trees, redwoods have surprisingly
shallow roots. But the roots are *wide*—they can stretch for hundreds of feet, intermingling with the roots of neighboring trees.

Whether or not they were gossiping about me underground, I'll
never know. But back at the visitor center, I learned of a much
more practical purpose for the long roots. Even though the tall redwoods are constantly at risk of toppling over, they rarely do, thanks
to a little help from their friends. The trees lock their roots together under the soil and hold each other tight.

That may be their most human quality of all. Like us, the trees
are stronger together than they are on their own.

When President Lyndon Johnson signed the bill establishing Redwood National Park, he remarked, "It is a great victory for every
American in every state, because we have rescued a magnificent
and a meaningful treasure from the chain saw. For once we have
spared what is enduring and ennobling from the hungry and hasty
and selfish act of destruction."

Fortunately, Johnson was exaggerating. These types of victories
have happened far more than just *once*. That's the story of our na-

tional parks, after all—each one is an example of how we have fought against our selfish, destructive impulses.

To save one tree—to save thousands—shows restraint. That makes them easily identifiable symbols of the responsibility that comes with our power. It is no coincidence that the most prominent feature on the arrowhead logo of the Park Service is a towering green sequoia. Look closely at a park ranger's "flat hat"—the iconic Stetson that's been part of the uniform since the 1920s—and you'll notice the brown leather band is adorned with two gold sequoia cones.

When advocating for the sequoias, Muir once wrote, "God has cared for these trees, saved them from drought, disease, avalanches, and a thousand storms; but he cannot save them from sawmills and fools; this is left to the American people."

If nature has a soul, it feels like it must be bound up in the bark and sap of our forests. There, older, wiser sentinels stand in silent judgment. Not just the ancient sequoias and redwoods—even regular pine and birch trees outlast us. *Every* tree is a witness tree—they see how we spend our time on earth, what we take and what we give.

7

MYSTERY

(Crater Lake, Congaree)

It wasn't that long ago when the rising of the sun, the lightning in the sky, the changing of the leaves, and the age of the earth itself were all mysteries to us. We would marvel at birds flying overhead without understanding the mechanics that made their flight possible, and we would die from illnesses brought on by microscopic killers we never thought to look for. We developed myths and legends and religions to explain our largely unexplainable world.

These days, it feels as if we're living in a world of know-it-alls—every question about our natural world has a neat and tidy answer. I think that's why, whenever we occasionally come across something that Google has no answer for, it fascinates us even more. There are fewer and fewer mysteries left to solve.

South Carolina's Congaree National Park is a park full of mystery. It is also full of mosquitoes. When I walked up to Congaree's visitor center, the first thing I noticed was a "mosquito meter" on the wall that tracks how bad the bloodsucking swarms are on a given day. The options:

1. All Clear
2. Mild
3. Moderate
4. Severe
5. Ruthless
6. WAR ZONE

Fortunately, I visited Congaree on a "mild" day. The park protects the country's largest remaining tract of old-growth bottomland forest, but the surrounding swamp (technically a "floodplain," the park emphasizes) can get very buggy very quickly.

While the lack of mosquitoes was welcome news, I was disappointed to learn I'd arrived slightly too early to catch a glimpse of another flying insect: *fireflies.*

Congaree is one of very few places in the world where you can witness the mysterious phenomenon of synchronous fireflies. Every year, for two weeks in the early summer, Congaree's floodplain lights up with the glow of thousands of tiny flickers, all pulsating at once. It's the most popular event at this relatively unpopular park—families will head out onto the trail at twilight, waiting for the magic show to switch on.

Even to biologists, that's what it feels like—*magic.* Nobody has any idea why the fireflies do this, although there are a number of theories. In most species of fireflies, flashing is thought to be a mating ritual—males repeatedly flash females to get their attention. (Don't try this at home.)

But why do the fireflies at Congaree flash *simultaneously?* There's speculation the males have synced up their mating Morse code so that females can spot them more easily. There's also a theory that this could just be a mistake. The males, all doing their best to stand out and flash *first*, have somehow accidentally ended up flashing in unison, each one now indistinguishable from the next. It's kind of like how nobody had that "long on top, shaved sides" haircut and then, all of a sudden, everyone did.

When I passed through Columbia, South Carolina, en route to

the park, I had seen a sign for their brand-new minor-league base-ball team: the Columbia Fireflies. (The team had just transferred from Savannah, where they—no joke—played as the Savannah *Sand Gnats.*) From the unpredictable timing of when the fireflies might sync up each year to the unexplained nature of what, ex-actly, they are doing out there in the woods, the bugs had capti-vated the local imagination.

Even without the fireflies, Congaree was an eerily enigmatic place. As I squished along the muddy trails, keeping an eye out for the water moccasins and copperheads I knew were common in the area, it felt like I'd entered *A Nightmare on Cypress Street.* The park is straight-up spooky.

Throughout the floodplain, misshapen knobs known as knees pushed out of the ground, like oversized versions of the sprouts you might find growing out of an old potato. The knees of Congaree's bald cypress trees are part of their root system. Pointing straight toward the sky, their stalks looked more like fingers than knees—weird little demon hands clawing their way out of the soil.

In 1819, botanist François André Michaux described cypress knees as "conical protuberances, commonly from eighteen to twenty-four inches, and sometimes four or five feet in thickness . . . No cause can be assigned for their existence." Amazingly, two cen-turies later, we *still* don't have a better explanation. Theories range from gas absorption (the root system for the cypress is generally underwater, so the knees poke up to grab some extra oxygen) to stability, adding some needed support in the squishy conditions, but scientists have never quite solved it. The knees were the ap-pendix of the plant world—perhaps they had an evolutionary pur-pose, or maybe they just existed to be weird-looking.

In their knots, I saw noses and lips—*is that one grinning at me?*—and the way they were clustered, in family-style groupings, made them look like a village of wooden trolls, ready to wrap around my ankles and drag me under the standing water. I fell in love with their strangeness, snapping picture after picture. In the absence of any concrete explanation for why the knees existed, I was able to ascribe all sorts of qualities to them—imagining powers and motives they might possess. Less than two feet tall, they somehow felt like they controlled the entire forest.

Around me, I heard subtle splashes and creaks, although I never whipped around quite fast enough to catch what was making the noises. In the distance, I could hear what sounded like the rapid-fire drill of a woodpecker at work. I wondered if it might be the ivory-billed woodpecker, a bird that was thought to have gone extinct, but now, according to some hopeful ornithologists, might still be alive. Nobody quite knows.

The only definitive footage of an ivory-billed woodpecker was shot in the 1930s. Decades would pass in between sightings. In 1994, the International Union for Conservation of Nature officially declared the bird extinct. But years later, they revised their assessment. Extinct animals don't come back from the dead, but perhaps this one had? People kept claiming they were seeing and hearing the woodpecker.

Various teams of researchers have captured what they claim is proof of the bird's existence—distant glimpses on video or possible birdcalls heard on audio recordings. Before he joined the Park Service, Kurt Fristrup—the scientist I'd met at Great Sand Dunes—had worked with a team at Cornell University that had collected hundreds of thousands of hours of audio recordings, searching for the woodpecker. Years ago, Kurt had come here, to Congaree, where the birds once lived, and set up his microphones.

He told me the material he recorded back then has only been partially skimmed—there's just too much to listen to. He still wonders if, somewhere in those recordings, a few seconds of an ivory-billed woodpecker's call might be hiding.

The woodpecker is like a birder's Bigfoot—tourists armed with zoom lenses have hunted for it across the Southeast, following leads that sometimes sound more like legends. After a kayaker claimed to have seen one near Brinkley, Arkansas, the town started marketing itself as "the home of the ivory-billed woodpecker," selling woodpecker merchandise to the visitors who had flocked there in search of the elusive, allegedly extinct bird.

A good mystery is hard to resist. In 1853, a mystery in the Oregon mountains led a group of treasure hunters to a priceless find: a place so beautiful, it became one of our earliest national parks.

Lost gold was the bitcoin of the 1800s, and everyone wanted in, no matter how ridiculous the story. When a group of Californians heard rumors that there might be a cabin full of lost gold just beyond Medford, Oregon, they headed north.

On their journey, they stopped at a local bar. After a few too many shots, one loose-lipped prospector accidentally spilled the beans about his group's covert mission. A gang of greedy Oregonians overheard him.

As soon as the Californians headed off into the mountains, the Oregonians organized their own squad and followed close behind. For days, they played what was later described by Oregon prospector J. W. Hillman as "a game of hide and seek."

As the gold hunt dragged on and both groups ran low on supplies, Hillman eventually approached the Californians he was tailing and suggested that the two groups split the profits. But even after they joined forces, the combined team never did find any gold. Instead, they unexpectedly stumbled upon a massive expanse of *blue*.

High up on Mount Mazama, surrounded by steep black slopes of cooled lava, they saw a giant pristine bowl of unbelievably bright-blue water, glistening in the Oregon sun.

"Every man of the party gazed with wonder at the sight before him," Hillman later wrote. The lake they had found was massive—six miles across—and yet none of the men, not even the Oregonians, had any idea it was up there. It wasn't a true discovery—the local Klamath tribes certainly knew of the lake—but Hillman's expedition marked the first written account.

"We discussed what name we should give the lake. There were many names suggested, but Mysterious Lake and Deep Blue Lake were most favorably received," Hillman wrote. "On a vote, Deep Blue Lake was chosen."

That name proved to be more accurate than the men could have possibly known. With a depth of 1,949 feet, Deep Blue Lake was the deepest lake in the entire country.

By the time William Gladstone Steel read about Deep Blue Lake, it had been renamed Crater Lake.

Every day before heading off to school in Kansas, Steel would wrap his lunches in newsprint, never quite knowing what bit of random knowledge he'd end up getting along with his sandwich. One day in 1870, when Steel was just fifteen years old, he came across a small article at lunchtime describing a sunken lake that had recently been discovered in Oregon. Decades later, at a national parks conference in D.C., Steel recalled how what he'd read that fateful day changed his life:

> It was said to be 5,000 feet below the surface of the surrounding country, with vertical walls, so that no human body could reach the water. In its center was an island 1,500 feet high, with an extinct crater. In all my life I never read an article that took the intense hold on me that that one did and I then and there determined to go to Oregon and to visit that lake and to go down to the water.

When Steel arrived in Oregon two years later, it took him ages to find anyone else who had even *heard* of Crater Lake.

> I was told there was something of the sort in southern Oregon, but my informer was not sure. Nine years later, I found a man who had actually seen it and gave me a good description of it that greatly increased my desire to see it.

Finally, in 1885, Steel was able to make it to southern Oregon to see Crater Lake for himself. Even after so much anticipation, it was more beautiful than he could have imagined.

On the west side of the lake, Steel noticed an oddly shaped island. It was a volcanic cinder cone, with a pointy top stretching 755 feet above the lake's surface and an unseen bottom extending all the way down to the caldera's floor. The conical island, covered in hemlock trees, had merited a small mention in the article Steel had read as a child, but it was not given a name. Steel decided to call it Wizard Island. The very tippity-top had been indented, a mini crater he named Witches' Cauldron.

Steel, who later served as the first president of the Oregon Geographic Names Board, seemed to revel in putting a bit of mystery in "Mysterious Lake." He named a rocky island on the southeast end Phantom Ship. Depending on the fog and the position of the sun, its jagged ridgeline sometimes disappeared from view. Steel had a marketer's eye, and he knew that ghost ships and wizard hats and witches' cauldrons would help add to the lake's mystical allure as he worked to sell Congress on his master plan—he intended to make Crater Lake a national park.

Steel's plan succeeded—Crater Lake became a park in 1902. That same year, the park's first geologist, Joseph Diller, wrote about a tree that he had noticed floating around the lake in an "erect position." He described the bobbing log as "a spectacle curious enough to excite the imagination."

It certainly was curious. The physics of it all didn't seem possible. Wood was supposed to float horizontally. But somehow, this one piece defiantly shot straight up toward the sky. And it *moved*. In a single day, the log would travel miles across the lake. Year after year, it refused to sink. Eventually, park rangers gave Diller's log a name: the Old Man. The stump just seemed like one of those things that must have *always* been old, like Morgan Freeman or Maggie Smith.

Eventually, word of the possessed stump in southern Oregon reached Washington, D.C., and a request was made for a formal study of its movements. In the summer of 1938, scientists at the park decided to track the log's path. For three months, its every movement was, for lack of a better word, *logged.*

The park published the findings in that fall's edition of *Nature Notes:* "During the period of observation 'The Old Man' traveled a total minimum of 62.1 miles, the distance between locations being measured in straight lines as indicated on the sketches." A map also showed the Old Man zigging and zagging across the water, seemingly at random, as if he had a mind of his own.

Despite all of the pictures I'd seen, nothing had prepared me for how jaw-droppingly blue Crater Lake was. When I arrived at the lake's dock to meet Mark Buktenica, the park's aquatic ecologist, I first had to scoop a handful of water out just to confirm that the liquid *itself* was not actually blue. Miraculously, the water in my hand appeared to be just as clear as water you can find anywhere else—or clearer, it turns out. A sign at the visitor center explained that the water's remarkable clarity allows sunlight to penetrate so far into Crater Lake's depths that the longer wavelengths of light get absorbed and shorter wavelengths—like blue—get reflected back to the surface. It was the bluest lake I'd ever seen.

Mark had agreed to take me out in search of the Old Man. A century after he was first documented, the Old Man is still careening across the lake. The park's research and tour boats stay in radio contact with one another, so they can keep tabs on where the Old Man has wandered off to each day. They don't want to accidentally crash into him.

"Yesterday, he was seen over by Pumice Castle," Mark told me, pointing in the direction of a bright orange-brown rock formation on the east rim of the lake. "So we'll try over there first. But I'm not sure exactly where we'll find him."

While Crater Lake can be admired from its rim year-round, there's only a brief season in which the lake itself is accessible, thanks to the long-lasting high-elevation snows. Mark is typically the first person out on the water each June, making him the first one to sight the lake's cantankerous wooden guardian.

"Every year there's a little bit of anticipation when we come out on the lake for the first time," he said. "And for the last two years, we went two weeks before we saw the Old Man. So . . . by the end of the two weeks, we were all a little bit anxious."

After a lengthy search around the lake, Mark and I finally found where the Old Man had been hiding. He was hugging the shoreline, perhaps feeling a little camera-shy. We pulled up alongside so I could pay my respects. As I tapped him gently on the head, a little spider peeked out of one of his cracks. She had been enjoying a free shuttle ride across the water.

Park Service VIPs used to get their pictures taken standing on the Old Man, although everyone is too nervous to do that now—whatever might be keeping him upright could shift. A day may come soon when the Old Man doesn't show up during the summer. When he finally decides to retire.

"That will be a sad, sad day," Mark said.

Mark clearly had a soft spot for the Old Man. When I referred to him as a stump, he took offense.

"I don't . . . *love* that term," he protested. "*Stump* seems a little degrading."

Mark had reason to be reverent. In 1988, he and a crew of researchers camped out on Wizard Island, working around the clock collecting water and sediment samples. Mark was one of just three people who got to pilot a one-man submarine, a revolutionary "Deep Rover" that allowed him to travel all the way to the lake's bottom to collect rocks and take photos.

At night, as the submarine batteries charged, another team would speed across the lake on a boat, collecting water samples using other specialized equipment. Time was of the essence, and it was difficult to navigate in the darkness. There was no way of knowing where the unpredictable Old Man might be. He had been hanging out on the eastern shore in the morning, but he could have decided to take a midnight stroll.

"You would think that the four feet above the water would act as a little sail and guide him around the lake," Mark said. "But sometimes he'll move all the way across the lake *against* the wind."

To make sure that nobody would accidentally crash into the Old Man, the crew decided to temporarily tie him up to the shore.

He didn't take kindly to the restraints.

"It wasn't long after he was tied up that a storm blew in," Mark remembered. "And the surface of the lake got too rough for us to deploy and recover the submarine."

It was August, and yet it had suddenly started *snowing* at Crater Lake. The entire expensive expedition was put on hold. As the storm raged, a thought crept into the minds of some of the scientists—a thought they dare not say aloud, because it sounded so unscientific. *Could... could the Old Man have something to do with this?*

It seemed ridiculous—no stump can control the weather—and yet the tied-up tree was the only variable that had changed.

"So our senior scientists at the time, Dr. Collier and Dr. Diamond, went out quietly one evening and released the Old Man from his bondage," Mark said.

As soon as the Old Man went back to freely roaming around the lake, the clouds broke and the weather returned to normal. *Probably* all just a coincidence, right? But nobody has ever tied up the Old Man again.

"What I really love about that story is that it shows that even scientists don't know what they don't know," Mark said, laughing.

There is still a surprising amount we don't know about the Old Man. We don't even know exactly what kind of tree he is. He's *probably* a mountain hemlock, but that's never been officially confirmed. A few years back, Mark was able to carbon-date a piece that had fallen off the Old Man—he now estimates the tree is over 450 years old. But in terms of the biggest mystery—why and how the log has stayed floating upright for all these years—*nobody* really knows.

The most popular theory is that rocks were once tangled in the

Old Man's roots, waterlogging the bottom part of the tree while the sun dried out the top. I asked Mark what *he* thought had happened.

"I've heard explanations," Mark said. "Some of 'em could be plausible. But not really testable."

Doesn't that bother him as a scientist? Not knowing?

"I think, maybe some questions should remain unanswered," he said. "Maybe it's part of the human condition to believe in a little bit of mystery and the interconnectedness of all things."

Scientific explanations can be awe inspiring. The true story of how a hemlock grows from a seed to a sapling, sprouts branches and leaves, and uses sunlight to transform carbon dioxide into the oxygen that we breathe is more spectacular than anything we could dream up. It's evidence of the "interconnectedness of all things" that Mark thinks we all want to believe in. But we also want to believe in mystery, and that's harder to do as we explain away more and more of our world.

The Old Man is old school in that respect. A plucky little piece of wood with a personality and powers that we can't quite describe—and don't really want to. He's a reminder that sometimes, it's fun . . . to be stumped.

8

BORDERS

(Big Bend, American Samoa)

Every day, more than eighty thousand people cross between El Paso, Texas, and Juarez, Mexico. But head close to 350 miles southeast, and the border has a bit of a different feel.

Fewer than *forty* people a day cross between the United States and Boquillas del Carmen, Mexico. The all-time record is 427—more than the entire population of Boquillas.

Electricity didn't come to Boquillas until 2015. But American tourists have been coming for decades, crossing over for an afternoon of shopping and eating. When they do, they begin their day in Big Bend—a national park that borders another nation.

"This land was once Mexico," ranger Jennette Jurado explained, gesturing to the grove of cottonwood trees where Efrain had set up his camera equipment—a rare bit of shade in Big Bend's eight hundred thousand acres. "There were Mexicans who lived here, and they helped establish the culture down in this area."

We were standing in the southeast corner of the park, near the dividing line between what was *once* Mexico, and what still *is*

Mexico. For 118 miles, the Rio Grande twists and turns through this part of the Chihuahuan Desert, forming the border of the national park, the state of Texas, and the United States of America. Big Bend takes its name from the river's "big bend," the section where the flow abruptly changes from southeast to northeast.

I hadn't seen Mexico yet, but I had already heard it. The trees were blocking our view of the river, but somewhere on the other side, I could hear a voice booming out, singing the chorus of "Cielito Lindo." The song's name may not sound familiar, but if you've ever eaten at a Mexican restaurant with a mariachi band, you know its chorus. It's the one that goes "Ay ay ay ay . . ."

"That must be Victor," Jennette said.

As much as a village of a couple hundred can have a local celebrity, Victor Valdez, or "Don Victor," is the most famous man in Boquillas. Jennette described him as the town's one-man welcoming committee, singing old Mexican songs to visitors from the other side of the river, hoping they might come across and put a tip in his jar.

It used to be easy to cross into Boquillas. Tourists and park rangers would take a rowboat over, have a couple of beers, and then come right back. Mexicans would regularly come to the park's grocery store to shop for food. Like most park grocery stores, the one at Big Bend was overpriced and understocked, but it was still way easier than shopping in Mexico. On the Boquillas side of the river, the nearest grocery store was more than 160 miles away.

The informal, back-and-forth crossings used to happen dozens of times a day. Nobody caused any trouble, and nobody really paid much attention to Boquillas. Not until 9/11.

Afterward, border security tightened all across the country. While the new, tougher measures were mostly meant for busy ports of entry like Tijuana, the government decided it could no longer ignore unenforced, unofficial crossing points like Boquillas. In May 2002, the Department of Homeland Security put an end to the daily Boquillas crossings. Overnight a hundred-foot journey was transformed into a 240-mile one—anyone wanting to visit Boquillas was required to go the long away around, through an official port of entry. Which meant that nobody did.

"Most of those families had to move away because there wasn't a way for them to legally support themselves anymore," Jennette said. Without the easy access to resources across the border, Boquillas quickly transformed from a tourist town to a ghost town. The park rangers watched from across the riverbank, helpless, as their neighbors to the south all moved away.

When I talked to Border Patrol officers about this, they argued that the 2002 "closure" wasn't really a closure. And they were technically right—the area around Boquillas was never legally "open" in the first place. But decades of crossings had established a way of life. Anytime before 2002, if an American family had stopped in the Big Bend visitor center and asked a ranger what there was to do, the US government employee behind the counter would have likely *recommended* a trip into Mexico. Access to another country was part of what made Big Bend unique.

Today rangers are finally able to make that recommendation again. In 2010, President Obama and Mexican president Felipe Calderón issued a joint statement urging more cooperation in the Big Bend region. In 2013, U.S. Customs and Border Patrol opened an *official* entry station in the park. After more than a decade of being shut off from the United States, Boquillas could finally welcome tourists back. This time, they'd be coming legally.

I followed Jennette toward the water. As we emerged from the trees, the river finally came into view. I stopped, stunned. Instead of the mighty, raging rapids I had anticipated, I was faced with a slow-moving, shallow brown creek. Jennette looked over and smiled.

"Smaller than you were expecting?"

"I guess I thought The Rio Grande would be a little bit more . . . *Grande*," I said, trying not to sound too disappointed.

Jennette laughed and waved to singing Victor, who, given his booming baritone, was also smaller than I was expecting. He was short and stout and seemed to be in his mid-sixties, relying on a tall walking stick to keep himself upright as he serenaded us from the other side. He smiled and belted out "Allá en el Rancho Grande," an old Mexican song I later learned was basically the "Despacito" of 1939, when whiter-than-*White-Christmas* Bing Crosby recorded an American version that shot up the charts.

As Victor sang, a younger man in a boat paddled across the river to pick us up. I could hear his oars occasionally scrape the river's bottom. At its deepest point—which is officially the dividing line between the two countries—the Rio Grande still wasn't waist-high.

The man's name tag read ADRIAN VALDEZ. OPERATIONS MAN-AGER. BOQUILLAS INTERNATIONAL FERRY, which seemed a little formal for the captain of a rowboat making a fifty-second journey across a shallow stream. Efrain explained in Spanish that we'd need to go separately, so that he could film me crossing from the other side. Adrian agreed, and took Efrain into the boat first.

It was early, and Jennette still had a full day of work ahead of her, so she wished us well on our "expedition" across the river. As she left, she reminded us that we should keep an eye on the clock. The Boquillas crossing is only officially open from 9 A.M. to 6 P.M., Wednesday through Sunday. Miss that last rowboat back and you have to spend the night in Mexico, or risk crossing illegally back into the United States.

Adrian came back to pick me up. His English was much better than my Spanish, and on our short ride across he told me how much life had changed in Boquillas since the crossing had been legalized. "Many, many families have come back," he said. "Much more business for us."

As I climbed out on the other side, Victor was waiting with his tip bucket. He smiled at our camera and told me he was on "the YouTube." He was very proud of this, even though I wasn't sure if he had seen the videos himself; there was only one house in Boquillas with internet access. A few tourists had apparently posted some clips, and Victor told me to make sure to look him up when I got home. I told him that we were filming a TV show, and that, after the segment had aired, our footage of him would also end up on YouTube. This made him very happy.

"You want me to sing for you again?"

I told him we had probably gotten enough singing footage, but we'd see him when we came back. Right now we were hungry.

There are only two restaurants in Boquillas. The one on the right side of the road, and the one on the left. We chose the left: José Falcon's.

The burrito "Grande" I ordered seemed to have been named by the same person who named the tiny river we'd just crossed. It was plenty tasty, though, so I ordered a second. I asked our waiter if there was a real José Falcon.

"He died," the waiter told me. "But you can talk to his daughter if you want."

After I finished my meal, I went back into the kitchen to meet Lilia Falcon. She showed me a picture of her father, a handsome man in a cowboy hat, sitting in a wheelchair.

"He was in a pickup truck accident," Lilia explained. "Broke his spine, ended up in a wheelchair. He ran the business from a wheelchair for thirty years."

I noticed a kid standing beside José in one of the photos.

"Is that . . . you?" I asked.

Lilia smiled. "I'm the little girl right there. I'm very proud of him."

Lilia's English had been strengthened by the time she'd spent in the United States. After the border closed in 2002, she and her family could no longer afford to keep the restaurant open.

"It completely changed our lives," she said wistfully. "A lot of people from town had to leave, too. To find work somewhere else."

Lilia first moved to Kansas City to work in a meat-processing plant, and then to Atlanta to work in construction. She moved back to Boquillas in 2011, to care for some family members who had stayed behind. Not long after, she heard the news that tourists were finally going to be able to cross again. She knew what she had to do: She reopened the family restaurant.

In 2015, when new solar electric panels arrived in Boquillas, Lilia was finally able to do something her parents never had: serve meat.

"For thirty-two years, my parents only served tacos and burritos made out of beans. We didn't have good refrigeration here in town. We only had a propane refrigerator," she said.

Today it's still a pretty limited menu, but beef and pork and cheese and sour cream are all part of José Falcon's offerings. For many of Lilia's customers, it's the first Mexican food they've ever had *in Mexico*.

"What they really like is that we have a very safe town here. It's nothing dangerous," she emphasized. She knows how Mexico is typically perceived, and she wanted to make sure I got the message. "Everybody takes care of the tourists here."

Boquillas is so far from the rest of civilization, it would be an odd choice for drug-runners to pick as a crossing point. The journey to get here from anywhere else on the Mexican side is long and treacherous. There's also nowhere to hide. If shady characters ever *did* show up in Boquillas, the entire town would know, and it would be in everyone's best interest to report them. The last thing anyone wants is for the border crossing to close again—there's far too much to gain from keeping Boquillas open and accessible.

In 1935, Texas senator Morris Sheppard wrote to President Franklin Roosevelt, suggesting that Big Bend be established as an *international* park. It would be a "peace park," jointly managed by the United States and Mexico.

It's hard to imagine any sort of international peace park happening with Mexico today. Not with all the talk of building a "big, beautiful wall" that would divide our two nations. But as I discovered at Big Bend, a big beautiful wall *already* exists on our southern border.

Lilia said we had to visit Santa Elena Canyon before leaving the park. After saying our goodbyes and heading back across the Rio

Grande, Efrain and I drove an hour and a half southwest until we came upon a pair of massive limestone cliffs stretching fifteen hundred feet to the sky, framing the river below. Solid and serene, the walls were built for free by Mother Nature, millions of years ago. Today, one side belongs to Mexico, the other, to the United States.

As we exited the park and began our long drive back to the hotel in Alpine, Texas, I noticed Efrain was being unusually quiet.

"Everything okay?" I asked.

"Yeah, yeah, everything's fine," he said. "I was just thinking about today. It feels like . . . I don't know. Like somehow I just crossed the line between what my life *could have been* and what it is."

Efrain was born in Durango, one of Mexico's most rural states. Five hundred or so miles southwest of Boquillas, over half the population of Durango lives below the poverty line. Durango was once a popular Hollywood filming location—John Wayne shot a few pictures there—but today the old movie sets are considered too dangerous for most tourists to visit.

"You've been back before, though, right?" I asked. "To Durango? Isn't that where your grandmother lives?"

"Yeah, but never back across that river," he said. "I just had my first-ever rowboat ride, dude."

Back in Biscayne, as we were debating whether or not the plywood-covered inner tube Efrain entered America on counted as a boat, I hadn't really considered the geography of his childhood journey. But now, as I thought more about it, I realized it didn't add up.

"Wait. So if your family was trying to get to Phoenix, then why go so far out of your way to cross through Texas? Was it somehow safer?"

"No, no, it definitely wasn't safer." He laughed. "After Durango, my mom and brother and I lived in *Juarez* for a year."

Efrain had never mentioned Juarez before. Whenever someone asked where he was from, he always said Durango. All of his stories about his abuela's enchiladas and the scorpions he would find in her backyard were set there.

"You lived in Juarez?" I asked. I only knew of the city from its reputation as the onetime winner of the "world's most dangerous city" title. "What was that like?"

"I remember I cried all the time," he said. "It wasn't a good place for a kid to play. The tops of the walls were always covered with broken glass, and I would just sit and play in the dirt. Juarez was a city where the sun had washed out all the color. That's what I remember. Just being surrounded by a bunch of brown and dirt and . . . *bullshit.*"

Efrain was only five when he came to the United States. He got amnesty and a green card in the '80s thanks to Reagan, but he arrived in the country as what we might today call a "dreamer." A little kid who didn't speak a lick of English, brought by his mother, unable to comprehend the significance of the journey he was making.

"What all do you remember about the day you crossed?" I asked. "Were you scared?"

"Honestly, I thought it looked super fun," he said with a laugh. "I saw my brother go first. He was older, so he got to go by himself. There was a guy standing on our side, and then a guy standing on the other side. In between them, they'd stretched a piece of me-cate, this cheap Mexican rope. And then you just sort of pulled yourself across on the raft."

"What did you pack?"

"You know, I don't remember carrying anything," he said. "I don't think I had anything I *could* carry. Maybe my mom brought a suitcase? She must have brought something. I do remember that when I sat on her lap, she squeezed my hand. I could tell that *she* was scared, so then that made me scared."

Efrain called his mother every day while we traveled. They were not always long calls, but he always called. Sometimes I would find him out by the car in the hotel parking lot, chatting in Spanish while waiting for me to come out to meet him for dinner.

"Ma says hello," he would say. "And she wants to make sure we're not playing Pokémon Go."

"What? Why? How does your mom even *know* about Pokémon Go?"

"She saw something on Telemundo about it. I guess a few people got robbed trying to catch some Pokémon? Or whatever you do with them, I don't know. Now she's freaking out. I told her that we're mostly in places where there's no cellphone service anyway, so we're not using our phones. That made her feel better."

Big Bend had been one of those cellular dead zones. We stayed to film the sunset, and it took two hours to drive back to where we were staying in Alpine, Texas. As we finally rolled into town, I pulled up to the one restaurant still open, a diner that was packed with a visiting school group.

"Do you mind if you go ahead and put our names in and I come back?" Efrain said as he jumped out of the car. "It will be too late to call if I wait until after dinner. I won't be long."

Twenty minutes later, I had just gotten a table when he came back inside and sat down.

"Did you tell her about your rowboat ride?" I asked.

"Yeah," he said, quietly. "She started *crying*. She was proud. I think it made her reflect on her own journey. I mean, she's come a long, long way, and she sees my success as her success. Which it is. One hundred percent it is."

Maria Robles had brought her son to the United States so that he could have a better life, and on this day this poor kid from Durango, the land of movie sets, crossed back across the same river he had crossed as a child, carrying a camera and lenses that cost more than what most families in Boquillas earn in a decade. Twenty-seven years earlier, Efrain may not have understood the significance of his crossing, but it was all too apparent now.

"Do you remember those first kids we saw?" he asked. "The ones trying to sell us trinkets?"

"Yeah, of course," I said. A group of adorable kids greet all the visitors on the banks of the Rio Grande, waving cheap scorpion sculptures made of wire and beads.

"I look at those kids and think, I could have *been* those kids. *Easily*. My life could have looked a lot like that. You just think of all of the potential that's inside them that might never have a chance to develop, right?" he said. "Over something that seems so small. When I saw the river, I had the same reaction you did. I couldn't believe how rinky-dink it was. I had built it up to be this huge thing in my head."

"Well, for you, it was," I said. "It changed everything."

The frazzled waiter finally came to our table, and we ordered what ended up being one of the worst meals of the entire year. Somehow, our earlier lunch at a tiny restaurant that had just gotten its first *refrigerator* managed to blow this crappy diner out of the water. I thought how proud that would have made Lilia Falcon's dad.

Several of the people in Boquillas had been curious about our camera, and what we were doing there. When they asked, Efrain did most of the talking. I could make out a bit of the Spanish, enough to know that they were also asking him about where he had grown up, where he lived now, and where his family was from.

"What do you feel like the people in Boquillas made of you?" I asked him. "Do you think they see you as Mexican? Or as an American?"

"You know, there's this saying in Spanish," Efrain said. "*Ni de aquí, ni de allá*. You're neither from here nor from there. That's how I feel. I go back, and I'm not a foreigner, necessarily, but I'm that guy who left. So I really don't fit in. And here, well, you know."

From Efrain's daily struggles to help people pronounce his name (*eff-rah-EEN*) to the extra attention he would occasionally get from suspicious gas station clerks when we stopped for snacks— glances I witnessed but never got myself—his experience in America was often that of an outsider. His trip across the river had come with a lifetime of baggage, whether he wanted it to or not.

Efrain's driver's license says Arizona, but his passport says Mexico. He is a lawful permanent resident of the United States, but he has never applied for citizenship, although I was sure he would ace the test. When we would meet up each morning, he would brief me on all the news he had watched the night before on TV. He was exceptionally well versed in American politics and had been following the daily drama of the presidential election much more closely than I had been. And yet, since he wasn't a U.S. citizen, he wouldn't be voting for president.

Ni de aquí, ni de allá.

As we left the restaurant in Alpine, Efrain mentioned that when he got back to Phoenix, he might talk to an immigration attorney so that he could finally go through the process of becoming a naturalized citizen. It had never really mattered that much to him before, but the political climate had convinced him that it was time to make his relationship with the country he had called home for nearly three decades official.

"Who knows," he said. "Maybe one day I won't even be allowed to, you know? If I'm going to do it, might as well do it now."

Close to a million people a year apply for naturalization, including people like Efrain, who were born on one side of a line and now legally live and work on the other. Often the emotional ceremonies conferring citizenship are held inside national parks—the Park Service has a partnership with U.S. Citizenship and Immigration Services. Congaree, Rocky Mountain, Glacier, Grand Teton, and Petrified Forest national parks have all hosted citizenship ceremonies.

But the National Park of American Samoa never has. Over seven thousand miles from our nation's capital, American Samoa is unquestionably U.S. soil. And yet, the people who are born there—including many of the rangers who work at the park—are not actually United States citizens.

When I first plotted out the parks on a map, it was obvious that the National Park of American Samoa was going to be the farthest I would have to travel to complete my list. It is the most remote unit in the entire National Park System.

After overnighting in Honolulu, I caught a second flight to take me twenty-six hundred miles farther into the Pacific. When the capital city of Pago Pago finally appeared out my window, it seemed crazy that, after two days of traveling, I still hadn't left America. I was south of the *equator.*

But sure enough, when I got to baggage claim, the signs were in English and the snack bar took dollars. A few blocks away, a McDonald's was buzzing with activity. This was America, all right, and any lingering doubts went away when I drove past the building next to the airport. Surrounded by palm trees and flowers, there was a sign for the UNITED STATES ARMY RESERVE CENTER.

Per capita, American Samoa frequently has the highest military enlistment rates of any U.S. state or territory. And yet, by default, none of the local servicemen and -women can choose their commander in chief.

Just like Guam, Puerto Rico, the U.S. Virgin Islands, and the Northern Mariana Islands, American Samoa can send delegates to the party nominating conventions, but its residents don't have the right to vote in the final presidential elections. It sends a delegate to Congress, but that delegate can't actually vote on legislation, although he or she can participate in debates and vote in committees. Members of Congress from the territories often seem as if they're in Washington to remind the rest of America that they exist. *Hey, you know those laws you're voting on? Those wars you're starting? Don't forget—they affect us, too.*

But American Samoa is different in one key respect from our other permanently inhabited territories. While the residents of the other territories are all considered U.S. citizens, the people of American Samoa are not.

"You're born owing allegiance to the United States. But you're not a citizen. America doesn't owe its allegiance *back*. That doesn't make any sense," attorney Charles Ala'ilima lamented when I met him in his office next door to a juice bar in the island's main shopping plaza.

Charles was barefoot, wearing a bright-blue floral print shirt—tropical island business casual. His small office was stacked high with books and papers. There was a cot down the hall where he occasionally slept if he was working late. It felt like I was in an episode of *Better Call Samoan*.

It's tough to have much of a specialty when you practice law in American Samoa, so Charles ends up being a jack-of-all-trades. Sometimes that might mean a local property dispute. Sometimes it's a suit against the U.S. government.

Charles was representing a group of American Samoans who were arguing that they should have birthright citizenship as provided by the Fourteenth Amendment, which guarantees citizenship to "all persons born or naturalized in the United States."

Fanuatanu Mamea, one of the plaintiffs in that case, had swung by the office to say hello. Born in American Samoa, Fanuatanu had served in the army for twenty years. He'd been awarded two Purple Hearts while serving in Vietnam. But this seventy-five-year-old veteran had been told he'd have to apply if he wanted to become an American citizen.

"It's not fair," Fanuatanu said. "Why should I have to fill out a ton of paperwork that they might not even approve?"

The legal status of our territories hinges on a series of Supreme Court decisions from the early 1900s known as the Insular Cases. In one of those cases, Justice Henry Brown argued that "those possessions are inhabited by alien races, differing from us in religion, customs, laws, methods of taxation, and modes of thought."

"Basically, Brown's opinion read, 'They are savage races that would not understand the concepts of English common law,'" Charles said, shaking his head in disgust. "Well, I'm a lawyer. I have a hard time with it, too."

The Supreme Court argued that the territories were "foreign in a domestic sense," whatever *that* meant. Ever since, for primarily economic reasons, the U.S. government has found it beneficial to treat the territories as separate but equal-ish possessions, refusing to recognize a constitutional guarantee of citizenship.

Puerto Ricans later acquired birthright citizenship through a separate act of Congress. Guamanians got U.S. citizenship in 1950, when President Truman signed the Organic Act of Guam into law. In every similar case, citizenship has required special legislation.

But American Samoa never got its citizenship law. It probably still could, but Charles's point was that the people there didn't *need* to. The Fourteenth Amendment should already apply, and it should have applied in all of the other territories as well.

Here's why all of this matters today: If you're a U.S. "national," which is what is stamped on the passports of those born in American Samoa, and you later move to the mainland United States, you're *still* not a citizen. In addition to being unable to vote, noncitizen nationals are often ineligible for federal programs and can be disqualified from holding certain jobs. To become a citizen, an American Samoan would have to go through essentially the same process as someone born in Mexico. They have to apply, pay a fee, and take a test.

A few months before I met Fanuatanu, the Supreme Court had declined to hear his case, meaning an earlier U.S. District Court of Appeals ruling that American Samoans had no claim to birthright citizenship would stand.

"I feel betrayed," Fanuatanu said, close to tears. "I feel I don't belong."

It wasn't like Fanuatanu had a loyalty to any *other* country. He was born in America. He took a *bullet* for America. If he's not fully American, then what is he?

Ni de aquí, ni de allá.

Park ranger Pua Tuaua had also served in the military, then traded in his army fatigues for a slightly different shade of government green. His Park Service uniform was the coolest I'd ever seen—instead of the traditional stiff ranger pants, Pua was wearing a park-issued lavalava, a green skirtlike garment worn by men and women of all ages across the island.

"I joined the U.S. Army so I was able to get out and leave this island, but my heart was always back home," he told me as we looked out over beautiful Amalau Bay. "I grew up with this culture, and I wanted to come back to it."

The national park, established in 1988, is spread out over three separate islands. The bulk of it is on Tutuila, the largest island, where 95 percent of the population lives. It protects miles of beautiful, rocky coastline and a lush tropical rain forest, full of fruit bats and colorful crabs. The coral reefs are teeming with aquatic life, and the islands are internationally famous for having some of the cleanest air in the world.

It's a small park overall—the second smallest park I'd see all year—but you do get a lot of scenic bang for your buck. All told, it protects close to ninety-five hundred acres of land. None of which, it turns out, the Park Service actually owns.

American Samoa is the only national park that's *leased.* The U.S. government agreed to rent the land from the tribal chiefs, who had no intention of offering it up for sale. Communal landownership, passed down through a system of families, chiefs, and tribes, is part of the Samoan way of life: "fa'a Samoa."

"The culture here is based on respect and love," Pua explained. "The fa'a Samoa is the way of life."

Fa'a Samoa encompasses everything from local religious customs to family hierarchies to the system of how land is shared and managed by the matai, the powerful chiefs who run the villages. Pua told me 90 percent of the land in American Samoa was owned this way, controlled by villages and extended families.

As it stands now, when the fifty-year lease runs out on the national park, it could cease to be a park. The matai could change their minds and decide to find another use for the land. But when

I started asking around, that didn't seem likely. The locals were *proud* they had a national park. It meant American Samoa had something half the *states* didn't even have.

And it was gorgeous. The entire island was. Before I learned the phrase *fa'a Samoa*, I learned *Motu o Fiafiaga*. It was written atop every American Samoa license plate. It meant "Island of Paradise."

And yet, as beautiful as the land was, my memories of American Samoa are not of the scenery. They are of the culture, the people, and the fa'a Samoa. At a park like Big Bend, unless you cross over to Boquillas, it is entirely possible to visit and leave without ever even considering the land's link to Mexico. If you fly to Maui, stay at the Hyatt, and pay for a shuttle to take you touring around Haleakalā National Park, you could leave Hawaii without ever once thinking about what it means to be Hawaiian. But it's impossible to spend a day in American Samoa without absorbing at least some sense of a culture that's more than three thousand years old. The bus stops, the markets, and the church services (I got invited to four) weren't technically part of the national park itself, but they were all part of the experience.

American Samoa was also the only park that advertised a "homestay program." On the park's website, there were names and cellphone numbers of a few local islanders who had agreed to occasionally host visitors needing a bed or a meal. The word *program* makes it sound a little more organized than it actually was—the park didn't have anything to do with it other than posting the names of people who may or may not pick up their phones—but it was suggested that a home visit was "an opportunity for visitors to become acquainted with Samoan people and culture in a village setting."

On a Friday night, I headed over to the home of Chief Satele-Lilio Aliitai and his wife, Evelyn, to have dinner. I wasn't given an address—I was just told to drive to the end of one of the island's few main roads and I'd eventually find their driveway. Surrounded by giant palm trees, their small white ranch-style house was constructed out of cinder blocks, designed to stand up to the harsh tropical storms that frequently blow through the island.

Dinner was cooked outside in an umu, or earth oven, in which sizzling stones were covered with banana leaves to seal in the heat. The family had been hard at work on the preparations long before I showed up, and when dinnertime came we all peeled off the giant leaves together. It felt like unwrapping a mysterious, delicious present. Underneath were servings of pork and fish and breadfruit—a fruit that, when cooked, resembled a cross between a potato and fresh-baked bread. My favorite dish was palusami—taro leaves filled with a sweet coconut cream.

After dinner, we went out into the yard to watch their fourth-grade son do a fire dance. We talked late into the evening, about life, politics, travel, the national parks, and what it meant to be American.

I remained confused about how land gets divvied up in American Samoa. How do you decide who gets to live where? How does inheritance work? What happens when someone who lives on a property dies or leaves? When everybody owns the land, I couldn't understand how anybody could. The best and ultimately most satisfying answer the family gave me was, "Here, it just works."

I had been approaching the idea of communal land like it was some bizarre foreign concept, but then it finally dawned on me—you know another place that has a lot of communal land? Nevada. More than 80 percent of Nevada is public land. Well over half of Utah and of Idaho are. The national parks are communal land, land we all own and manage together. Every American is an equal shareholder in our mountains, rivers, valleys, and streams—places we pass down through the generations.

It's an audacious system, but most of the time, *it just works.*

The sights we come to see in the parks exist because of lines we cannot see. The giant trees and the wide-open spaces on one side of a line are considered sacred and special. On the other, civilization is allowed to creep in. The lines mark the difference between the bustle of Jackson Hole and the quiet of Grand Teton, between the coastal resorts of Miami and the protected beaches of Biscayne.

Traveling across the country, I had been crossing back and forth across these invisible lines, and so many more that divide one state, town, and time zone from the next. In most cases, the distinctions seemed arbitrary. In a year in which there was so much talk of red states and blue states, it was tempting to think of the people who lived inside a certain set of artificial boundaries as belonging to some monolithic group. But thanks to the conversations I'd been having at truck stops and on trails across the country, I knew that wasn't even remotely accurate.

The amped-up rhetoric surrounding the Mexican border had turned it into a conflict that was often talked about in terms of "Us" versus "Them." At a park like Big Bend, it didn't feel like that—it was easier to think in terms of what *We* might have in common.

At dinner with the Satele family in American Samoa, they introduced me to their two dogs: Mitt Romney and Barack Obama.

"Wait, you're kidding, right? You named your dogs Obama and Romney?"

"Yup, that's them!" Evelyn said, laughing. "They were born during the last election, so we thought we'd have one of each."

"Do they fight all the time?" I asked.

"You'd be surprised," she said. "They get along great."

The word *insular*—as in the Insular Cases that determined what life would be like for those who live in the territories—was merely referencing the fact that the territories were islands. But *insular* has another definition: "ignorant of or uninterested in cultures, ideas, or peoples outside one's own experience." Borders—perceived or actual ones—come with the capacity to make us insular. Crossing them—at parks like Big Bend and American Samoa—helped remind me of the equally invisible threads that bind us all together.

9

VOLCANOES

(Lassen Volcanic,
Hawaii Volcanoes, Haleakalā)

If you got the word *volcano* in a game of Pictionary, you would not draw California's Lassen Peak. Lassen is just a little too rounded, a little too humpbacked to ever stand in for the volcano emoji.

Lassen is a plug dome volcano, a rare type of volcano formed by a thicker, stickier lava that doesn't flow as far from the source, thus forming a shape that's more mound than mountain. The classic volcano we all think of—a jagged, pointy triangle with red shooting out of the top—is known as a stratovolcano, or composite volcano. The largest percentage of the world's individual volcanoes are stratovolcanoes, including Mount Fuji, Mount St. Helens, and every elementary school science experiment ever made.

Volcanoes can also come in wide, flat shield varieties and in squat, loose cinder cones. The four different types can be found spread across the world, but there are very few areas where you can actually find all four clustered together in the same place. Three hours northeast of Sacramento, California, Lassen Volcanic National Park has them all.

Lassen's explosive potential makes itself known all along the park's main road—the Volcanic Legacy Scenic Byway. Driving in from the south, I passed mounds of minerals that steamed like kettles, then wound through an area known as "Fart Gulch." As in, that's what the *park website* calls it. To my knowledge, it's the only mention of farts on a dot-gov. "The sulfur smells make this area easily identifiable," says the brief blurb on Lassen's page.

Though the park's many volcanoes are currently dormant, they fart in their sleep. (Volcanoes—They're Just Like Us!) Lassen gurgles and rumbles and *reeks*. I rolled my windows up.

I was headed to the park's largest hydrothermal area, Bumpass Hell. There boiling pools, bubbling mud pots, and plumes of sulfuric steam cover the ground. It was named after Kendall Vanhook Bumpass, a cowboy guide who stepped a little too close to a mud pot in 1865 and accidentally broke through the thin crust. The acidic, boiling-hot water scalded Bumpass's leg, which eventually needed to be amputated.

Today the park has placed a sign near the entrance to the area with a warning to all hikers: DON'T LET THIS INFERNAL WONDERLAND BECOME YOUR HELL.

I gingerly stepped onto the wooden boardwalk, determined not to be a Bumpass. The narrow planks laid down by the Park Service promised me safe passage as long as I stayed on track, winding my way through small rocky hills stained orange and yellow by the mix of chemicals in the hot water. To the left and right of the trail, steam rose from pools that churned like mini Jacuzzis.

Lassen's ground seemed unsettled, uninviting—as if it were constantly angry. The brilliant-blue and emerald-green pools along the trail were pretty, but the gas rising out of them irritated my eyes. I took their hiss as a warning—*stay away*.

I passed Big Boiler, one of the hottest fumaroles in the world. A fumarole is an opening in the earth's crust that releases hot steam, and the steam chugging out of Big Boiler like the exhaust from an engine had been measured to be 322 degrees Fahrenheit. Even from the safety of the boardwalk, I could feel its heat.

High above me, Lassen Peak didn't look particularly menacing, but a century earlier the plug dome had "unplugged," shooting hot bits of lava and ash into the air. From 1914 to 1917, Lassen's intermittent eruptions devastated much of the nearby area, so much so that there's a part of the park just named Devastated Area. There, it's possible to wander among boulders blown miles from their original homes by the force of Lassen's eruptions and the mudslides that followed.

The eruptions are what inspired Congress to designate Lassen as one of our earliest national parks. With so many natural wonders to protect, the one that was actively *exploding* in California seemed like a solid place to begin.

August 1916 was a big month for volcanoes. Just one week before Lassen Volcanic National Park was established, Congress had extended federal protection to *another* collection of volcanoes, thousands of miles away in the Pacific.

Kīlauea, on the Big Island of Hawaii, is one of the most active volcanoes in the world.

When Mark Twain visited in 1866, he described its twisting lava flows as looking like "a colossal railroad map of the State of Massachusetts done in chain lightning on a midnight sky."

Hawaii wouldn't become a state for nearly another century. Today Kīlauea—protected when Hawaii was still a territory—is the fiery star of Hawaii Volcanoes National Park.

Hawaii's Mauna Loa volcano—also part of the park—last erupted in 1984. But over the past hundred years of recorded activity, Kīlauea has been oozing lava nearly nonstop—its only extended break came during a stretch between 1934 and 1952. When it eventually woke up from that eighteen-year nap, it was very, very cranky. Over the next several years, a series of large eruptions led to evacuations across the Big Island. In 1955, an eighty-eight-day eruption destroyed twenty-one homes and covered thirty-nine hundred acres of the island with lava.

That's where Robert Trickey wanted to build his house.

Robert owned an upholstery business in San Francisco. When he told his friends he was thinking of moving to Hawaii, they assumed he would be living among palm trees on white sandy beaches. But the site Robert had picked out was jet black. That was the look he wanted. He loved the lava.

The 1955 eruption had killed all of the plant life, and the vegetation had only barely started to come back when Robert started looking at properties in the late '90s. The landscape was black, jagged, and desolate. And cheap, for good reason. The lava that had come there before would almost certainly come there again.

Every lot on the Big Island is ranked on a scale from 1 through 9, with 1 being the most likely to see lava. The summit of Kīlauea is in Zone 1. The Puna District, where Robert had found his lot, was in Zone 2.

As I pulled up Robert's street, I realized the photos I had seen online of his home didn't come close to doing it justice. It was one of the coolest houses I had ever seen.

A wide rectangular structure of glass and concrete, the home was all clean lines, large windows, and bright, open spaces. I got out of my rental car and waved to Robert, who was waiting for me in his living room that was . . . outside? Inside? I couldn't exactly tell.

There was a roof overhead, but I didn't see a wall in front. From the room's gray concrete floor, you could dive straight into the adjacent thirty-thousand-gallon pool. The bright-blue water was a startling pop of color set off by the field of deep-black lava that bordered its right edge.

The home was designed by renowned San Francisco architect Craig Steely, who ended up falling in love with the lava so much after visiting Hawaii with Robert that he and his wife built their own vacation home a few streets away. There are now seven Steely-designed homes in the neighborhood, part of what he calls his

On January 1, the summit of Acadia National Park's Cadillac Mountain is the first place in the contiguous United States to see the sun rise. I knew it was going to be a busy year— I wanted to get a head start. *Courtesy of the author*

From the top of a mountain to the bottom of the ocean, it was a journey of constantly shifting scenery. Biscayne National Park is 95 percent water—its "Maritime Heritage Trail" tells the story of wrecks like the *Lugano*, which sank off the Florida coast in 1913. *CBS News*

While our early parks were set aside for their scenic wonders, ranger Alan Scott told me the Everglades was the first national park set aside for "what is alive." At least I think that's what he said—I was half-listening. Something alive had just slipped past my foot. *CBS News*

Friends in low places: video journalist Efrain Robles at Death Valley—the lowest, hottest, and driest place in the country. *Courtesy of the author*

Despite its name, Death Valley contains a surprising amount of life. The park is home to one of the rarest fish in the world—the Devils Hole pupfish. *CBS News (above); Olin Feuerbacher/USFWS (right)*

Scientist Kurt Fristrup measures the silence of Great Sand Dunes, one of the quietest places in the country. *CBS News*

At Katmai National Park, hikers are instructed to constantly make noise on the trail—bears will usually avoid humans as long as they can hear us coming. Sneak up on one, though, and you might end up like this salmon.
Courtesy of the author

(above) My love of nature began in my home state of West Virginia. I've been hugging trees for as long as I can remember.
Courtesy of the author

(left) It would take a circle of twenty people to properly hug *this* tree. Sequoia National Park's General Sherman Tree is the largest living thing in the world.
Courtesy of the author

One of Redwood
National Park's
cathedral-like groves.
If nature has a soul,
it feels like it must
be bound up in the
bark and sap of
our forests.
*Courtesy of
the author*

"Everybody needs beauty
as well as bread, places
to play in and pray in,
where nature may heal
and give strength to
body and soul alike."
—John Muir, THE YOSEMITE
Courtesy of the author

"A spectacle curious
enough to excite the
imagination." The first
written description of
the "Old Man" of Crater
Lake dates back to 1902.
Today, the log is still
mysteriously floating
upright in our country's
deepest lake.
*Courtesy of
the author*

For more than two centuries, biologists have wondered why the bald cypress trees of Congaree National Park have "knees." While much of our natural world has been explained away, there's something especially thrilling about stumbling across a mystery that Google can't solve. *Courtesy of the author*

(left) The 1,500-foot-high walls that already exist on our southern border. One half of Santa Elena Canyon is in Big Bend National Park, the other half is in Mexico. *Courtesy of the author*

(below) The Rio Grande is surprisingly pequeño. From Big Bend's Boquillas Crossing Port of Entry, it's possible to wade into Mexico. The area was originally intended to be an international park. *Courtesy of the author*

South of the equator and over 7,000 miles away from our nation's capital, American Samoa is our most far-flung national park.
Courtesy of the author

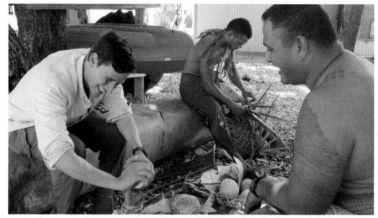

Controversially, the Americans born in this remote territory are not legally considered American citizens. Unlike the residents of Guam and Puerto Rico, American Samoans must apply for citizenship.
CBS News

Like all of the Hawaiian Islands, Maui was created by volcanic activity. Today, Haleakalā National Park looks like Mars on Earth.
Courtesy of the author

Mother Nature was giving birth, and I got to hang out in the delivery room. I arrived at Hawaii Volcanoes National Park just as the Kīlauea eruption began pouring into the sea, making the Big Island just a little bit bigger. *CBS News*

The lava has served as a blank canvas for architect Craig Steely, who designs homes—like this one for client Robert Trickey—on the sites of past eruptions. It's a rare opportunity to build on some of the newest land in the entire country. *Courtesy of the author*

By 2030, Glacier National Park is predicted to have no glaciers left. I hiked with geologist Dan Fagre to view the remnants of the park's once-legendary Grinnell Glacier. *CBS News*

(above left) This photo was taken in 1938. *T. J. Hileman, courtesy of Glacier National Park Archives*

(above right) Dan took this photo the day we visited. *Dan Fagre, USGS*

Alaska's Wrangell–St. Elias National Park is home to the largest system of glaciers in the country, but they too are rapidly shrinking. Former Park Service director Jon Jarvis has said that climate change is "fundamentally the greatest threat to the integrity of our national parks that we have ever experienced." *Courtesy of the author*

Lavaflow series. The lava has served as a blank canvas, offering a rare opportunity to build on some of the newest land in the entire country.

While other homes in the neighborhood had paved or planted over the rocks, carting in dirt from elsewhere on the island, Craig and Robert had decided to leave everything natural, the same as it had looked when it cooled after the '55 eruption. The house didn't just bring the outside in, it brought the underside . . . up.

"It makes you understand that we live on this giant burning cinder," Robert said, looking out his windows. "When you walk around New York, you don't think, *There's lava, like, way way below me*. But here, you remember that."

Robert was right. I definitely don't spend much time thinking about how I'm constantly standing on a crust separating me from the molten hot rock flowing underneath my feet (technically magma, not lava—it only becomes lava when it reaches the surface). But I also don't think about how I'm constantly flying through space at sixty-seven thousand miles an hour, since neither fact has much of an impact on my daily life. If I lived in Robert's neighborhood, though, I wouldn't just think about lava all the time, I'd have nightmares about it. I would worry that it was going to come and burn down my dream house.

"Doesn't that scare you?" I asked.

"Well, you just make your peace with it," he said. "You simply know that it's part of life. I think in some way, it makes you remember life is passing. You know, it's not permanent."

Robert pointed at me. "You're not, like, permanently here."

I knew that, but I still didn't know if I could build a home on land that's inherently so dangerous. Then Robert reminded me that California, where I'd lived for the past decade, wasn't exactly safety central.

"You don't really think about the earthquakes, do you? I don't think about them in San Francisco. And really, they're much more sudden," he said. "At least with the lava, you have some warning. You can pack up everything and leave before it makes it here."

Robert was about as Zen a guy as you can imagine. He looked like a tan, relaxed, gray-haired Tom Hanks. He was wearing swim shorts, no shoes, a partially buttoned short-sleeved shirt, and hadn't stopped smiling during our entire conversation. The guy got to wake up every day with a view of the ocean from his second-floor bedroom, then eat his breakfast looking out on a dramatic black moonscape. He never had to mow his lawn. Sure, it might all go away one day, but for now it seemed like paradise.

The timing of my Hawaii visit was especially fortuitous—the day before I arrived, Kīlauea had started dumping lava into the ocean for the first time in three years. I found a couple of guys with a boat—a six-seater catamaran—who agreed to take me out to watch the show.

Kanoa and Kainoa were native Hawaiians, and it took them saying their names three times before I realized there was actually a one-letter difference. Kanoa means "the free one." Kainoa means "father's namesake." Kanoa piloted the catamaran while Kainoa and I chatted up front.

As the lava came into view, we both grew quiet. Maybe he would eventually get tired of running these tours, but only a few days in, Kainoa was as stunned as I was to see the lava pouring down the steep black cliffs.

It looked like the center of a half-eaten chocolate cake had been doused in a heavy, orange syrup, and the excess topping was drizzling off the sides. The neon arteries split and twisted, covering the cliff. As the lava eventually made its way into the ocean, it hissed, spouting massive clouds of steam. It was literally boiling the seawater, then quickly cooling into rocky chunks that sank below the surface. We were a safe distance away (at least I assumed we were—I had placed my trust in the locals), but I could still feel the wave of heat pressing hard against my body. When I dipped my hand into the ocean, it was hot, warmed by the twenty-one-hundred-degree fuel that was steadily filling it up.

On our boat ride out to the flow, we had passed several homes on the cliffside, homes that were even closer to the lava flow than Craig Steely's Lavaflow homes. I asked Kainoa if he often thought about the risks of living here.

"We know the risks. If She decides to come and take our land, we welcome Her with open arms," he told me.

The "She" he was referring to was Pele.

Her full name is Pelehonuamea, She Who Shapes the Land, the Goddess of fire and volcanoes. The internet is full of supposed Pele sightings—Her long, flowing hair is seen in the wisps of orange clouds or in tendrils of hot lava.

Pele is frequently referred to as Madame Pele, a sign of reverence and respect for Her power. When you live here, your home—your life—is all in Pele's hands.

"If She decides to come and take your house, you clean your house, you get your house ready for Her," Kainoa said. This sounded insane to me. In the midst of an evacuation, people are going to take the time to make Pele preparations?

"Yeah, you rake your yard. You make everything presentable for Her," he said.

"And *then* you run to safety?" I asked.

"Then you get out of there," he said, laughing.

Hot lava is thought to be the kinolau, the physical embodiment of the Goddess. And if a Goddess wants to pay your house a visit, well—that is not the kind of invitation you can refuse. You can only hope that your place is tidy enough that, after She leaves, She won't bad-mouth you to the other deities at brunch.

Pele's home is said to be inside of Kīlauea's Halema'uma'u Crater. There's where I'd caught my first glimpse of Her—on my first night at the park, I'd joined hundreds of other tourists on an observation platform on the edge of the crater to peer into the lava lake that bubbled just below the rim. Its soft orange glow lit up the sky like a distant, foreboding fire.

But I was determined to get even closer—closer than even a boat tour would allow. I'd been told that, all the way at the end of the park's Chain of Craters Road, there was a path that would lead me straight to the lava.

The six-mile hike out to the flow felt even longer. The terrain wasn't steep, but it was slow going—navigating the spiky, uneven landscape required my full concentration.

As I walked out to the lava, I could smell the sulfur. Not quite Fart Gulch bad, but definitely a sign that I was getting closer. I began to hear creaks, cracks, and sizzles—the sound of something slowly cooking. I started to feel the heat on my boots, radiating up to my face. Finally, I could see it. A bit of orange peeking out below gaps in the black rock, flowing underneath my feet. How far underneath, I couldn't tell.

I was attempting a "hot crossing," walking across a field of recently cooled lava. The hard rock I was standing on had, perhaps just hours before, been liquefied and orange.

Had no one else been standing out there, I would have absolutely turned back. It felt like I was marching into hell. How on earth was this allowed? It couldn't possibly be safe. Walking across a field of lava felt like driving over downed power lines or skating to the center of a newly frozen river—a totally reckless thing I definitely wasn't supposed to do.

But up ahead of me, I saw groups of tourists in the distance. There were even a few rangers walking around, answering questions. I had to zig and zag to get to where they were standing, avoiding bits of fresh, bubbling lava that had risen to the surface. It felt like dodging puddles on a sidewalk, except in this case a misstep wouldn't mean soggy socks, it would mean *burning my foot off.* It was insane, thrilling, and easily one of the best experiences I've ever had in a national park.

Other parks have beautiful mountains, impressive sandstone formations, and mighty trees. But there is only one park where you can witness land being created right in front of your eyes. It was transfixing. After an hour or so of watching the lava slide down slopes and weave through narrow crevices, I wandered away from the small crowd to a remote section of the field, recently cooled. I knew with certainty that, at that moment, I was standing on ground that nobody had ever stood on before. How often do you get a chance to do that?

I had walked out to the lava before sunset, and I stayed until well after dark. I knew this was something special, and I wanted to soak it in as long as possible. Mother Nature was giving birth, and I got to hang out in the delivery room.

All of the Hawaiian Islands were created by lava. They all began as volcanoes, each taking their turn in the center of what's known as the Hawaiian hot spot. The Big Island, the youngest island in the chain, currently sits on the hot spot. It won't always. The island is currently moving northwest at a rate of five to ten centimeters a year. Five million years earlier, Kauai occupied the same exact bit of the Pacific—then Oahu, Molokai, and Lanai all took their turns before they cooled and drifted farther out to sea.

Maui, the second youngest Hawaiian Island, now lies twenty-six miles northwest of the Big Island. There, high above the clouds, Haleakalā volcano towers over the luxury resorts down on the coast.

When honeymooners pack for Maui, they typically bring suitcases full of flip-flops and board shorts, T-shirts and sundresses. It's only after they arrive on-island that they finally glance at the forecast for Haleakalā National Park. The summit of the park's namesake mountain, ten thousand feet above sea level, can be a good thirty degrees chillier than the beach. At 5 A.M., it's downright freezing. So under the cover of darkness, tourists flee their hotels under their covers, hanging DO NOT DISTURB signs to keep their temporary burglaries secret from housekeeping.

I'd invited my sister Kathleen to come join me in Maui, and we laughed as carload after carload of these amateur criminals arrived at the summit, all bundled up in teal fleece and floral bedspreads to keep warm while they waited for the sunrise. We dubbed them the Blanket Bandits.

We'd come prepared with jackets, hats, and gloves. Kathleen had flown in from San Francisco, where she works for the Golden Gate National Parks Conservancy, a nonprofit group that assists with managing the park units in the Bay Area. Back when I decided to spend a year visiting the parks, she was the first person I called for advice. Kathleen majored in environmental studies and once spent a summer tracking moose in the Tetons. She had worked as a seasonal ranger at Yosemite, chasing bears away from campsites, and served on a trail-building crew in the Marin Headlands. She was far more qualified for my new gig than I was.

When I told her I was going to spend a year hitting the parks, she was both very jealous and very supportive, giving me gear recommendations for my journey. She also vowed to come meet me at one. The park in paradise was an easy choice.

I was glad to have the company. Living on the road, I'd abandoned any semblance of a normal social life. I was constantly meeting lots of *new* people, but it was nice to spend time with a person I knew so well. The past few days had been comfortable and familiar in all the best ways.

It was pitch dark when we arrived at the park's rocky summit after the nearly two-hour drive from our hotel. People come to Kīlauea volcano to see the lava, but people come to Haleakalā volcano to see the sun.

Haleakalā literally means "house of the sun." According to Hawaiian legend, this is where the sun-god La begins his journey across the sky each day. Demigod Maui is said to have once climbed to the top of the volcano to trap La in his lasso, refusing to release the deity until he promised to move more slowly across the sky. Native Hawaiians—Kanaka Maoli—don't have to pay entrance fees if they're coming to the park to conduct cultural practices at sunrise.

It felt strange to be standing so high up, as if Kathleen and I were waiting for morning from the window seat of an airplane. The sky had brightened significantly since our arrival, but La still hadn't come into view. Any second now, it seemed. A hush fell over the chatty Blanket Bandits. Whether or not you believed in La or Maui, it was easy to feel there was something sacred about standing on the black rocks waiting for an orange ball of fire to begin a new day.

Finally, a little sliver of sun peeked over the curtain of clouds, checking out what the crowd looked like for this day's performance. My sister gasped. It was finally here.

In a matter of seconds, La raised the rest of himself into the sky. I had never seen the sun like this, illuminating nothing but the clouds below it. It set fire to the sea of white stretching out in the distance, wavy and jagged, with peaks that looked simultaneously fluffy and sharp. They resembled the actual sea, crashing against the shore, except every single wave was frozen mid-break.

To watch La begin his journey across the sky that day, I had somehow found my way to a spot that had started growing out of the ocean on a day two million years earlier. I was shivering ten thousand feet above the earth's surface thanks to molten hot rock twelve hundred miles below it. I couldn't begin to comprehend the insane series of geological processes that had all come together to create the summit of this volcano, the most obviously perfect place to view the dawning of a new day. It all seemed impossible and yet somehow inevitable.

Kathleen and I spent the rest of the day hiking Haleakalā's dramatic lunar landscape, traipsing through a desert of cinder where colorful mounds of varying shapes provided a glimpse into the dormant volcano's past. We passed Haleakalā's rare silverswords—wispy, almost white plants that have returned to the summit, improbably popping up out of the rocky soil. Even on the slopes of a volcano, life finds a way. And then, in an instant, everything can change.

.   .   .

We're going to begin tonight with breaking news from Hawaii. A magnitude 5.3 earthquake has hit the Big Island not far from the Kīlauea volcano, which began erupting yesterday. More than fifteen hundred people have been ordered to evacuate as red-hot lava bubbles up from the ground and snakes through forests and neighborhoods.

That's how Jeff Glor began the *CBS Evening News* on May 4, 2018. "At least two homes have burned so far," he reported. Two months later, the total had risen to more than six hundred.

The images coming out of Hawaii were astonishing. The cable channels played them multiple times an hour, alternating shots of gushing rivers of lava with slow creeps down suburban streets. Camera crews stood just feet away, unable to help, as the orange-and-black ooze steadily advanced down the road, engulfing any vehicle or home that might be in its way. As the eruption continued, the lava's path snaked and shifted. New warnings were released each day. Residents who initially thought they were safe were forced to evacuate.

Before they fled, some of the homeowners left behind carefully arranged leaves and flowers in their yards. I thought of Kainoa back on the boat, and his story of raking the yard to make it presentable for Pele. At the time, I was skeptical that anyone would ever go to such lengths. Less than two years later, I saw proof that people did.

"Everywhere else in your life you see destruction," Kainoa had told me when I asked why he loved the lava. "Things getting destroyed. Here you finally get something being created."

But creation itself can be destructive.

When a hurricane or a tornado or an earthquake hits, there are still signs of life in the aftermath. Residents return home to find waterlogged family photo albums, children's toys, and broken furniture strewn across their lawn.

But lava doesn't leave anything behind. It engulfs it all. The slate is wiped clean.

When I saw the news, I checked in on Craig and Robert. Their homes, and the rest of the Lavaflow homes, had been spared. But hundreds of others were gone forever.

The eruption also caused Halema'uma'u Crater to collapse. The lava lake inside drained, feeding the eruptions that poured into the East Rift Zone. The observation platform where I'd once stood broke apart—tons of rocks and debris fell into Halema'uma'u, sealing its orange glow off from view.

Even Pele's house could not withstand the unrelenting forces of change that are constantly reshaping our planet. Robert was right. *None of this is permanent.* Nothing is.

10

ICE

(Glacier Bay, Glacier, Kenai Fjords, Wrangell–St. Elias)

Glacier Bay National Park in Alaska and Glacier National Park in Montana may have similar names, but the glaciers they protect couldn't be more different. The bay in Alaska features giant tidewater glaciers—magical fortresses of frozen water, more blue than white. Approaching them by boat, they look like something straight out of *Game of Thrones*—massive walls of ice stretching a mile wide and soaring hundreds of feet high, impossible to scale. Not that you'd ever want to try climbing one. Giant chunks of ice regularly "calve" and break off into the sea below, a regular highlight and threat for the boats full of tourists forced to stay thousands of feet away.

The small terrestrial glaciers hiding out high in the Rocky Mountains of Montana aren't going to break apart and kill anyone. They're barely surviving. Some of the patches of ice are only just large enough to be *classified* as glaciers anymore. As of this writing, there are twenty-five glaciers in the park, but some models predict that, by 2030, they'll have all disappeared, and an asterisk may need to be carved into the Glacier* National Park sign. Even now, most decent ice sightings require substantial, strenuous hikes.

I was willing to do whatever it took to get to one. I'd watched Hawaii Volcanoes' volcano erupt, I'd boated across Lake Clark's lake, and, no matter what, I was determined to see at least *one* of Glacier's glaciers. I knew it might be my only chance.

To reach the park's Grinnell Glacier, I hiked twelve miles round trip and climbed the equivalent of 160 flights of stairs. When I finally made it up to the ice, it felt like my thighs were on fire. I plopped down onto the nearest rock, took out my lunch, and gazed out at the sheet of white that spanned the ledges of the mountain peaks, dripping down into the turquoise lake below.

George Bird Grinnell—the glacier's naturalist namesake— described this region as the "Crown of the Continent." The glaciers are the jewels in the crown—acres of ice with dense centers that remain frozen year-round. My shirt was drenched in sweat from the hike—it was borderline *hot* outside—but the ice in front of me was a relic from seasons and centuries past.

As I ate my sandwich, geologist Dan Fagre set about roaming the base of Grinnell, trying to find just the right place to position his tripod. Like most photographers, Dan was obsessed with getting the perfect shot. He spent ten minutes wandering from spot to spot, peeking through his lens, futzing with the zoom. First it was a little too close, then it was a little too far, then it was too close again. I could tell he was frustrated. It still wasn't quite good enough.

As I watched him at work, I noticed all the amateurs with iPhones kept glancing over at Dan. *What's that guy seeing that we aren't?* He wasn't even facing the obviously "pretty" direction.

But Dan is not an artist. He's a scientist. When he finally settled in and clicked the shutter, he wasn't focusing on the scenery. He was trying to take a picture of what *wasn't* there.

What was missing was the *ice*. Tons and tons of it have disappeared from these mountains. In 1850, there were an estimated

150 glaciers on the land that now makes up Glacier National Park. Today there are a sixth of that.

Back in his office at the U.S. Geological Survey, Dan has charts and graphs and spreadsheets that show the rising temperatures, the retreating ice, and the increase in humankind's greenhouse gas emissions. Thesis after thesis, study after study has documented how our climate is changing. And yet this PhD was out taking snapshots with me. He needed photos to drive his point home.

The park has an impressive archive of old images, some over a hundred years old, including black-and-white photos taken to promote Glacier after President Taft designated it a park in 1910. Dan had brought some of these old prints to serve as his guide. He would hold each one up, then try to approximate where it might have been taken from. It was harder than it sounds. Everything looked so *different.* In one photo from the 1930s, there was a man standing on a giant block of ice. Today that man would be floating seventy feet above the ground. It's shocking, and that's the point.

"It speaks to our biology," Dan said. "We get a lot of information visually, and we tend to trust that even more than what we hear."

The lack of trust surrounding climate science has never made sense to me. I can certainly get why people don't *want* to think that climate change is happening—it's terrifying—but to not believe that it actually *is?* That means that, in the face of a mountain of evidence presented by every major credible scientific organization out there, a layperson is somehow able to look at all of that information and think, *Meh. It's probably a bunch of bunk.*

If this frustrates *me*, then I assume it must infuriate Dan. But he remained calm and rational when I asked him about it. He's a scientist, after all.

"Our role as the U.S. Geological Survey is to provide the information. We're not policy makers," he said.

"Yeah, but . . ."

"We try to make people understand what we are seeing, what

we are measuring. And we hope that our data gets used in better societal decisions."

I hoped he was right. Dan was setting up again for another shot—he was the only photographer I'd ever seen take several pictures of his own *tripod*. He was marking its location, so that when the next re-photographer comes out here, they will be able to find this spot. Because after Dan is done, there's at least one more picture that will have to be taken. The final "after" shot, when this glacier disappears for good.

Former Park Service director Jon Jarvis has said that climate change is "fundamentally the greatest threat to the integrity of our national parks that we have ever experienced." No park is immune from its effects. A century from now, Joshua Tree is expected to have no more Joshua trees—long-lasting droughts and warmer winters will have likely killed them off. Wildfires are ripping through Yosemite. Warmer waters are bleaching Biscayne's beautiful coral reefs.

Really, if it weren't all so depressing, it would be fascinating—climate change is an excellent way to understand how connected everything is in nature, and how even the subtlest shifts can have large impacts.

Take the Dall sheep found in the Alaska national parks. Dall populations don't migrate, which makes them fairly straightforward to study. The Park Service considers the sheep an "indicator species"—by tracking their health, scientists are able to gain insight into other changes in the ecosystem.

In the high elevations of Alaska's Wrangell–St. Elias National Park, thousands of Dall sheep roam free, eating alpine grasses and lichens. While a warming climate doesn't necessarily mean those plants can't grow anymore, it does mean *other* plant species can start thriving for the first time—shrubs and woody plants that have never existed that high up in the mountains. As those new plants grow, they start casting shadows on the lowly grasses favored by the Dall sheep, which means the grasses will die out, and potentially so will the Dall. Indicator species are the canaries in the coal mine—they remind us of the bigger picture.

Flying into Wrangell–St. Elias, it appeared the sheep climbing the mountains in the distance were nothing more than white dots—part of one *enormous* picture. Wrangell–St. Elias is larger than Yellowstone, Yosemite, Everglades, Rocky Mountain, Big Bend, Great Smoky Mountains, Zion, Shenandoah, Crater Lake, and the Grand Canyon *combined.* Officially known as Wrangell–St. Elias National Park and *Preserve* (sport hunting is permitted in the preserve), it encompasses more than thirteen million acres, home to the largest system of glaciers in the country.

My pilot pointed out Kennicott Glacier—a long, winding glacier that seemed to be gliding down from a nearby mountain, covering 149 square miles below it. It took me a moment to even realize it *was* a glacier—it just looked like a giant, white highway.

The next morning, I joined two German tourists for a hike out to the park's Root Glacier, one of Kennicott's tributary on-ramps. The men told me Germany is down to its final few glaciers—a reminder that global warming is, well, *global.* The Germans said they wanted to visit Alaska "while it still looked like Alaska."

When I arrived to check in for the hike, our guide asked if I'd brought my own crampons or wanted to borrow some. I didn't know what crampons were—they sounded like Tampax that somehow made your period *worse.* I stammered until the guide pulled out a pair of chains and spikes that were meant to clip underneath my hiking boots.

"Oh *those*," I said. "Yeah, I'll borrow yours if that's okay."

After a two-mile walk on a gravel trail, we all strapped into our crampons and stepped out on the ice. The metal teeth bit down into the glacier, providing stability as we walked across the surface. Standing right on top of the ice, I could hear it melting beneath me—it creaked and crackled like a muted rainstorm broadcast on a distant radio. Little bright-blue pools of water had formed across the surface, creating miniature waterfalls where trickling streams fell down through the cracks.

I knew that the little bits of water beneath my feet didn't prove anything. Glaciers *always* melt in the summer—that's what they do. But not this much. Not this fast.

I can get why melting glaciers are imperfect messengers for someone who doesn't understand—or doesn't *want* to understand—climate science. We're *used* to ice vanishing. The ice that arrives in our Chipotle cup isn't meant to stay in there forever. The ice on our driveway goes away on a sunny morning. Where most of us live, ice isn't a constant—if anything, it's a nuisance. It performs the same magic trick again and again—it disappears, then it comes back. But the ice in Alaska isn't coming back.

Perhaps the most obvious signs of climate change are the actual signs on display at the entrance of Alaska's Kenai Fjords National Park. There, little brown wooden rectangles line the side of the pavement, each painted with four white digits. Driving into the park, you see numbers long before you see ice.

The first one I noticed—1815—looked like it might be an elevation marker, except there's no way I had ascended close to two thousand feet since I'd left my hotel back in Seward. I soon passed another one—1899. They definitely weren't distance markers—the ice was still well over a mile away.

After parking the car, I kept walking toward the glacier in the distance. The small signs continued to line the trail. 1926. 1961. I finally realized what they represented, but I couldn't believe it—they were markers of where the ice I'd come to see *used* to be.

Kenai's Exit Glacier was not named for how quickly it's *exiting*, or retreating. That's just an unfortunate coincidence. The name comes from a 1968 skiing expedition, during which a group of cross-country skiers—including, fun fact, pop singer Jewel's grandfather Yule Kilcher—exited the Harding Ice Field at this very spot on their journey from Homer to Seward.

The ice the skiers would have seen in the 1960s was long gone. I passed another sign—1978—and was still thousands of feet away from the start of the glacier.

I met up with ranger Fiona North, which is, remarkably, the name of an actual real person and not the heroine of a breezy novel about an Alaskan park guide's fantastic life. As much as I wanted to hear about *The Arctic Adventures of Fiona North*, I'd asked her to walk out to the glacier with me to help me understand what I was seeing—or, more accurately, what I *wasn't*.

"Since 1835, the Exit Glacier has retreated, on average, about forty-six feet per year," she said. "And more recently, say 2014, it retreated 151 feet. So a *huge* increase in the rate of retreat.

"Keep in mind . . . the glacier is flowing downhill." Fiona nodded toward the glacier. "So it moves *forward* about ten inches a day, but it's retreating from its original spot."

Basically, it's two steps forward, ten steps back. What neither Fiona nor I knew at that moment was that the glacier in front of us was retreating faster than it ever had before. By the end of the summer, Exit Glacier was measured to have retreated an estimated 262 feet—the most significant year ever recorded.

The year before, President Obama had toured Kenai by land and by sea, marveling at icebergs he proclaimed "the size of a Costco." There's a video of Obama goofing around with a GoPro in the park—it's pretty clear the president was having a blast.

But his message—and the reason for his trip—was serious. Obama had come to Alaska to give a speech at the Conference on Global Leadership in the Arctic: Cooperation, Innovation, Engagement and Resilience. GLACIER, for short.

In his remarks, Obama compared a gigaton of ice to the size of the Washington Mall.

"Now imagine seventy-five of those ice blocks," he said. "That's what Alaska's glaciers alone lose each year. The pace of melting is only getting faster. It's now twice what it was between 1950 and 2000—twice as fast as it was just a little over a decade ago."

He went on to warn the crowd full of native Alaskans and foreign dignitaries that "if we do nothing, temperatures in Alaska are projected to rise between six and twelve degrees by the end of the century, triggering more melting, more fires, more thawing of the permafrost, a negative feedback loop, a cycle—warming leading to more warming—that we do not want to be a part of."

It was a speech full of dire predictions, but there was just enough hope to keep it from becoming too gloomy. Obama closed by encouraging the crowd to get out there and see the ice for themselves.

> I hope you have the chance to visit a glacier. Or just look out your airplane window as you depart, and take in the God-given majesty of this place. For those of you flying to other parts of the world, do it again when you're flying over your home countries. Remind yourself that there will come a time when your grandkids—and mine, if I'm lucky enough to have some—they'll want to see this. They'll want to experience it, just as we've gotten to do in our own lives. They deserve to live lives free from fear, and want, and peril. And ask yourself, are you doing everything you can to protect it?

The New York Times described that Alaska visit, near the end of Obama's second term, as the president in "legacy building mode." But as I stood in Kenai's Glacier View Pavilion, a structure built in the 1980s that no longer even offers a view of the glacier, it was obvious to me I was looking at *our* legacy. The parks are our indicator species. Living laboratories where we can see—sometimes in something as simple as a photograph—that trouble is coming. If glaciers continue to melt at their current rate, then one day soon entire Alaskan villages will be underwater. People are already dying from wildfires caused, in part, by the longer, hotter summers brought on by climate change.

"We're making a difference, but we have to keep going. We

are not moving fast enough," Obama told the Alaskan crowd that day.

It must have been tempting to describe the pace of our response as "glacial," although I can understand why he didn't. That word doesn't carry the same weight it used to. Today the pace of glaciers is anything but slow.

11

PEOPLE

(Arches, Bryce Canyon, Zion)

I arrived at Zion National Park just as a shipment of porta potties was being delivered.

"They are new for this year," Superintendent Jeff Bradybaugh said of the row of toilets, which were being set up in a parking lot near a popular trailhead.

"It's kind of a test. We're going to measure each time those doors open and close. Each time they're pumped out, we'll have a *volume* measurement."

"Wow. That's a . . . fun job," I said, grimacing.

"Yeah . . . That's one we like to contract out."

Hiring a private company to measure the amount of visitor crap was just one of several projects Zion was undertaking that summer. The park was tracking wait times at the entrance stations, surveying random hikers on popular trails, and holding "listening sessions" in the adjacent town of Springdale, Utah. The data collected would hopefully help Zion finally come up with a solution to a problem that had been plaguing it for years: The park was being loved to death.

. . .

When I first visited Zion in 1995, as part of a ten-day trip out west with my family, Zion "only" got 2.4 million visitors a year. I'm sure I was one of the most enthusiastic ones. I was fourteen years old, and I was having the time of my life.

Until that trip, the farthest west I had ever been was Kentucky. It was the first time I'd ever traveled on an airplane. When we landed in Phoenix, it felt like I had arrived in a whole other world.

My siblings and I had each been given our own Kodak FunSaver disposable camera. Rationing my twenty-four exposures for the week was even harder than making my Halloween candy last. I wanted to photograph *everything*. I wonder if that's why the memories of that trip are still so vivid for me—at each stop, I had to carefully consider what amazing view I wanted to remember forever.

My family first drove our rental van north to the Grand Canyon, then started to make our way to California through Utah and Nevada, stopping for a night each at Zion and Bryce Canyon.

I had purchased a special journal adorned with an M. C. Escher print to serve as my diary for the trip, but I ended up having so much fun that I only filled a few pages. Looking back now on what I *did* write, there are several references to the crowds. At each park we visited, I commented on how the hotels and restaurants were booked solid. I remember it feeling stressful back then, but it was nothing compared with what the parks are like today.

In 2010, fifteen years after my first trip to Zion, visitation had only increased from 2.4 million to just under 2.7 million. But five years after that, it *skyrocketed*. In 2015, more than 3.6 million visitors showed up at Zion. By 2016, the number had climbed to nearly 4.3 million. Think about that. In the space of just a year's time, an extra 646,281 people showed up. Over half of the national parks don't see that many people *total* in a year.

"The word is out," Bradybaugh told me. "Zion is a beautiful place."

The word got out largely thanks to Utah's Mighty 5 campaign.

Launched in 2013, the series of scenery-soaked advertisements promoted the state by promoting its five national parks—Arches, Bryce Canyon, Canyonlands, Capitol Reef, and Zion—as a bucket-list-worthy itinerary, something akin to the Seven Wonders of the World.

"Five iconic parks, one epic experience," the voiceover in the commercial said.

That's exactly what Jennifer Lam and her friends were hoping for when I met them on the Emerald Pools Trail at Zion. They had flown all the way from Hawaii to tackle the Mighty 5 in just six days. Their itinerary was insanely ambitious, and also included stops in popular spots like Horseshoe Bend and Antelope Canyon, but the Mighty 5 were the mightiest draw.

"I kept seeing them mentioned on a bunch of travel blogs," Jennifer said. "I wanted to come see them in person."

In 2016, visitors spent a record $8.54 billion in Utah, translating into more than a billion dollars of tax revenue. The Mighty 5 ads aired everywhere from Germany to China. From a financial standpoint, the campaign was a tremendous success.

But for the parks, the massive increase in interest has not translated into a noticeable increase in federal funding. Year over year, park budgets have barely budged, despite dealing with nearly twice as many visitors. The entrance fees that all of the Utah parks charge at their gates don't come anywhere close to what it actually costs to maintain and staff them.

Sometimes tourists aren't even able to *get into* the gates. In 2015, in what *The Times-Independent of Moab* called an "unprecedented decision," the Utah Highway Patrol shut down the entrance to Arches National Park for part of Memorial Day weekend. Traffic had backed up for miles and was creating safety issues for other motorists along U.S. Highway 191.

At Bryce Canyon, an hour-and-a-half drive away from Zion, the park website cautions road-tripping visitors that just one parking space exists for every *four* cars entering the park. Arrive early, they warn, or you might be circling all afternoon.

Automobile traffic is banned altogether at Zion during peak season. Five years after my family drove through the park, Zion instituted a shuttle system to ferry visitors back and forth along the main road.

At first, the shuttles were a success, bringing peace and quiet back to the park. A fleet of fewer than twenty buses took the place of thousands of cars. But now even the buses have become overwhelmed. Today, instead of circling and circling to find a parking space, tourists might spend even longer waiting to catch a shuttle.

"At the visitor center, the wait can be forty-five minutes, even longer sometimes," Bradybaugh said. "And there might also have been that long of a wait at the entrance station."

"So before someone even sets foot on a trail, they've been waiting an hour and a half?" I asked.

"Yeah, it's not the ideal experience, for sure," Bradybaugh said. "And we want people to have that *exemplary* Zion experience."

But what even constitutes an "exemplary" experience in a national park? To find out, Bradybaugh suggested I visit an office park on the outskirts of Denver.

The Denver Service Center does not offer official tours, although I wish it did. For anyone interested in the Park Service, I'd argue that a visit to that nondescript office provides a more illuminating look into how the parks actually operate than a trip to Teddy Roosevelt's old cabin in North Dakota.

Situated among the strip malls of Lakewood, Colorado, the red-brick-and-glass building looks like it might be the headquarters of an SAT prep company or an e-commerce site that sells scented candles. The windows offer views of an Advance Auto Parts store and a Sonic Drive-In across the street.

But inside, a staff of more than two hundred employees shapes how Americans spend time in some of the most scenic spots in the country. When I visited, I did not see a single ranger in uniform, but instead found cubicle after cubicle filled with social scientists, landscape architects, cultural resource managers, contracting experts, and transportation specialists. These were the people *behind* the parks, focused on all manner of operational and ecological concerns across the Park Service.

Inside a conference room that looked straight out of Dunder Mifflin, I met with Kerri Cahill, an expert in visitor use management.

"It's about making the experience as high-quality as it can be," Cahill told me. "Typically, if you ask people, overall, did they have a good experience, they're largely going to say yes, because they got to see the Grand Canyon or Yosemite or Yellowstone or these gorgeous, beautiful, iconic places. But when you dig a little deeper, you might find out that there were things that could've been better."

Any ordinary company would be thrilled to have the customer satisfaction rates that a place like Bryce Canyon or Arches has. But as much as the Denver Service Center might look like a business from the outside, it does not run like a business inside. "Good enough" can't be good enough for the Park Service, where the mission goes far beyond just getting bodies in the door. Cahill and her team are most concerned with the intangibles. For them, it's more than just giving people the chance to *see* the Grand Canyon—it's giving them the chance to be *inspired* by it.

Ensuring those inspirational moments survive an influx of visitors is no easy task. Take the shuttles at Zion. Within the park, they have successfully reduced noise and cut air pollution. Everyone agrees that's been a good thing. But they've also created intense bursts of visitors arriving at popular trailheads all at once, which has created a new problem: Instead of people starting out on a hike one or two small groups at a time, now a group of fifty or so all unload simultaneously. There's nothing inspirational about a mass of shuffling, shoving people.

At Zion, Bradybaugh had shown me a picture taken in a section of Zion Canyon known as the Narrows. The water there is only knee-deep, so it's possible to walk for miles straight up the middle of the river—it's one of my favorite hikes of all time.

But I barely recognized the Narrows in Bradybaugh's photo. It was packed with people. A mass of hikers in tank tops and sun hats seemed to fill every available inch of the riverbed.

"Holy crap," I said. "That looks like Coachella."

It was crowded and chaotic and *gross*. Nothing about the picture looked like the tranquil, beautiful hike I remembered.

"Was that like, one *particularly* terrible day?" I asked hopefully.

"There are a lot of days like that now," Bradybaugh said, shaking his head.

The people in that photo looked like they could have just as easily been at Six Flags Hurricane Harbor. Is that what national parks are destined to become?

The Organic Act of 1916, which established the Park Service, specified that parks must be preserved "in such manner and by such means as will leave them unimpaired for the enjoyment of future generations." In other words, we are not just sharing the parks with millions of visitors each year, we are sharing them with the billions of people who have yet to be born.

Thus far, preservation has mostly been thought of in terms of keeping the parks wild. Don't chop down all the trees, don't pave over every available space, et cetera. Let the parks be sanctuaries where people can enjoy unspoiled nature.

But the mere act of enjoying that nature can spoil it. Bradybaugh told me Zion had well over twice as many miles of "social trails" as it had official trails. Never as well planned or resource-conscious as the trails planned by the park, social trails are created when hikers, frustrated with crowds on the main path, find their own way. Unfortunately, in the process, they trample vegetation and damage the fragile soil. Bryce Canyon, a park created by erosion over millions of years, is very vulnerable to the type of erosion caused by a summer of people walking where they shouldn't.

At some point, with enough people, crowded parks don't just become unpleasant, they become *unsafe*. The most famous trail at

Zion is Angels Landing, a steep climb full of switchbacks that eventually leads to one of the best views in the park.

The last half mile is the tricky part. Hikers must scramble up a narrow cliff, holding on to chains nailed into the rock for support. At least nine people have slipped and fallen to their death since 2004.

In 1995, on my first visit to the park, my dad wouldn't let my siblings and me climb the final bit. I remember being so upset with him, telling him he was being overly cautious. We argued as other hikers, some with even younger kids, passed us by.

"This will be my only chance, Dad," I pleaded. "Pleeeease. I'll probably never be back here again." He held firm, and I sulked on my way back down the trail.

Two decades later, after I finally did the hike on my own, I called him to apologize.

"You were so right," I said that night. "There's no way we should have gone to the top as kids. That was crazy. I probably shouldn't have gone *now*."

The day I finally hiked Angels Landing, the narrow trail was teeming with hundreds of other visitors—tour groups wearing flip-flops and twentysomethings paying more attention to their GoPro shots than to their foot positioning. On a mountain where there's already so little room for error, there was barely enough room to stand—one misstep by anyone could have inadvertently sent an entire group off the edge. The view at the end of the trail was spectacular, but I think there's just too many people today for it to be worth the risk.

So what's the Park Service to do? A quick and easy way to ease overcrowding would be to raise prices. That's what any business would do. Charging more—maybe a *lot* more—would help pay for infrastructure improvements and would finally uncover what the "market rate" is for an exemplary national park experience.

When I talked to Superintendent Bradybaugh, Zion was charging thirty dollars per car for a one-week entry pass. The rate has now increased to thirty-five dollars per car.

It very nearly went up to seventy. In 2017, then interior secretary Ryan Zinke proposed a significant price hike at the most popular parks like Zion, Yellowstone, and Yosemite, but the plan ended up being so widely criticized that he had to back off and settle for a more modest increase. Over one hundred thousand public comments, most of them negative, poured into the NPS website. People worried that if parks got more expensive, then the Americans who could least afford them would no longer visit.

"These parks belong to the people," Bradybaugh had told me back at Zion. "We want to be careful that we aren't pricing out certain folks."

The vast majority of park units don't charge entrance fees at all. For those that do, an eighty-dollar annual pass provides unlimited entry into every park in the country for an entire year. (By comparison, one *day* at Disney's parks costs well over one hundred dollars.) The national parks are a good deal by design.

In Denver, Kerri Cahill told me that establishing timed entry reservations was one of the options under consideration at popular parks like Zion. Show up without one, and you won't be let through the gate. It's a strategy that's worked well for museums. The Getty Villa in Malibu is free to enter, but visitors must first reserve a specific time and date online.

Somehow, though, being told when we can and can't go to our parks just feels . . . *wrong*. "The mountains are calling and I must *go*," John Muir wrote. Not "the mountains are calling and I must go next Thursday at 3 P.M., because that's the only ticket I could snag that was available."

And yet several parks already have reservation systems in place for backcountry permits and tours and popular campgrounds. It's hard to imagine a future in which *some* kind of reservation system doesn't continue to spread across the more popular parks. Especially if the goal is to preserve some of that intangible inspiration.

What's better, ten thousand people a day all having a miserable time? Or seven thousand people a day all having a fantastic one?

I don't want to paint too gloomy a picture. In the overall scheme of things, the story of overcrowded parks is really only the story of *certain* parks. The Park Service manages more than four hundred units, but over half of all visitation occurs at less than thirty of them. Even with the Mighty 5, it's really more like the Giant 3, with Utah's Canyonlands and Capitol Reef still not quite bursting at the seams. In a year in which Yosemite saw five million visitors, a park like Pinnacles, less than two hundred miles away, received closer to two hundred thousand. There's still plenty of room to roam out there.

Even at the most popular parks, I was shocked by how the crowds would disappear the moment I wandered away from the parking lots. The vast majority of visitors spend mere hours at the parks. They don't have time to take long hikes in between driving to lookouts, snapping photos, and visiting the gift shop.

Utah's license plate features a picture of Delicate Arch, which makes a strong case for it as the mightiest attraction in all of the Mighty 5. While it's definitely worth seeing, there are more than two thousand other arches at Arches National Park. My four-and-a-half-mile round-trip walk out to the far less crowded Double O Arch was one of the best hikes I did all year. Wake up a bit earlier, walk a bit farther, and you can still have the views to yourself.

Also, none of these overcrowding concerns are particularly new. In 1869, when David Folsom—part of the first official expedition to explore the Yellowstone region—saw its largest body of water, he wrote, "We felt glad to have looked upon it before its primeval solitude should be broken by the crowds of pleasure seekers which at no distant day will throng its shores."

In 1953, back when the national parks received less than a tenth of their current visitation, essayist Bernard DeVoto published a piece in *Harper's Magazine* titled "Let's Close the National Parks." Alarmed by the poor conditions he'd observed at parks where "there are not enough rangers to protect either the scenic areas from the depredations of tourists or the tourists from the consequences of their own carelessness," DeVoto suggested we shut them down altogether.

"The national park system must be temporarily reduced to a size for which Congress is willing to pay," he wrote. If the Park Service, the "impoverished step child of Congress," couldn't be properly funded and staffed, DeVoto argued, then the parks should be "temporarily closed and sealed, held in trust for a more enlightened future."

At Bryce Canyon, I got a preview of that future while being reminded of my past. As I walked through the parking lot at Inspiration Point, I saw a family with three kids who seemed to be around the same age as my brother, sister, and I were when we first visited Bryce. The kids were speed-walking around the rim carrying a Junior Ranger pamphlet, occasionally bending down to grab something off the concrete. I could tell from their excitement that they were on some sort of scavenger hunt.

At every park, the Junior Ranger program gives kids (or really, anyone who wants to participate) a certificate or a merit badge for completing a series of activities meant to connect them to the place. It's generally stuff like "spot a prairie dog and a lizard," "complete a word search of Native American words," or "interview a volunteer about what they do at the park."

As I got closer to the family at Bryce, I finally noticed what the kids were doing. They were picking up *trash*.

"Seven, eight . . ." the little girl crowed as she snatched up what looked like gum wrappers near a bench. To become a Junior Ranger at Bryce, one of the requirements is to "dispose of at least ten pieces of litter."

Our best weapon for protecting the parks from people has always been *people*. Even if it were possible to somehow lock our national treasures away, preserving them for some "more enlightened future," how would that enlightenment ever arrive unless people had a chance to experience these places for themselves? The more people who visit the parks; the more people who see, first-hand, what needs to be addressed; the more kids who are able to feel that same feeling of inspiration at Inspiration Point I felt when I was a kid, the more chance we stand of protecting the parks.

Perhaps the record-breaking popularity of the parks will help us love them back to life. In addition to significant staffing short-ages, the Park Service currently has a massive twelve-billion-dollar maintenance backlog. With enough political pressure, Congress could take this on. Finding funding gets easier when there are 330 million visitors out there cheering you on.

Stephen Mather, the first director of the National Park Service, firmly believed that as many people needed to visit the parks as possible. To Mather, the parks represented our greatest source of national pride. They were places with a unique capacity to soothe our "national restlessness." Once, when asked if he was concerned that more visitors meant more trash, he replied that "the parks belong to everyone."

"We can pick up the cans," he said. "It's a cheap way to make better citizens."

12

HOME

(Mesa Verde, Great Smoky Mountains)

Mesa Verde bills itself as the first national park created to "preserve the works of man." Established in 1906, the park was once the home of the Ancestral Pueblo people, former nomads who settled in what's now southwestern Colorado around AD 550. For more than six hundred years, they lived on the top of Mesa Verde, the mighty "Green Table," transitioning from a lifestyle of hunting and gathering to one of farming.

As the population grew, the Ancestral Pueblo people constructed villages to serve as the centers of their communities, overlooking the valley below them from the eight-thousand-foot-high clifftops. And then, for reasons we still don't understand, they decided to move into the cliffs themselves.

Built straight into the side of the mountain, Mesa Verde's cliff dwellings would be impressive if they were built *today*, but they're mind blowing considering they were constructed sometime in the late twelfth century. When cowboys passing through in the 1800s looked up and saw them for the first time, they rushed home with tales of the abandoned cities they had glimpsed high above them.

Ranger David Franks had agreed to give me a tour of Cliff Palace, the largest cliff dwelling in the park. Standing directly above it, you would have no idea the "palace" was there—the buildings are hidden under an overhang. Take a running jump from the top and you'd fall right past this entire little world, sandwiched into an alcove.

To get to the dwellings, I followed David down a series of precarious ladders—modern additions to this ancient place. The hundred or so people who lived here are thought to have free-climbed to the top of the mesa to farm.

"Their commute to work was just amazing," David marveled. "We really are incredible creatures . . . It makes you proud to be a human being."

David grew up nearby, and as a child he would come to the park with his family to wander around the ruins.

"I've always had a healthy imagination," he said. "I would just sit there, close my eyes. You could hear ravens; you could hear other birds floating around. You'd feel the wind. And my mind just started seeing people *living* here . . . what they were doing. You know—laughter, crying, sweating, arguing . . . everything that we do today."

David smiled, thinking back on those early visits.

"That hooked me. I just wanted to be here."

Archaeologists can only speculate as to why the inhabitants of the cliff dwellings decided to move down from the mountain into a place that seems far more inconvenient. Were they protecting themselves from their enemies? From the elements? Were the cliffs in a better school district?

"That's part of the fun of it." David smiled.

The dwellings feature kivas, large circular underground rooms said to have been used for ceremonies and religious practices. In the center of each circle, there's a second, smaller circle, a hollowed-out indentation about the width of a manhole cover. In the Hopi language, it's known as a sipapu. The Hopi, descendants of the Ancestral Pueblo people, believe the sipapu represents where *all* humans came from.

"You're in what some refer to as Sky World or the Fourth Earth," David explained. "Three other earths were cleaned prior to this earth."

According to the legend, the First Earth was destroyed by fire. The second froze into solid ice. The Third Earth was destroyed by a massive flood. In each case, the humans had forgotten what was important. We forgot to honor and respect our Creator. The few who remembered were saved, emerging into the new world, in their new forms, from the sipapu.

Staring into the kivas, walking around Cliff Palace, it didn't take long before I began to feel the wonder David must have felt as a child. This was a place where people *lived.* This was a community.

Inside one of the towers, I could see a few paintings on the wall. Triangles and squares and squiggly lines with little notches poking out. They were abstract, but were arranged in a way that couldn't have been random. Was it a map? Art? A way of recording historical events? I asked David, but he didn't want to venture a guess.

"I think I'm always careful when I interpret things like this, because I know seven hundred years from now they're gonna talk about *us,* and they're gonna say something like, 'Hey, in the '70s, those people must have been really attuned to the earth because they all decorated their homes with wood paneling and avocado-green shag carpeting.'"

Point taken. It's fun and a little terrifying to wonder what future historians might get wrong about our culture. The ruins of an abandoned Olive Garden in Des Moines, interpreted incorrectly, might leave the impression that the Tuscans once conquered the Midwest.

The cliff dwellings were barely occupied for a hundred years when the Mesa Verdeans vanished. It's a puzzle that's fascinated anthropologists and archaeologists. Was it a drought? A war? A religious calling? *Something* must have been significant enough to convince an entire culture to migrate away from the new homes they'd just risked their lives building.

David is happy to entertain various theories (it's the most common question he gets on his tours), but he said he tries to bring visitors back to the emotional angle.

"I share a story about my father," David said. "He passed. And he built this house that I have so many wonderful memories in. We got to a point where we had to sell that house, me and my brothers. And . . ." He trailed off.

"That was hard," he said, finally. "Because that's home."

"So you can focus on the *why* questions all you want, but remember, these are *human beings*. With heavy hearts, people left where they buried their family, where they met that special person in their life, where their child was born, to basically go to an unknown. That's an incredible risk and sacrifice."

In the early 1940s, hundreds of families left their homes in the Great Smoky Mountains. They didn't want to move, but they were told it was their patriotic duty. Helen Vance's family was one of the last to leave.

"We didn't have a place to go," Helen told me. "But then Daddy got a letter . . . Said, if you don't get out, we're gonna come down and have the sheriff set your things out. You have to get out."

Helen and I were sitting together at the edge of Fontana Lake, not far from the Tennessee/North Carolina border. Somewhere out in the middle of all that water was where Helen had grown up. Today her backyard full of apple trees is submerged forty feet deep.

The lake was created after the Tennessee Valley Authority began construction on nearby Fontana Dam in 1942. The dam was part of the war effort, built to provide hydroelectric power for Alcoa's aluminum plants and the then secret Manhattan Project site in Oak Ridge, Tennessee. The surrounding valley was flooded, and families like Helen's were forced to move. A few weeks after they got that eviction notice, they packed up everything inside their house. Then they packed up the *house*.

"Daddy and I tore our house down, board by board. We had every plank off it, every nail out of it," she said. By 1944, Helen's brothers had already gone off to war, so it was up to her and her sisters to help with the heavy lifting. "We stacked it all up and took the lumber with us. Took everything."

Everything they could. Helen's great-great-grandmother, great-grandfather, and a slew of other family members were buried high up in the mountains, and they weren't about to start digging up their relatives. Plus, they didn't need to. Helen and her family knew they would be seeing those gravestones again soon. They'd been given a promise.

"My dad would have never agreed to it any other way," Helen said. "I was *with* my dad in the front lawn of our house when a TVA man came around and told him there would be a road built back after the war. I remember how excited Daddy was."

After Helen and her neighbors moved out to make way for the dam, forty-four thousand empty acres were left behind between the lake and Great Smoky Mountains National Park. The park—brand-new at the time—was eager to add the parcel to its collection. When the Park Service took over the land, part of the agreement stipulated that, once the war was over, *they* would be the ones to build a road back to the cemeteries. Instead, they built a Road to Nowhere.

Officially, the six-mile stretch of pavement leading away from Bryson City, North Carolina, is named Lake View Drive, although nobody calls it that. Even the signs downtown say ROAD TO NO-WHERE, and after a short drive through the woods, I found out why.

As I rounded a bend, I came upon five waist-high brown metal posts planted in the middle of the road, clearly meant to stop any vehicle attempting to travel farther into the mountains. From the dents and scratches on the posts, it looked like some cars had tried to push through anyway. Ahead, the pavement stretched onward into a dark stone tunnel, clearly built to accommodate automobile traffic. I pulled over, got out of the car, and continued into the tunnel on foot.

When I finally reached the other end, I was in the forest. The paved road turned to gravel, then to dirt, then disappeared altogether. As advertised, the Road to Nowhere had led me straight to, well, nowhere.

After a series of delays, in the 1960s the Park Service had started building the road they'd promised the Vance family, but stopped here after an environmental study convinced them the road would cause too much damage. While later studies concluded that the road *could* actually be built safely, the cost to do so would have exceeded a hundred million dollars, money the Park Service claimed they didn't have. Even if they did, I'd imagine it was hard for anyone in Washington, D.C., to stomach the idea of paying so much money to help a small group of people in North Carolina visit some overgrown headstones in the woods.

In 2007, sixty-five years after the road was first proposed, the Park Service admitted they were never going to finish it. Instead, they agreed to pay Swain County fifty-two million dollars in its place, money that could be used to support local schools and programs—whatever might benefit the public. It took the Park Service over a decade to pay up. For most people in the county, the settlement was welcome news, but it still wasn't going to get Helen and her sisters home.

The day I met Helen by Fontana Lake, the parking lot was packed full of cars. Families were dragging coolers, chairs, and massive Tupperware containers of food over to a dock where, every twenty minutes or so, a pontoon boat would arrive to ferry a group across the lake. The Park Service now provides transportation for families who want to visit the once inaccessible cemeteries on the other side. I had arrived on the one Sunday each year when the descendants of the people buried in Bone Valley and Hall cemeteries were able to go back home.

"We're not legally mandated to do such a thing," ranger Dana Soehn told me as we rode across with the last group of families. "But it's the right thing to do."

On the other side of the lake, at the top of a steep trail, tents and picnic tables were set up, covered with more hot dog buns, deviled eggs, and green bean casseroles than anyone could possibly ever eat. Kids were running and playing, someone was strumming a guitar, and people were smiling and catching up. It looked like a big family reunion and, in a way, it was. Several *different* families had come together to reconnect with the place their ancestors called home.

I had been expecting something a little more solemn. This felt like a party. In the South, it's what they call a Decoration Day. Everyone arrived in high spirits with armloads of flowers to decorate the graves.

The headstones were chiseled with first names that clearly came from another era. CRATEN was born in 1849. NARCISSUS was born in 1815. I found a stone that hadn't been decorated—DELIA TURPIN—and bent down to place a flower on it. Then I noticed the dates: April 13, 1938–June 10, 1938.

Delia had lived for less than two months. Whoever her parents were, they weren't just leaving behind a cemetery where they had interred their ancestors. This was where they had buried their infant daughter, now left behind in the woods.

Helen, who had been dealing with some health issues, had to stay back on the shore, but I traveled over with her younger sister, Mildred, who was a spry eighty-six years old. She was fourteen when she left the mountains, old enough to remember what life in them was like. On our way up to the cemetery, she had pointed out where her old schoolhouse was and where the "baptizin' hole" used to be. This land was her home, until it suddenly wasn't.

"They pushed us out," she said. "We either had to leave or swim."

Of course, a century before Mildred's family was pushed out of the Smokies, the U.S. government had forcibly removed thousands of Native Americans from the same land. Everywhere east of the Mississippi, tribes were rounded up and made to march west toward Oklahoma.

There are few pieces of legislation in history with such horrible, literal names as Andrew Jackson's Indian Removal Act. If such a bill were drafted now, it would surely be called something like "Operation Enduring Relocation," but back in 1830, nobody really saw the point in beating around the bush. The act was meant to do exactly what it did—remove the Indians. Remove them from their homes in the American South to go someplace, anyplace, else. The treacherous westward journey on what became known as the Trail of Tears was ultimately responsible for the death of an estimated quarter of the Cherokee tribe.

There are Cherokee burial mounds in Great Smoky Mountains, but they're unmarked and, in many cases, unknown. In recent decades, though, the park has been making an effort to make sure they better emphasize the history of its first residents. In 2011, the Oconaluftee Visitor Center opened, the first new visitor center built at Great Smoky Mountains since the 1960s.

Oconaluftee, which features interactive exhibits on the history of the Cherokee, sits on the edge of the Cherokee Indian Reservation in North Carolina, a popular gateway to the park. There, I learned the land technically *isn't* a reservation—it wasn't "reserved." Instead the Eastern Band of the Cherokee had to buy it back in the 1870s. After the Indian Removal Act forced tribes west, less than a thousand Cherokee stayed behind in the Southeast. Some were able to negotiate an exception from the government's official removal policy, while others hid out in what's now Great Smoky Mountains National Park. While nearby touristy towns like Gatlinburg and Pigeon Forge would be unrecognizable to the Cherokee who once lived throughout the Southeast, today the land preserved inside the park is some of the last land left that would still look like home.

. . .

When I left Cherokee, I drove north out of North Carolina and headed toward West Virginia. Country roads, take me home.

I grew up a few miles outside of Charleston's city limits. The summer before my senior year, we moved closer to town, but most of my memories of home are gathered around that first house—the one my parents built not long after they got married. Built as in built *themselves,* with their own two hands.

If it weren't for the old photos of my dad in the driveway pouring concrete and my mom hanging sheets of insulation between two-by-fours, I would have never believed they actually did it. It's still hard to fathom. Shouldn't some of those genetics have filtered down to me? I can barely change a tire, and yet I grew up under a roof on which my parents had personally laid every shingle.

The lack of a big, busy neighborhood meant we had plenty of forests to explore and hills to sled down. We'd play entire football games in the middle of the street without ever having to stop for a car. Everyone knew everyone else, and when I would walk door-to-door to sell magazines or candy bars for school, every house bought something. As I got older, I got frustrated that I lived so far from my school friends, but even then I knew I was lucky to live somewhere I loved. My heart lifted every time we pulled onto our street.

Once we left that house, we never had much reason to return. It seemed so far away. But while visiting my parents after the Smokies, I was running a few errands on that side of the city and decided to head out and see the old place.

I was surprised that I still knew every twist and turn on the winding road that took me out of town. It was the road I had learned to drive on, and its bends were locked into my muscle memory.

But when I finally pulled up to the house, I hardly recognized it. There was bright-white aluminum siding where my parents had once nailed light-brown cedar boards. The bush in the front yard by the mailbox was gone. The garage had been renovated and the side yard had been cleared of the trees I used to climb.

The nostalgia I had been hoping would sweep over me was replaced with an uneasiness. That wasn't my house anymore. It *re-sembled* my house, but too much had changed for it to feel like home.

Home has been a moving target for me ever since we moved off that street. Today, when credit card applications try to verify my identity by asking me about my old addresses, I often struggle to pass the test. "Oh right . . . I *did* live in that crappy apartment on Franklin Street in San Francisco in 2005 . . ." By now that rickety old building has probably been turned into a steel-and-glass cafeteria for Twitter employees.

As I traveled through the parks, it was the one question I kept getting asked—"Where's home?" It had never been harder for me to answer. Home kept shifting every few days, so much so that I was constantly taking pictures of my room keys and parking spaces so that I'd remember how to get back.

But I knew that whenever I eventually put down more permanent roots, home would still be a temporary concept. My friends had started buying what they all called starter homes—places that, from the day they moved in, they had decided they would ultimately leave. Whatever memories were going to be created within those walls would one day be left behind, papered over until they looked entirely different.

But when I went back to Bryce Canyon National Park and hiked the same trail I'd walked as a kid over two decades earlier, it felt as if *nothing* had changed. Maybe a few more people had arrived, but otherwise the park looked exactly the same as it did on my first visit. Around every turn, I could feel fourteen-year-old me peeking out from behind the rocks.

It's comforting to know that, wherever I live twenty years from now, I can return to Bryce and see that same view again. There will be no shopping plaza, there will be no aluminum siding. Parks are the homes we've taken off the market. Despite their often painful origin stories, our national parks have become our collective sanctuaries, places that welcome us back through their gates with open arms no matter how long we've been away. An old tree may have grown taller since the last time—but those are like moments marked in pencil inside a doorjamb. The house stays the same.

After a few glorious days in West Virginia catching up with my folks, sharing stories of my adventures, and sleeping in my old bed, it was time to get back on the road. They had baked a bag of goodies for my drive, and we squeezed together for one last hug in the driveway. I told them I'd see them soon.

For now, it was time to head back out into the parks. Time to go home.

13

CANYONS

(Grand Canyon, Black Canyon of the Gunnison)

In 1903, Teddy Roosevelt visited the Grand Canyon for the first time. It was only a day trip, a brief visit that offered a preview of how most tourists would come to experience one of the seven wonders of the natural world. Today the average visitor spends less than six hours total at the canyon.

When Roosevelt visited, the Grand Canyon wasn't yet a national monument or a park, but he hoped it might become one soon.

"In the Grand Canyon, Arizona has a natural wonder which is in kind absolutely unparalleled throughout the rest of the world," he told the crowd that had assembled to hear his remarks. "I want to ask you to keep this great wonder of nature as it now is."

Roosevelt knew how tempting development would be—he'd seen what had happened at places like Niagara Falls—and so he was explicit in his warnings.

"I hope you will not have a building of any kind, not a summer cottage, a hotel, or anything else, to mar the wonderful grandeur, the sublimity, the great loneliness and beauty of the canyon," he said. "Leave it as it is. You cannot improve on it. The ages have been at work on it, and man can only mar it."

Less than a year later, construction began on the massive El Tovar Hotel, just twenty feet from the South Rim.

The El Tovar was designed by Charles Whittlesey, chief architect for the Santa Fe Railway. Whittlesey had never even visited the Grand Canyon when he sketched the plans for what the railroad touted as a grand resort "combining the proportions of a Swiss chalet and a Norwegian villa."

The hotel was an instant success, and remains so today, with reservations booked more than a year in advance. Perhaps the El Tovar should have never been built in the first place, but once it was, well, who *wouldn't* want to stay twenty feet from the rim of the Grand Canyon? Even Teddy Roosevelt, when he visited years later, slept at the El Tovar.

I, however, slept thirty-seven thousand feet away from the rim, way back at a Best Western down the road in Tusayan. For two hundred dollars a night, I had snatched up one of the last rooms left in town, walking distance to a consistently packed McDonald's and IMAX theater. The Grand Canyon is now the country's second most popular national park (after Great Smoky Mountains), and the town of Tusayan caters to the millions of tourists who pass through each year. The Best Western was in the process of adding on a brand-new fitness center and swimming pool to supplement its attached bowling alley and arcade. The mighty El Tovar seemed quaint by comparison.

In the morning, I joined the long line of cars on AZ 64 to head into the park. There, I met up with ranger Kristen Luetkemeier, who was waiting for me in the concrete plaza outside the El Tovar.

Kristen is an expert on the great *indoors* of Grand Canyon. She told me she wanted to show me what she described as "one of her favorite views in the park." Instead of looking out at the spectacular panorama of red and brown stretching out for miles in the distance, Kristen turned her attention to the buildings.

"Imagine yourself back in 1905. If you look to your left," she said, pointing to the El Tovar, "you see where U.S. architecture was coming from.

"But if you look to your right, you see where it was *going*."

To the right was Hopi House, a building that opened the same month as the El Tovar but looked like it had been built centuries earlier. Modeled after ancient Hopi pueblos, the three-story reddish rectangular building isn't nearly as symmetrical and precise as the El Tovar. Its haphazard roof heights and window shapes make it feel more organic and handmade, and its walls of locally quarried sandstone match the colors along the rim. The El Tovar was a bit of Switzerland imported to Arizona, designed to make a statement on the edge of the canyon. The Hopi House was subtler, meant to blend in with its surroundings.

The house was designed by architect Mary Colter, an employee of the Fred Harvey Company, a hospitality industry giant responsible for many of the shops, restaurants, and hotels that lined the railroads in the West. In her work for the company, Colter traveled throughout New Mexico and Arizona. When she got the assignment for the Grand Canyon, she drew upon her experience with the Hopi sites she'd visited.

"She wanted to create buildings that were of this region, that spoke to it, and that educated people about it," Kristen explained.

The Hopi House is at once completely fake and surprisingly authentic. It's the kind of project that could have easily crossed the line into kitsch—a sort of Native American Epcot Center—but somehow feels as if it genuinely belongs at the canyon. Colter fashioned the fireplaces and the chimneys out of broken pottery jars and used peeled log beams and local branches to create her ceilings. She designed the upper floors as residences, so that Native artisans could live and work on-site.

All told, it was pretty ambitious . . . for a gift shop.

. . .

From 9 A.M. to 5 P.M., seven days a week, the cash registers at the Hopi House chime with the steady purchases of Native blankets, pottery, and kachina dolls. Occasionally, a tourist might "tsk tsk" that such a beautiful structure in such a magnificent setting has been turned into such a blatantly commercial enterprise. It's a criticism that never ceases to amuse Bruce Brossman. Hopi House has *always* been a gift shop.

"These buildings were built to lure tourists to the Grand Canyon, frankly," he chuckled. Bruce works for Xanterra, the company that runs most of the Grand Canyon's commercial facilities. "They were marketing tools. Mary Colter just happened to be a genius."

After the success of the Hopi House, Colter was asked to build two more gift shops: Lookout Studio and Hermit's Rest. Whereas Hopi House was set back a bit from the rim, Colter's next two buildings were butted up along the edge, their rock walls appearing as if they were natural extensions of the canyon's own walls. While Colter was not the *first* architect to see the value in matching structures to their surroundings, she helped to popularize the practice at what would soon become one of the most popular parks, at a critical time in Park Service history. Her buildings became prime examples of an architectural style still employed today: National Park Rustic.

I drove with Bruce out to Hermit's Rest, seven miles west of Hopi House. A ramshackle collection of local stones and wood, it's not the kind of building for which the blueprints would necessarily wow you. It was designed to look like someone who didn't really know what they were doing threw it together in a hurry. But Colter knew *exactly* what she was doing—the chaos was all part of her plan. She liked to give her buildings a built-in backstory.

"She wanted it to look like a hermit actually lived there," Bruce said. "That, when people visited, they had just missed him."

The hermit of Hermit's Rest was entirely imaginary, but Colter pre-sooted the ceiling inside to make it look like a fireplace had been burning for ages. She brought in cobwebs and wore down the finish on the furniture. In 1914, when the store opened for the first time, it already looked used. It was the gift shop equivalent of a pair of pre-ripped three-hundred-dollar designer jeans.

Colter's most impressive work is the Desert View Watchtower. Near the East Entrance of the park, the watchtower looks as if it might have been part of some abandoned fortress, a tall cylinder of uneven rough stones sitting on a base of faux ruins. By the time it was built in 1932, Colter had gotten even more skilled at making the new seem old again, hiding the tower's supportive steel skeleton behind a weathered rock façade. Every stone was carefully positioned. Once, the work crew completed a couple of layers in Colter's absence, assuming she'd be pleased at their progress. When she returned from her trip, she made them tear it all down. Everything needed to be done according to her precise specifications.

Most Colter legends make her out to be an exacting taskmaster. She chain-smoked, she wore Stetson hats, she was prickly and unlikable. "A woman working in a man's world," Bruce from Xanterra said. I suspect her personality also got an unfair amount of attention *because* she was a woman. Plenty of male architects are exacting and irritable, and it barely merits a mention in their biographies.

Colter died in 1958, but her contributions to "parkitecture" have only recently been recognized. This, in part, is also due to a general lack of respect for female architects—and Colter was always an employee, never an independent practitioner, which also didn't help—but ranger Kristen offered another interesting perspective.

"People are always pretty happy to speculate that gender plays a role in Mary Colter's fame, or lack thereof," she said. "I think region plays an important role, too."

Snooty architecture critics on the coasts had no idea what Colter was up to in the Southwest. While she was a contemporary of Frank Lloyd Wright, who shot to fame while living in ritzy Chicago, Colter was an architect working in a flyover state before there were even cross-country flights. It wasn't until the late 1980s, long after Colter's death, that she began to achieve the fame that eluded her in life.

Today there are books about Colter for sale in the gift shops she designed. Rooms at the Colter-designed Bright Angel Lodge sell out over a year in advance. The interiors are trimmed in a shade called Mary Jane Blue, which sounds like a strain of pot you might find at a Denver dispensary but was named by the lodge painters in honor of their boss, who was as particular about the specific hue as she was about everything else.

I found a park pamphlet that described Colter as a "woman ahead of her time." But time takes on a different meaning at a place like the Grand Canyon. Colter was designing buildings meant to look six hundred years old on the rim of a canyon that's six *million* years old. First built up, then partially torn down, a canyon has construction delays that are measured in terms of eras—the Paleozoic and the Mesozoic and the Cenozoic.

While the Grand Canyon was famously carved by the Colorado River, its work can feel more like a mystery when standing in front of Hopi House—the Colorado winds and bends along a bottom that's largely out of sight. But the Gunnison River—the architect of Black Canyon of the Gunnison National Park—is easier to spot. A few miles away from the town of Montrose, Colorado, Black Canyon's walls are so jaw-droppingly steep that anyone brave enough to stand along the rim can peer straight down into our planet's ancient foundation.

The rare Precambrian "basement rocks" at the bottom of Black Canyon of the Gunnison are nearly two billion years old. That's so staggeringly long ago that it's almost impossible to comprehend. As author John McPhee wrote in his study of geology, *Basin and Range*, "Any number above a couple of thousand years—fifty thousand, fifty million—will with nearly equal effect awe the imagination to the point of paralysis."

I'm sure at least part of the paralysis I experienced at the edge of Black Canyon had to do with my fear of falling into it. While the Grand Canyon is far wider than it is deep, Black Canyon is often far *deeper* than it is wide—it's a sheer drop down to the bottom. Instead of the brilliant hues of red and pink and purple found in Arizona, Black Canyon's walls are—if not quite black—a dull sort of gray, made grayer still by sharp, long shadows. That's why they call it Black Canyon—it's very difficult for sunlight to penetrate its chasm. Parts of its interior only receive half an hour or so of sun a day. At the canyon's narrowest point, down by the Gunnison River, it's only forty feet across.

The river carves the canyon at the rate of one inch every hundred years. As the park points out on its website, that's the width of one human hair a *year*.

One of the most useful documents to ever detail the powerful forces responsible for the formation of Black Canyon is an in-depth U.S. Geological Survey bulletin written by Wallace Hansen back in 1965. (Even that seems like *ages* ago.) In his study of the canyon, Hansen acknowledges the "incomprehensible immensity of time" that a place like Black Canyon represents. But even more incomprehensible is that the canyon isn't really that old.

"In terms of relative geologic age, viewed in the vastness of geologic time, the canyon is very youthful indeed—it formed only yesterday," Hansen writes. "But in terms of man's experience, his short recorded history, and his even shorter life span, the antiquity of the canyon is staggering."

When thinking of a canyon's lifespan in relation to our own, I'm reminded of a fireplace I saw at the Grand Canyon. Inside Bright Angel Lodge, sandwiched in between two windows overlooking the canyon, Mary Colter had constructed a stone fireplace in the shape of one of the canyon's many buttes—wide at the bottom, sloping triangularly upward to its peak. The story of the fireplace was not of a fictional hermit—it was the story of the canyon itself.

The base of the fireplace is made out of Vishnu Schist, a

1.7-billion-year-old dark rock found at the base of the Grand Canyon. The next layer is composed of rock pieces from what's known
as the Grand Canyon Supergroup, a band of reds and blacks that
range from 800 million to 1.2 billion years old. As the fireplace
ascends, the stone gets progressively younger, mirroring the layers
of rock found at each layer of the canyon, until finally, at the top,
the light limestone of the canyon's rim makes an appearance. Colter had asked for stones to be hauled out at every level to construct
this replica. While today that would technically be illegal, her Geologic Fireplace is seen as a masterpiece.

Of all of the stories Colter tried to tell with her designs, this was
the one that had the most impact on me. Even though I could see
the layers of the canyon outside, it was only when standing right
next to a model, not much taller than I was, that I found myself
thinking more about the time it represented.

I know that the oceans are billions of years old, but they seem
ageless when staring at them from a beach. The Great Smoky
Mountains might contain more than two hundred million years of
history, but from a distance they appear as giant mounds of uniform green, something that might have been born, fully formed, at
some unknown point in the past.

But rivers cut canyons wide open, laying bare their insides for
us to see. Looking at a canyon's different lines and layers, we can
read its diary, seeing the various strata that made it what it is today.
The layers are stripes, not smears—they all seem so clearly delin-
eated. I wondered if, inside of each of us, those same markers exist.

When we think of personality, we tend to think of it like a soup,
a blend of traits and experiences that have been mixed together to
make us the people we are today. Over the years, more and more
gets added. The broth gets thicker, and the individual ingredients
become harder to discern.

It seemed to me that we might be more like that fireplace, like
the canyon. Full of layers with clear dividing lines, moments that
say, *From this point on, everything will be different.*

Maybe those lines mark deaths, births, loves, and losses—the moments we'd expect to define the different periods of our lives. Or maybe they correspond to days and events we would have never initially seen as important. Did I actually change as a person when I graduated from college? Probably not. Maybe a more significant shift happened midway through seventh grade, when my teacher told us to pick a college to do a report on and, instead of picking one that was good at sports, I chose Yale, a place I knew nothing about. Maybe your life changes on your wedding day, but I'd imagine the actual change happens on your fourth date, when the woman who will one day be your wife tells a joke that somehow tells you she's the one.

It's never clear a layer is over until the line appears and a new one starts. Looking past the fireplace, out to the canyon it represented, I began to think that I might be smack dab in the middle of an important layer, an era that was changing who I was as a person. There was the me before the parks, and there will be the me after them.

14

FORGIVENESS

(Dry Tortugas, Petrified Forest)

"The setting of a leg is no crime that calls for forgiveness."

On December 22, 1865, Sarah Frances Mudd wrote those words in a letter addressed to *His Excellency, Andrew Johnson, President of The United States.*

"I hesitate to address you," she began, "but love is stronger than fear, timidity must yield. I must petition for him who is very, very dear to me."

Sarah was writing to request a pardon for her dear husband, Dr. Samuel Mudd. A few months earlier, Dr. Mudd had been sentenced to life in prison and sent to a cell on a remote island in the Gulf of Mexico. He had been convicted of "conspiracy to murder," but he had not fired a shot. There was no concrete proof of his involvement in a murder plot. What Mudd *had* done, beyond the shadow of a doubt, was set the leg of a man who had broken his left fibula. His name was John Wilkes Booth.

At around 4 A.M. on April 15, 1865, Booth arrived limping at the Mudd residence. A few hours earlier, when he had leapt from the balcony of Ford's Theatre after shooting President Abraham

Lincoln, Booth had broken his leg on the stage. As Mudd would later argue, how could he possibly refuse to attend to an injured man?

The government argued Booth was not just some random patient in need. The two men had met before—a few different times—and therefore Mudd *must* have been part of the conspiracy to assassinate Lincoln. After initially lying to investigators, Mudd eventually admitted that yes, "on reflection," he had indeed met Booth before, but he didn't recognize him that night.

The military commission claimed that Mudd not only knew Booth, he knew of and supported his plans. The commission sentenced Mudd to life in what was then America's largest military prison. Today it's one of our smallest national parks.

I was speeding toward Dry Tortugas National Park on the *Yankee Freedom III,* a twin-engine catamaran that departs daily from Key West. On this day, I would end up spending as much time on the boat as I would at the actual park—I'd signed up for a four-and-a-half-hour round-trip journey to enjoy what basically amounted to a leisurely lunch break on less than fifty acres of land.

The islands were first named by Ponce de León in 1513. He called them Las Tortugas—the turtles—after the sea turtles he found on these lonely specks in the sea. Later, *dry* was added to the name, to warn passing mariners that there was no fresh water to be found on the islands.

To reach them, I had driven the length of the Florida Keys the night before. When I finally arrived in Key West, I took a picture of the concrete buoy that marks the SOUTHERNMOST POINT IN THE CONTINENTAL U.S.A. Dry Tortugas lies sixty-eight miles *farther* out into the ocean, closer to Cuba than to the mainland United States. It's one of our most inaccessible national parks. That's what made it a perfect prison.

I could hear folks cheering near the front of the boat. After two hours of nothingness, a bright-red hexagon had suddenly appeared on the horizon: Fort Jefferson. Everyone rushed to the deck to take pictures. We were in the middle of the ocean, and the fort we were fast approaching was a truly shocking sight, the kind of place pirates might whisper about. *Gather round, ye ... Way out in the middle of nowhere, I've been told there's an island ... An island full of bricks.*

Sixteen million bricks, to be precise, all of them imported. Fort Jefferson, originally intended to protect U.S. shipping lanes, is the largest brick masonry structure in the Americas. It was never finished. Still under construction when the Civil War broke out, it became a Union stronghold under Lincoln, who repurposed its forty-five-foot-high walls to contain traitors and deserters. After his death, those walls would imprison four of the men who were convicted of plotting to kill him.

Samuel Mudd wrote to his wife often during his imprisonment. His letters were massively depressing and he knew it, full of worry for his family and complaints about his new dreary existence on this "horrid island."

"I am sorry I have nothing entertaining and interesting to relate," he wrote. "Such would be a contradiction to this place of woe."

The worst part might have been the mosquitoes. They were relentless. "We can't rest day or night in peace for the mosquitos," Mudd wrote. But the mosquitoes were more than just annoying. They were deadly. In August 1867, Fort Jefferson logged its first case of yellow fever.

In the 1860s, scientists didn't know that yellow fever was spread by mosquitoes. So when prisoners and soldiers started dropping like, well, flies, the annoying pests weren't suspected as the culprits. The outbreak ripped through the prison—a month later, it claimed the life of the prison doctor.

Dr. Mudd volunteered to take over medical duties at Fort Jefferson. Day and night, he cared for the prisoners and soldiers alike. After years of pacing the yard and cleaning the bricks, Mudd was finally back doing what he had trained to do: help people.

Mudd managed to keep the mortality rate far lower than expected. By the end of the outbreak, three hundred soldiers signed a petition for his release. They were alive, they believed, because of him. Survivor Edmund Zalinski wrote to President Johnson that Mudd "inspired the hopeless with courage, and by his constant presence in the midst of danger and infection, regardless of his own life, tranquillized the fearful and desponding."

With one month left in office, Andrew Johnson officially pardoned Mudd in February 1869. The next month, after three and a half years in the Dry Tortugas, Mudd was able to leave the islands.

I spent my few hours at Fort Jefferson imagining how trapped those imprisoned there must have felt. I couldn't decide which was worse: being jailed near a town, where you know there are free people living their happy lives right outside your cell, or being held captive on an island in the sea, where you're miles and miles from the rest of the world.

Before I walked back to the boat, I discovered a plaque in Mudd's old cell, containing part of Johnson's pardon.

Samuel A. Mudd devoted himself to the care and cure of the sick, and interposed his courage and skill to protect the garrison . . . from peril and alarm, and thus saved many valuable lives and earned the admiration and the gratitude of all who observed or experienced his generous and faithful service to humanity.

Those words were written by a president about a man who, less than four years earlier, had allegedly conspired to assassinate the prior president. Johnson never admitted that Mudd was wrongfully imprisoned, just that he had redeemed himself through his selfless actions. The plaque hangs on the old prison walls to show that it is possible to forgive, and to ensure that we don't forget.

"Return these to the forest and forgive us for taking them," read the anonymous letter that arrived at Arizona's Petrified Forest National Park in 1976. The note came attached to shiny pieces of pet-rified wood that had been stolen from within the park boundaries.

Wood theft remains an issue at the park today, although the rangers have gotten better at warning tourists before they "break bad." Would-be wood burglars apparently have a guilty look to them, pacing around one area and then slowly trying to sneak a chunk up their pant leg.

"Our law enforcement rangers, they can tell when somebody's 'shopping,'" paleontologist Bill Parker told me as we walked past dozens of the softball-sized wood chunks. We were exploring a por-tion of the park's Chinle Formation, a colorful field of red and brown and white badlands, home to some of the most extensively researched Triassic dinosaur fossils in the world.

"Spielberg didn't use the word Triassic when he made the movie," Bill said. "If he'd used Triassic instead of Jurassic, every-one would know what this was."

Bill was smiling, but I could tell he was a little annoyed. He had spent his life imagining the lives of creatures that lived here 200 to 250 million years ago, and he knew I'd never heard of any of them.

"Probably our most famous Triassic animal is a dinosaur called Coelophysis . . ."

Uh . . . Sorry?

He patiently suggested a few other well-known ones. Nothing registered. Not the Camposaurus, not the Chindesaurus. Bill kept at it, putting the "try" in Triassic. The "ass," well, that was me.

Like most Americans, my dino knowledge went extinct after the "Fourth Grade Era." Perhaps back then, I could have recalled some of these creatures.

"It's one of those things that a lotta kids do," Bill said. "When you're little, you spout off all the dinosaur names. And then you're kinda supposed to outgrow that kinda thing." He paused, then smiled. "Some of us don't."

Hundreds of millions of years ago, this dry, red desert was lush and green and humid, full of all sorts of plant and animal life. Pterosaurs flew over groves of giant conifers, while birds and reptiles and proto-mammals beat the heat by hanging out together near flowing streams. The mural in the visitor center that imagines this long-ago scene is striking—both for how unbelievably *different* it looks from the landscape today, and for how hilariously chaotic and violent it is. Nearly every creature on the wall seems to be depicted mid-bite, captured just as it is thrashing about in the water, gnashing teeth, and chomping down on necks. It's as if an artist decided to portray life at a suburban Kohl's by choosing to draw what it looks like when the doors open on Black Friday at 7 A.M.

Scientists theorize that, at some point, massive flooding toppled all the trees and drove away all the animals. The downed logs traveled for miles downstream, before they were eventually buried in layers of sediment and volcanic ash. Drop by drop, groundwater began to seep into the wood, carrying some of that volcanic ash with it. One cell at a time, the trees' organic material morphed into silica. Beautiful, shiny silica.

With all due respect to my new paleontologist friend, the ancient trees were what I—and everyone else—had come here to see. It's not called "Obscure Dino-Bone Fragment National Park." The sign at the entrance promised a PETRIFIED FOREST.

After the flood, the wood took millions of years to resurface. When it finally did—carved out of the hills by the forces of erosion—it *glistened.*

Trace amounts of iron and manganese had combined with the silica to give the wood the brilliant, multicolored hues that make it so spectacular. The morning sun dazzled across the exposed cores of the trees, bringing the long-dead plants back to life.

The largest pieces looked as if they had just been chopped down yesterday, scraps left behind by a team of lumberjacks who had decided to call off work early. Instead, as Bill explained, the logs had broken apart back when they were still underground, collapsing under their own weight.

"Think, like, if you drop a piece of chalk, it breaks into smaller pieces of chalk, right? Well, that's what these logs do," Bill said.

You definitely would not want one of the pieces to drop on *you*. Petrified wood weighs up to two hundred pounds per cubic foot.

That heft didn't stop early visitors to this area from carting off shiny souvenirs by the wagonload. As early as 1895, the Arizona Territorial Legislature started worrying that too much wood was disappearing, so they asked Congress to create a park. In 1906, the Antiquities Act was used to preserve Petrified Forest as a monument. From that point on, if you took wood, you were stealing from the U.S. government.

You can ask anyone who's ever fudged a small deduction on a tax return how tempting *that* can be. Visitors kept right on taking the wood, despite warnings and signs and fines and an understaffed force of rangers determined to stop them.

The park is big—over two hundred square miles—and there's no way rangers can catch *everyone* in the act. Short of doing full Tijuana-style inspections of every car leaving the park, cutting open the upholstery while a pack of wood-sniffing dogs root around in the trunk, it's impossible to stop at least *some* wood from leaving the park. Rangers once claimed that a ton of wood a month went missing, a statistic that shocked everyone. But almost as surprising—to the park, at least—was how much of that wood would come *back*.

Matt Smith is the museum curator at Petrified Forest. Mixed in among his collection of fossils, there's a folder of all of the apology letters the park has received. Handwritten and typed, dating back to the 1930s, the letters are tales of remorse, written by reformed criminals.

"To Park Rager," one full of misspellings reads. "I am so so sorry for tackeing the petrified wood. I didn't know it was so speshall."

It is written in the unmistakable scrawl of a child's hand. As is another: "I am sorry I take the rock. I am returning it because it's the right thing to do. I feel very, very ashamed. I found it at the Giant log trail."

One can imagine the series of events that might have led to a letter like this. A curious kid picked up something shiny, then, after he got home, his parents noticed it in his backpack. An important life lesson about right and wrong was taught, and the kid was told to apologize. The wood was sent back, and all was right with the world.

But the majority of the letters come from adults. They're typed, double-spaced, and the return address is intentionally left off. These are not letters written under the watchful eye of a parent. They're multipage confessionals, apologizing for a long-ago theft. The authors want forgiveness—a clean conscience. In exchange, they offer up the wood, found in a closet, or perhaps collecting dust on the mantelpiece. The souvenir that was supposed to remind them of their trip now just reminds them of their flaws.

Some of the letters are laundry lists of the various misfortunes that have befallen those who dared take the wood outside of park boundaries. There's a popular theory that the wood itself is *cursed.*

"These items were located in the possession of my recently deceased wife," reads a note accompanying a box of fragments. "For the past decade, my family, mainly my wife, has been besieged by horrific events and occurrences, and just plain bad luck. Hopefully these can help clean the slate."

"We're good people, and never do wrong to anybody," says another. "But bad things keep happening . . . Unduly kicked out of college, identity theft, institutions lost our documents, health problems . . ."

I can't help but think that "institutions lost our documents" doesn't actually sound that bad, but I get the point. In letter after letter, misfortunes great and small are blamed on the wood.

"I don't know how much I buy that," Matt said as we pored through his collection. "If you're the kinda person who would take something from a national park, *maybe* you just have poor judgment skills."

Demonic wood is nonsense, of course, but the popularity of the curse is, in part, the park's own doing. When the first of these letters started coming in, the park displayed them in the visitor center. A kind of *See? This is what could happen to you* warning. If you were to take the wood like those poor souls did, even if the park didn't catch you, the curse would.

But it didn't seem to do much good. Seeing those letters—proof that others were stealing—might have actually emboldened visitors to take a piece or two themselves.

"We may have just been encouraging people unwittingly to do the wrong thing by emphasizing it, you know? *Overemphasizing* it. Saying, you know, *Bluefin tuna are going extinct, so you better eat some sushi,* or something like that," Matt said.

The message was basically *Get the wood while the gettin' is good.* Before it all disappears.

So the park decided to switch strategies. They took down most of the letters and removed some of the more intimidating signs throughout the park. They started selling polished petrified wood in the gift shop, wood that was sourced from *outside* the park boundaries. (Plenty of private land has petrified wood—it's found in every state. The park just has an especially significant collection.) Perhaps, they thought, if people had a chance to *legally* buy some wood, they'd be less tempted to smuggle out souvenirs.

Morale-wise, Matt mentioned, it was also a bummer to be known as the "strict park." Petrified Forest staff felt like they were always lecturing everyone.

These kinds of crimes happen at all the parks. It's just as illegal to pick a bouquet of flowers at Yosemite as it is to take wood from Petrified Forest. Both are federal offenses. It's just that the flowers grow back. Once the wood is stolen, it's gone forever.

Even, as it turns out, when it is sent back.

What most of the penitent thieves don't realize is that, once the wood is moved from the spot where it was found, it loses all of its scientific value. It *can't* go back in the park. Some of the wood deposits are 208 million years old. Some are 217 million years old. Mixing and matching wood from different eras is bad science.

"If we don't know exactly where on the ground that came from, we can't put it back," Matt explained, showing me a softball-sized piece that had been mailed back. "Because somebody who's going out to study that stuff could inadvertently pick up something that has no reason to be there and botch their results."

So where does it all go? Into the "Conscience Pile."

Tucked away down a service road, there's a giant pile of returned wood. Hundreds of pieces—maybe thousands—that can't go anywhere else. It's not on the map, it's not a visitor attraction. It was named by the rangers who would drive out to dump the new arrivals on it, emptying out boxes that often cost forty or more dollars to ship.

When I saw the pile, I couldn't decide if it was depressing or beautiful. It's probably a bit of both. It's a monument to our desire to do the right thing, but it's also proof that, sometimes, doing the right thing doesn't matter. Sometimes it can be too little, too late.

In Matt's office, we picked up one last letter, written in a language I didn't recognize.

"Navajo," Matt said.

Nahasdzáán,

Shaa nidini ahh

Ahéhee'

Several of the park employees are Native, so Matt asked around for a translation. One suggested: "To whom it may concern. Please forgive me. Thank you."

But another coworker offered a different translation. *Nahasdzáán* could also be interpreted as "Dear Earth."

Dear Earth,

Please forgive me.

It's a letter perhaps we all should write.

.   .   .

After my trip to Petrified Forest, I drove south to Phoenix, where I spent the better part of a week running errands and plotting the next stages of my journey. After so much constant newness, I was looking forward to being back in a familiar city.

But everything that made Phoenix familiar was also what made it painful. Driving down Camelback Road, I passed that parking garage with the little javelina pictures. I drove by St. Francis, the restaurant where my ex-fiancée and I had gone on our second date, and The Phoenician, the fancy resort we had snuck into after dessert to sit by the pool and look up at the stars.

While being back reopened some of those old wounds, I knew that *whatever* city I went to, there would always be some hidden land mine waiting to trip me up. A favorite song of hers that might suddenly come on the radio. A guy with a passing resemblance to her brother standing in front of me at an airport Starbucks. Any mention of the television series *Glee* or the scent of the lavender laundry soap she liked.

It was useless to try to forget her. I'd been trying, and it hadn't worked. But in order to let occasional memories come and go as fleeting blips and not morph into all-consuming day ruiners, I knew I finally needed to forgive her.

I hadn't done that yet, partially because I wasn't even sure what, exactly, I was forgiving. It wasn't like not wanting to marry me was some terrible crime. Honestly, if you were to ever watch me eat corn on the cob or listen to me sing in the shower, you would be surprised that anyone ever even temporarily agreed to do such a thing.

But I was still angry. I was angry that my family had been hurt—I could deal with my own heartache, but it had killed me to see my parents, who had already welcomed her into the family, upset. I was also angry on behalf of a woman I hadn't even met yet. It felt like something meant for her one day had been snatched away.

In a moment of weakness while packing up in Pasadena, I had sent one final email. I didn't want a reconciliation or an apology, I told her, I just wanted clarity. The whole thing had turned into a chapter of my life I wished never existed, but as long as those final few paragraphs remained full of omissions, it was hard for me to turn the page.

I never received a response.

I no longer wait for that letter, but I have considered the possibility that, at some point in the future, I might receive it anyway. Maybe one day she will want to clear the air—time can change things. But should that letter arrive, it won't be for me anymore. It will have been written for her.

I decided to do my forgiving back in Phoenix. I was determined to leave my resentment right there in the desert. I knew I wasn't done being sad, but I was done being angry.

There hadn't been some grand conspiracy to hurt me. By continuing to hold on to my anger ever since, I had only been hurting myself. And that was one thing I had control over. I could let it go. A letter couldn't change things anyway—the change had already occurred.

Like that stolen wood at Petrified Forest, once a piece of you has been taken, it can't be put back.

15

CAVES

(Wind Cave, Carlsbad Caverns, Mammoth Cave)

"Wind Cave is the sixth longest cave in the world!"

The beaming ranger's announcement was met with a round of applause from our tour group, as if we were congratulating her personally for carving the three-hundred-million-year-old passageways underneath the South Dakota soil. Or perhaps everyone was congratulating themselves for being there to witness such a marvel. I suppose seeing the world's sixth longest cave *is* pretty dang impressive. Unless, a few months earlier, you had just seen the world's longest.

Seeing fifty-nine of the country's most stunning places back-to-back inevitably leads to some comparisons. Sure, the sunset in Joshua Tree was spectacular, but not as spectacular as the one in Big Bend. Laurel Falls—one of the star attractions of Great Smoky Mountains—pales in comparison with Yosemite Falls. And yes, Wind Cave is long, but it's nothing compared with the four-hundred-plus miles of Mammoth Cave National Park, by far the world's longest. While I'd been doing my best to push these types of comparisons out of my head—it's not a competition, after all—there's a commonality to caves that makes them easy to lump together.

Caves may be my least favorite "genre" of parks, primarily because you're usually forced to experience them on an organized tour. From a practical standpoint, I understand this. Caves are dark and dangerous, and people can be careless and clumsy. Even the oils from our fingers can damage the delicate formations, so metal railings keep much of the cave off limits. But, traipsing down defined passageways and squeezing through tight crevices with thirty-nine other chatty tourists, I find that all of the blissful solitude, the quiet, and the ability to roam free that I've come to treasure in the parks disappears.

The Park Service manages more than forty-seven hundred caves across the country, most of which are parts of other parks. Only three have been deemed impressive enough to merit their *own* national park distinction: Along with Wind Cave in South Dakota, there's Carlsbad Caverns in New Mexico and Mammoth Cave in Kentucky.

At each, the tour guide will explain what particular gypsum-y geological feature makes their cave unique. At Wind Cave, it's the collection of boxwork—thousands of strands of calcite that crisscross the ceiling, like the hardened leftovers of a massive Fraggle Rock Silly String fight. The boxwork is extremely rare, as is Wind Cave's age—portions of the cave are more than three hundred million years old.

New Mexico's Carlsbad Caverns National Park is much younger—the oldest areas of the cavern are about six million years old. While on a tour there, the ranger asked our group if anyone knew who first explored Carlsbad. After five awkward seconds, a kid beside me raised his hand and said in a trembling voice, "Um . . . Carl?"

The limestone walls echoed with the knowing laughter of adults. But of course, none of us knew the right answer, either. As it turned out, the first explorer of Carlsbad was a kid not that much older than the one who had spoken up. He was a curious teenage cowboy named Jim White.

Standard disclaimer: It's highly unlikely this White, or any "white," was the first person to "discover" Carlsbad. Native people lived in New Mexico for thousands of years and certainly knew of the cave's existence. The Zuni Pueblo people called it Eshotsi an' Alak'kwa: Bat Cave.

Cowboy Jim found out why. Wandering the Chihuahuan Desert in 1898, he thought he saw smoke. And where there's smoke, there's usually fire—a wildfire, most likely, burning off in the distance. He galloped over to get a closer look.

As Jim got closer to the smoke, he couldn't smell anything. *That's strange,* he thought. And then he finally saw it. It wasn't a cloud of smoke. It was a cloud of . . . *bats.* Thousands and thousands of bats.

The bats he saw were Brazilian free-tails, heading out for their nightly feast of insects. As Jim watched them swarm overhead, he wondered where they had come from.

"The more I thought of it, the more I realized that any hole in the ground which could house such a gigantic army of bats must be a whale of a big cave," he later recounted in his self-published booklet, *Jim White's Own Story.*

Jim was right. After his initial shock, he came back to the cave and started to explore it, mapping and naming its various features: places like Witch's Finger, Devil's Armchair, King's Palace, Fairyland, and Papoose Room. The caverns are still being explored today—in 2012, a team of spelunkers stumbled upon a large, previously unmapped section of Carlsbad and called it Munchkinland.

That's another cave commonality—the subterranean world is *full* of whimsical names. Aboveground our mountains and lakes are in relatively short supply, so we tend to reserve naming rights for presidents, explorers, and geologists. Underground, anything goes.

At Wind Cave, there is a room called Aguilera's Attic, named after Christina Aguilera. There's a thirty-foot-deep chasm named

"What! Yeah!" because those happened to be the Lil' Jon lyrics that came to mind when explorers discovered it in 2006. There's also the Cheese Whiz Room, Bagel Ballroom (a room where a 1987 group of explorers stopped to eat bagels), Hairy Hooter Room, and Pee Wee's Playhouse, so named because—and keep in mind I'm taking this straight from the park's official record—"the night before the group had all watched the movie *Pee Wee's Big Adventure.*"

The insides of caves are full of inside jokes. They're also frequently decorated with the names of past visitors. Entire passageways at Kentucky's Mammoth Cave National Park are covered with scribbled names dating back to the 1800s, written into the rock with candle smoke.

"Only the wealthiest people could afford to be here," ranger David Kem told me as we walked through Mammoth's Register Room, a passage where the low white limestone ceiling made for especially easy smoke writing. "Being able to leave your mark and indicate that you were here was a status symbol."

David's interest in Mammoth's history had been sparked by the smoke writing. He discovered a relative's name burned into the ceiling of the cave, dated 1843. Do something like that today, and you'd be fined or arrested. But the old high-society graffiti at Mammoth is federally protected. It tells part of the cave's story.

Once a prime source of saltpeter, used to create gunpowder during the War of 1812, Mammoth was turned into a tourist attraction after the war ended. It wasn't long before its wonders became world-famous. Visitors would travel by train to Kentucky to take private tours. When the local farmers saw how lucrative Mammoth had become, they started hunting for caves in their backyards. Kentucky is *full* of caves.

"If you could get paid by building a few steps, and buying a few lanterns, and telling some stories underground, then—people were willing to try it," David said.

At first, the only successful caves were the ones located right along the rail line. But when the automobile arrived at Mammoth, it ushered in a chaotic, competitive free-for-all—an era known as the "Kentucky Cave Wars."

Everyone with a hole in their backyard started trying to convince passing motorists to come visit. Mammoth Cave was the region's big-name draw, so signs touting caves with suspiciously similar names started popping up to divert traffic. This way to "COLOSSAL Caverns!" Turn left for "Mammoth ONYX Cave!" It was like those rip-off DVDs you used to see on the shelves at Blockbuster. It was easy to accidentally go home with *Transmorphers* instead of *Transformers,* or to spend half an hour watching *The DaVinci Treasure* wondering why Tom Hanks hadn't popped up yet.

"By the time you figured it out, you'd already paid your tourist dollars, and they've got your money in their pocket," David told me. " 'Sorry about your luck ... you can go see Mammoth Cave down the road.' "

Tourists were more likely to stop at the caves at the beginning of the road: It was all about location, location, location. As someone who has stopped at many an Arby's just because of its proximity to an interstate exit, I can understand. Unfortunately for Kentuckians Leonidas and Martha Collins, their cave was at the *end* of the road. Their son Floyd had discovered "Crystal Cave" on their property in 1917, but it was hell trying to convince folks to schlep out to see it.

If only they had a cave closer to the start of the road, they might be able to siphon off more of Mammoth's traffic. A cave like *that* could make them rich. So Floyd set off to find one. If anyone was going to be able to do it, it would be him.

"He was perhaps the greatest cave explorer of his era," David told me. Floyd was fearless, and he had his family's livelihood motivating him. He made a deal with some farmers farther up the road: If he found a cave worthy of showing, they would all split the tour profits.

Sure enough, he did find a way into one. He just never made it out.

Floyd squeezed through the tight tunnels of what was known as Sand Cave. It looked promising, but after a few hours of exploring, his lantern started to run out of kerosene. As Floyd crawled back to the surface, a rock fell from the ceiling, pinning his leg. He was alive, but he was badly injured. As hard as he tried, he couldn't wriggle himself free.

He was stuck in an almost impossibly narrow passageway. The rock—while not large—blocked off access from the way he'd come. The rescuers who were called in couldn't figure out a way to reach him. As they strategized, news of Floyd's predicament started to reach a larger audience. The story of the farmer trapped alive in a cave became national news.

"In January and February of 1925 the whole nation watched. Radio was new. Congress was halted several times so they could listen to what was happening to old Floyd down in Kentucky," David said.

According to David, Floyd's ordeal was one of the first media circuses—if not *the* first. Long before Baby Jessica got trapped in that well in Texas, Floyd Collins was trapped in a cave in Kentucky. For seventeen days, rescuers attempted to reach him. While they worked, Cave City turned into a madhouse. Reporters and thousands of fans flocked from around the country to take part in the spectacle. A tent city sprang up. Vendors sold hot dogs and balloons and liquor to curious onlookers.

One man, William Burke Miller, was actually able to squeeze into the cave opening and talk to Floyd through a small crevice. Miller was nicknamed "Skeets," because, so they say, he wasn't much bigger than a mosquito. He eventually won a Pulitzer Prize for the interviews he conducted underground, until the tiny passageway he was talking through collapsed, and all contact with Floyd was lost.

The happy ending everyone had been rooting for never came. When rescuers finally reached Floyd, on February 16, he was already dead, most likely from a combination of thirst and hypothermia. It was a three-column front-page headline in *The New York Times,* and a heartbreaking conclusion for all who had been following the story.

Floyd Collins's death brought more attention to Mammoth Cave, but it also brought shame to this part of Kentucky.

"Those that weren't aware of just how nasty the competition had gotten suddenly saw that now *lives* are being lost," David told me. "It was an ugly scene. Tens of thousands of people watching a man die in a cave is just *not* something you want to be known for . . ."

Poor farmers risking their lives for a bit of tourist money was a sad story. Couldn't someone come along and buy up all of the competing caves? Someone like . . . Uncle Sam?

The East had already come down with a case of national park envy. All of these majestic places they kept reading about in Muir's writings—they were all so *far away*. While the vast majority of the population lived in the eastern states, the vast majority of the parks were out west. It just didn't seem fair.

The East was anxious for some parks to call their own, and Mammoth Cave was the easiest to make a case for. There really wasn't another place like it in the country or, as researchers would later confirm, in the world. Mammoth is almost *twice* as long as the world's second longest cave.

In 1926, a year after the death of Floyd Collins, Congress finally authorized the Park Service to start acquiring land for three new eastern parks: Shenandoah, Great Smoky Mountains, and Mammoth Cave. Mammoth wasn't officially dedicated for another two decades—it took some time to negotiate cave contracts. It took even longer for geologists to eventually discover that most of the competing caves, the ones that tourists were sometimes tricked into thinking were actually Mammoth Cave, *were*, in fact, Mammoth Cave. The caves were all connected underground. As it turned out, most of those feuding farmers owned different parts of the same thing. Today it belongs to us all.

While I may not be able to fully appreciate the geological differences among Carlsbad and Wind Cave and Mammoth, or any of the dozens of other caves I've seen in my life, I always come back to the surface different than when I went down.

There's something primal about entering a cave, walking back into the gaping mouth of the earth that provided humankind's first shelter. In a cave, you are simultaneously outdoors and indoors, protected from the elements and yet exposed to all sorts of new dangers.

Caves can be *scary*. They're full of bats and stalactites and stalagmites that look like gnashing teeth ready to swallow you whole. And while the bats have adapted to life underground, we have not. For me, walking through a cave is a little like diving down to the ocean floor. Something always seems a little off—I know I don't belong, and as wondrous as what I'm seeing is, my mind is always on the surface. I do not want to end up like Floyd Collins—I know I eventually need to leave.

Caves—even the longest ones in the world—still manage to be one of the few places where nature can feel claustrophobic. Maybe it's the indeterminate length that's unsettling. Every acre of Acadia has been accounted for, but scientists believe Mammoth Cave might actually be *twice* as long as we think it is. By now even the ocean floor has been mapped—caves are still a twisting, final frontier.

There's a moment in every cave tour I've come to recognize. By the time I got to Wind Cave, I could tell exactly when the ranger was about to attempt it. She waited until our group was all in the same place—it would be dangerous to leave a straggler—and then, reaching over to a central switch . . . she turned off the lights.

Someone screamed. It was *shockingly* dark. Close your eyes. Now cover them with your hand. It's darker than that. Way darker.

Jim White once described the darkness of Carlsbad Caverns as feeling "as though a million tons of black wool descended upon me. The darkness was so dense it seemed smothering—choking me."

It was only after all the lights had gone off that we were given a glimpse of what the early cave explorers would have seen: a pitch-black nothingness. No signs, no marked passageways, no strategically lit columns. A flickering lamp might have barely illuminated the way ahead, but glance back in the other direction and there would be no trace of where you had just been. You wouldn't see *anything.*

The crowd was starting to squirm. Perhaps they thought their eyes would quickly adjust to this. I remember thinking that the first time. Now I know they're not going to. They can't. It's no surprise that several of the creatures that live in caves are blind; having a functioning pupil underground is a waste.

In the darkness, I momentarily found the solitude I had been missing during the tour. It wasn't until my third cave of the year that I was finally able to lean back and ease into the nothingness without fear. To stare as hard as I could into the oblivion and for a moment, instead of feeling smothered, feel embraced. To know that there was beauty all around me, even if I couldn't see it.

Then someone checked their iPhone, and the moment was ruined.

16

LIGHT

(Great Basin, Saguaro)

In July 1986, *Life* magazine described U.S. Route 50 as the "Loneliest Road in America."

Underneath a single depressing photo, the magazine featured this description of the two-lane highway:

> "It's totally empty," says an AAA counselor. "There are no points of interest. We don't recommend it." The 287-mile-stretch of U.S. 50, running from Ely to Fernley, Nev., passes nine towns, two abandoned mining camps, a few gas pumps and an occasional coyote. "We warn all motorists not to drive there," says the AAA rep, "unless they're confident of their survival skills."

It was a colossal diss, but Nevada tourism officials couldn't have been happier. All of a sudden, *Life*'s non-endorsement of their depressing little highway had given it a *brand*, and in so doing managed to popularize the road among a certain set of gloomy travelers. The state put up signs advertising the new name—HWY 50, THE LONELIEST ROAD IN AMERICA.

Just three months after that article was published, U.S. 50 got an attraction that even the most jaded AAA counselor would have agreed at least counted as a *point of interest.* Set back a few miles from the highway, a seventy-six-thousand-acre plot of land was given a branding upgrade of its own. In October 1986, Congress passed a law establishing Great Basin National Park.

The park was intended to serve as a representative sample of the entire Great Basin region—a massive watershed spanning five states, including almost all of Nevada. All the water found in the Great Basin drains or evaporates internally, never making its way to the Pacific Ocean or the Gulf of Mexico. Put another way, what happens in Vegas stays in Vegas.

The park itself is less than three hundred miles away from the Las Vegas Strip, the brightest spot on our entire planet when viewed from space. But the country's loneliest road doesn't see many head-lights. The closest town to Great Basin—Baker, Nevada—is home to just sixty-eight people.

"We're pretty rare," ranger Annie Gilliland told me when I met her near the visitor center. "This is one of the—if not *the* darkest place in the Lower 48."

Annie is a "Dark Ranger," part of an elite squad of park staff who lead regular astronomy presentations.

"I love it," she told me, smiling. "It makes me sound like a superhero."

The Dark Rangers are real-life Guardians of the Galaxy, tasked with ensuring that the lighting inside the park stays low so that visitors aren't distracted from the sky up above. At Great Basin, the stars are the star attraction.

Before my meeting with Annie, I had spent the day hiking a few short trails and drove up the park's Wheeler Peak Scenic Drive. The scenery I'd seen was pleasant enough, but most of it, to my eye at least, was the same type of pinyon-juniper woodland that can be found all throughout the Great Basin region.

If one were to go home when the sun goes down, then Great Basin might merely seem as "Great" as the Great Plains. That's why rangers like Annie encourage visitors to stick around. Here, they have a saying . . .

Half the park . . . is after dark.

I'd heard about Great Basin's skies, and I'd timed my visit so that I would arrive on the night of a new moon—the darkest possible night. It was also a weekend night, which meant Annie would be hosting one of her popular astronomy talks. As the sun set, a small crowd began to form in the parking lot. Flashlights were forbidden—Annie wanted our eyes to adjust naturally.

When the stars finally made their debut, the canopy shining overhead did not strike me as something that should be referred to as a "dark sky." Wind Cave was *dark*. This was the brightest sky I had ever seen.

Rising up from the east, the Milky Way slowly streaked across Great Basin's horizon—it looked like the heavens had been ripped apart. This wasn't some faint constellation where you have to struggle to connect the dots just to see a shape that vaguely resembles a bear chasing after twin crabs. This was an unmissable interstellar Grand Canyon, a massive band of light so brilliant it cast shadows on the ground.

I was transfixed. It was hard to comprehend that all of these thousands of stars had all been up there all along, hiding in plain sight. I realized that all other supposedly beautiful starry nights of my life had been symphonies with notes missing. At Great Basin, I was finally able to appreciate the full composition.

An astronomer would tell you that I was still only seeing a tiny fraction of the universe. The human eye, under the best of conditions, can see fewer than five thousand of the billions of stars that shine in our galaxy alone. As I tried to take them all in, I wondered if the limiting factor was not the eye, but the human brain. Throw in even a few dozen more bright-white pinpricks and it felt like my head would explode.

When I occasionally lowered my gaze to rest my neck for a few minutes, I could see the heads of a hundred other tourists craned skyward, their eyes wide with wonder. Annie had set up telescopes in the parking lot for anyone who wanted to take a closer look. When I walked over to one to peer at Jupiter, I met a troop of Boy Scouts from Farmington, New Mexico, who had come to the park to earn their astronomy merit badges. I asked one of the Scouts if the sky was different than what he was used to seeing back home.

"I can't see any of this back home," he said. "It makes me think, our world is so small, and the galaxy out there is so *big*."

At an age when most kids think they're the center of the universe, the stars of Great Basin helped remind this kid that he wasn't. That none of us are.

For most Americans, those types of cosmic insights are increasingly hard to come by. More than two-thirds of the country lives in areas where the Milky Way can't be seen from their backyards. While today we know far more about the cosmos than any generation in history, we *see* far less of it.

When the International Dark-Sky Association announced in 2016 that it was recognizing Great Basin as a "Dark Sky Park," program manager John Barentine told the *Las Vegas Review-Journal* that Great Basin was "as close as you can get to what the night sky might have looked like before the invention of electric light."

It's easy to forget that the era he was referring to wasn't actually that long ago. Lights have only been obscuring our view of the sky for a century and a half—Thomas Edison's company didn't start selling bulbs until the 1880s, and it took a long time for cities to turn into the glistening metropolises we know today. But our world keeps getting brighter and brighter. The direst predictions estimate that, by 2025, there may be no dark skies left in the Lower 48.

Before it could be certified as a Dark Sky Park, Great Basin first had to adjust its lighting fixtures to all point downward. The bulbs around the visitor center were retrofitted to use low-wattage red lights, a color that allows our eyes to stay better adjusted to the dark. (That's why everything from the numbers on digital alarm clocks to the insides of submarine control rooms are illuminated red.)

Most important, the park strove to never use more light than was necessary. When something wasn't in use, it was switched off. That's how easy it can be to address light pollution. It literally can go away with the flick of a switch. Light pollution is *reversible.*

Parks, with their charge to preserve, "unimpaired," our natural resources, have an ecological responsibility to consider the impact of light. Artificial light sources can cause massive disruptions to the circadian rhythms of animals in the parks and impact the relationship between nocturnal predators and their prey. Lights can also disorient species that rely on the moon and stars for navigational cues.

Every year in Florida, millions of sea turtle hatchlings die when they waddle off in the direction of artificial light sources along the beach, mistaking the glow of condos for the light of the moon. Frogs, who croak at night to find a mate, may never *realize* it's night if it's too bright outside. If the males can't get in the mood to make their baby-makin' music, then the females don't mate, and the frog population dies out.

Beyond the environmental impact of light pollution, seeing the stars at Great Basin reminded me that the night sky *itself* is a resource worth preserving. The view of what lies beyond our world can be just as powerful and transformative as any of the scenery found on its surface. Unfortunately, protecting that view is beyond the power of a few Dark Rangers. The real star wars are being fought in cities, towns, and backyards across the country.

Kitt Peak Observatory, on the outskirts of Tucson, Arizona, is where astronomers Vera Rubin and Kent Ford first discovered that the universe is full of "dark matter." But by the 1970s, Tucson's skies had grown so bright that researchers were worried that the city's glow might impact future discoveries.

A group of concerned scientists approached the city council and made their case for the importance of keeping the skies dark. Astronomy was, and still is, big business in Tucson—the city is known as the "astronomy capital of the world." Losing observatories would mean losing jobs, the scientists argued. In 1972, the city passed a groundbreaking ordinance regulating outdoor lighting.

Today, for a metro area of nearly one million people, Tucson is surprisingly dark. The city has adopted lighting "curfews," preventing stores from running their bright signs long after they're closed for the day. There are strict rules governing lumen levels and light-shielding, and all streetlights face downward. The city has gotten brighter since 1972, but it's far dimmer than it *might* have been.

A park like Great Basin stays dark because it's in the middle of nowhere. But Tucson's Saguaro National Park is in the middle of a city. Or more accurately, the city is in the middle of *it.*

Downtown Tucson splits Saguaro into two sections—the Rincon Mountain District to the east, and the Tucson Mountain District to the west. The terrain in each is slightly different, but both sections contain an abundance of the park's namesake plant—the saguaro cactus.

Saguaros look like lanky aliens, and the squadrons of them dotting the park's hillsides resemble a bright-green invasion, stopped suddenly in its tracks. Turn your head for a moment, then turn back, and you'll swear ten more have appeared. Arms raised to the sky, most appear to be waving hello—others seem to have paused mid-Macarena.

The main scenic drives in both park districts close at sunset, gates padlocked until the next morning. When I asked a ranger about this—it's fairly uncommon for parks to shut down their roads—I was surprised at her answer. Just like Petrified Forest, Saguaro has a problem with theft.

While I can understand the temptation to pick up a loose, smooth piece of shiny wood, who would possibly want to steal a spiky, giant cactus that's planted into the ground? A saguaro isn't something you can casually slip into your pocket or your trunk—the plants can grow to forty feet tall.

"Yeah, but they also sell for a hundred dollars a foot," the ranger told me. Poachers have been known to drive their trucks into the park at night, wrap blankets around the plants' sharp needles, and cart them off to sell to homeowners looking to spruce up their yards. Rangers have started implanting the most attractive cacti with microchips so they might later identify the ones that go missing.

Even though the park's main roads close each night to cars, it's still possible to enter Saguaro on foot or on bicycle twenty-four hours a day. I've been to the park several times—it's a fun getaway from Phoenix, and easy to experience in an afternoon—but the few hours I've spent there in the dark have been the most memorable.

As soon as the sun goes down, the desert comes alive. All sorts of creatures that have spent the day hiding from the sun come out to hunt and explore. The saguaros themselves come alive—cacti breathe at night. Desert days are so hot that, to conserve water, the plants keep their pores closed until nightfall, then finally open them up for a quick gulp of carbon dioxide.

The Sonoran Desert, beautiful in aggregate, appears eerie in isolation. On my first midnight walk through the park, a series of strange, unfamiliar shapes took their turn in the spotlight of my headlamp. I was experiencing the world one illuminated circle at a time, constantly wondering what might be lurking in the shadows. I eventually took my headlamp off and held it in my hand so that I could swivel it faster, wielding light as if I were wielding a weapon.

The faint glow of Tucson in the distance served as a reminder that this desert—as ideal a spot as any to bury a body, it seemed—was within half an hour of hundreds of thousands of people. What if a few of those people were out here with me? What if I accidentally stumbled upon some gang of cactus bandits on my walk? I doubted the backyard gardening mafia got to where it is today by leaving witnesses alive.

Every creak and croak brought a rapid-fire onslaught from my light. I would spray an area with my bright LED to see what might have caused the noise, and then I'd whip around in the other direction to make sure nothing had snuck up on me. It was exhausting—far from the fun nighttime stroll I had hoped for. Walking with the light, it felt like I always had to be aiming it at something, so I finally decided to just stay in one place. I wandered to the middle of a wide, sandy trail, took a deep breath, checked for snakes, and turned off my beam.

Almost immediately, I wanted to flick it back on. But I forced myself to wait. Slowly, without the distracting shine of my light, my eyes started to adjust to the night. Within ten minutes, it felt like I didn't even need it anymore. When my light was turned on, the saguaros had turned into a series of individual, frightening beings. With it off, I was once again able to see the field of cacti as a unit, connected and coexisting with one another.

The same was true for the brilliant stars twinkling above me. For thousands of years, our instinct has been to look for links when we look up at the night sky. We see familiar shapes in the stars just like we see shapes in the saguaros. There's Orion and his belt, there's Aquarius and his jug. We want to think that the bright white lights—millions of miles away from one another—are somehow tied together, and are somehow tied to us.

The visitor center at Saguaro lies on almost the exact same line of latitude as Jackson, Mississippi, and Benghazi, Libya. On any given night, the same constellations, planets, and galaxies pass over all three places. The sky is what links us together.

It's a concept I first learned from the renowned animated astronomer Fievel Mousekewitz. In 1986, the same year that Great Basin became a national park, the year that Highway 50 was declared the loneliest road in America, Universal Pictures released *An American Tail* in theaters. I was five.

The film's hit song, "Somewhere Out There," points out that no matter how lonely and distant we might feel, "it helps to think we're sleeping underneath the same big sky." Somewhere out there, someone else might be wishing on the same star.

But that's only true if they can *see* the same star. When I looked up at the sky while at Great Basin, I wished that such a magnificent view weren't so rare. There's something about a night sky that has the power to simultaneously ground us and lift our spirits.

Recently, we've started to think more about how the bright lights from our screens are affecting our bodies. But I wonder how the lights from our cities might be affecting our souls. As people, we arrived on the planet with a "dark mode" pre-installed, but for the past century, we've been turning it off. In an effort to see our own world more clearly, we have obscured our view of other worlds and—quite possibly—of the divine.

Fortunately, somewhere out there, there are more and more towns like Tucson working to bring a bit of the sparkle of the sky back. Torrey, Utah; Ketchum, Idaho; and Dripping Springs, Texas, have all become International Dark Sky Communities, not because they were worried about professional astronomers leaving, but because they wanted amateur astronomers to come *visit*. A beautiful night sky is the one "attraction" that every town technically has, but only some offer. National parks might be some of the last places left to see one—but they don't have to be.

It's easy to feel small when looking up at the constellations. That night in Arizona, while standing alone in a massive field of cacti under a field of stars, I certainly thought of my own insignificance in the universe. But I also thought about how my view of the Milky Way that night came courtesy of an entire city working together. And that knowledge made me feel *big*. Tucson hadn't just found a way to show off the stars—it had shown that seemingly inconsequential actions, done by enough people, can make an enormous difference.

17

TRAVELERS

(Theodore Roosevelt, Voyageurs, Denali)

In late 1906, Theodore Roosevelt became the first president to travel to a foreign country while in office. His international trip—a more-than-two-week journey down to Panama to see how that canal of theirs was coming along—was a first for America, but it was hardly a first for Roosevelt. When he was just ten years old, Roosevelt's wealthy family had taken him abroad on a yearlong European tour.

Ten, it turned out, was not *quite* old enough to fully appreciate an international adventure. As Roosevelt later chronicled in his autobiography, he and his younger siblings largely hated their family vacation. "Our one desire was to get back to America, and we regarded Europe with the most ignorant chauvinism and contempt," he wrote. "Four years later, however, I made another journey to Europe, and was old enough to enjoy it thoroughly and profit by it."

By fourteen, young Teddy had seen more of the world than most Americans see in a lifetime. His family cruised up the Nile in Egypt, then toured Syria, Turkey, and Greece before eventually making their way north to Germany. There the Roosevelt children were left with a family in Dresden for an entire summer, in the hope they would learn German language and literature. The trip, Roosevelt wrote, "formed a really useful part of my education."

As he got older, Roosevelt sought out trips that provided him with a physical challenge. In college, he traveled to Maine to climb Mount Katahdin. While honeymooning with his beloved Alice in Europe, he climbed the Matterhorn in the Swiss Alps. On September 13, 1901, he had just climbed Mount Marcy in the Adirondacks when he received a message that President William McKinley had taken a turn for the worse.

A week earlier, McKinley had been shot by an assassin in Buffalo, New York, but he had recovered so promisingly that then vice president Roosevelt decided to leave his bedside to go hiking upstate. Roosevelt rushed back to Buffalo, but by the time he finally arrived, McKinley was dead. Roosevelt was sworn in as our twenty-sixth president.

While that was the day Roosevelt officially became president, he later remarked that "I would not have been president had it not been for my experience in North Dakota." The Dakota Territory—where Roosevelt had gone to grieve Alice's death—is where he ultimately found his strength and sense of purpose. After he died in 1919, the U.S. government set about preserving tens of thousands of acres near Roosevelt's North Dakota ranch in honor of the man who had preserved so many millions of acres across the country. Of all of our national parks, Theodore Roosevelt is the only one named after a person.

Today the park may be best known for its wildlife. Ten minutes after I drove through the entrance gate, I saw my first bison, wandering by itself on a distant hillside. Watching the mighty beast lumber along, it was strange to think that this mammal could have been as foreign to me as a woolly mammoth had it not been for the conservation efforts of a man whose initial instinct, upon seeing a bison, was to shoot it.

Roosevelt traveled west to kill his first bison in 1883. But by

1889, he started to think more about how quickly the giant animals were disappearing. After a hunt, Roosevelt lamented that "few indeed are the men who now have or evermore shall have the chance of seeing the mightiest of American beasts, in all his wild vigor, surrounded by the tremendous desolation of his far-off mountain home."

He was right to be concerned. When Roosevelt took office in 1901, the bison was nearly extinct—an estimated three hundred remained in the entire country. Thanks to protections he put in place as president, well over three hundred thousand of them now roam across North America.

The bison have become so plentiful in this part of North Dakota that they actually make it a little difficult to follow the official trails at the park. I frequently found myself wandering off in the wrong direction, accidentally following a path that I only belatedly realized had been stomped into the grass by a two-thousand-pound animal and not mowed by a human. It felt like there should have been a wooden sign to point the way, and there likely once was— the bison use them as scratching posts and knock them down.

Of course, when Roosevelt explored this land, there were no human-made trails at all. Had there been, I doubt he would have fallen so hard for this landscape of "savage desolation." Time and again, Roosevelt planned his trips around the paths less traveled. In 1903, he went to Yosemite to go hiking for three days in the backcountry with John Muir. After Roosevelt left office, when he could have easily been enjoying a life of speaking engagements and fancy dinners like a proper ex-president, he instead opted to spend several months exploring an uncharted river in South America. It was an absurdly long, dangerous journey, full of piranhas and snakes and rapids and whirlpools—an *adventure*.

It should come as no surprise that the Dakota Badlands spoke to Roosevelt. They represented a challenge. As Roosevelt wrote in *Hunting Trips of a Ranchman*, "This broken country extends back from the river for many miles, and has been called always, by Indians, French voyageurs, and American trappers alike, the 'Bad

Lands,' partly from its dreary and forbidding aspect and partly from the difficulty experienced in travelling through it."

For Roosevelt, a trip that wasn't difficult wasn't a trip worth taking.

The "French voyageurs" Roosevelt referred to have since been largely forgotten by modern Americans, but they would have been legends back in the 1800s. *Voyageur* is the French word for "traveler," and from the late 1600s to the late 1800s it was the name given to the thousands of French Canadian fur trappers who traveled across the continent.

Europe had come down with a bad case of beaver fever. Prized for their soft, warm fur, beavers had been hunted to near-extinction in Europe. When the animals started disappearing, the Old World looked to its colonies in the New World for a fresh supply of pelts. To feed the rampant demand, the voyageurs would set off from Montreal and paddle over a thousand miles to where beavers were plentiful, arriving in what's now northern Minnesota, home of Voyageurs National Park.

The *u* in the park's name often goes unnoticed. The park does not honor the 1977 NASA spacecraft or the 1995 *Star Trek* series or any of the other countless American "Voyagers." It is a national park named in honor of travelers exploring a different kind of frontier.

International Falls, Minnesota, is a full day's drive from Theodore Roosevelt National Park. Within hours of arriving at my lodge, the small town had already lived up to its name. The only person who came up on Tinder turned out to be in *Canada.* My dating radius was set to twenty miles, but that was twenty miles as the crow flies. I soon realized my match was staying at a lodge on the opposite side of the water, so the only way we could have gone out (without a four-hour round-trip drive) was if I had a boat.

I did not have a boat. I started to wonder if I was the only person who had ever come to Voyageurs without one. Every car on the road seemed to be towing some sort of watercraft. With all the bait shops, the lodges, the marinas—this was clearly a park meant for boaters.

Around 40 percent of Voyageurs National Park is water, although that's a deceptively low number. Most of the parkland is *in* the water—a massive peninsula and close to nine hundred islands stretching to the Canadian border. To access them all, you need to find your way onto what the park calls its "interconnected water highways."

Those were the water highways the voyageurs once crisscrossed by canoe. Much of our modern-day border with Canada traces their historic route. Each voyageur boat would hold several men, supplies, and as many beaver pelts as could possibly fit.

The voyageurs never could have done any of this without the help of the tribes who lived along their routes. The Ojibwe of Minnesota traded with the Europeans, providing them with food, furs, and key knowledge of the waterways and beaver-trapping locations and methods. While a far more accurate name for the park would be "Merci Beaucoup, Ojibwe," Voyageurs stuck.

The voyageurs managed to capture the popular imagination. They were like a crew of fashion-forward cowboys—in most depictions, they're seen wearing their signature red knit "toque" caps, loose long-sleeved white shirts, and flowing, bright-red sashes. It was hard but prestigious work—the men were famed for their speed and strength. And, according to a volunteer I met at the national park visitor center, for their *singing*. The men paddled to a beat, belting folk songs with each stroke. "Better singers made for better voyageurs," the volunteer said.

I tried to picture my college a cappella group cramming into a canoe together. Much like the voyageurs, we wore matching outfits and toured around the country, although I fear that's where the similarity ends. Had we ever been forced to survive outdoors in a Minnesota winter, I am quite certain we would have all been dead within a week.

The voyageurs mostly subsisted on pea soup and pemmican, a

dried mixture of beef and fat that could last for up to a year. They were on a tight schedule and had no time to stop for hunting or gathering on their journey. They needed food that wouldn't spoil.

Chewing on my own stale piece of beef jerky as I traveled across the park's Lake Kabetogama, I was disappointed by how little snacks had evolved over the last three hundred years. But, like the voyageurs, I didn't have time to stop for lunch. This noon boat ride was my only shot to make it out on the water.

I had been in a grouchy mood all day. I was convinced I had screwed up Voyageurs. My constant traveling had finally caught up with me—this park clearly required more advanced planning than I had devoted to it. I regretted not renting my own boat, one that would have allowed me to explore the hundreds of islands at my leisure. Perhaps I could have camped on a couple—every single one of the park's campsites is only accessible by water. At the very least, I should have booked a room at the Kettle Falls Hotel, a legendary lodge that's a boat ride away from everywhere else.

But by the time I finally turned my attention toward Voyageurs, everything was either booked, too expensive, or too complicated to arrange. I was told I was lucky to have even found the bed I'd secured in a run-down bunkhouse near one of the lakes, although I hadn't felt quite so lucky the night before when a bat had flown down from the rafters and chased me through the hallway toward the communal shower.

I didn't say anything about the bat at breakfast—I was busy buttering up the lodge owner into taking me to the other side of the lake so I could at least explore *something* out in the water. She agreed (or rather, she agreed to have her husband do it), and so at noon I hopped into his speedboat for a quick trip over to the edge of the Kabetogama Peninsula, where I would hike one of the park's few maintained trails. After a few hours, her husband would come back to the dock to pick me up. Or would he? I had no way of contacting him if he didn't show. That small bit of uncertainty at least made it feel like I was having somewhat of an authentic voyageur adventure.

Part of the reason the voyageurs wore hats and long-sleeved shirts was to keep away Minnesota's relentless mosquitoes. Bug repellent has advanced far more than jerky over the last few centuries, but when I reached into my backpack, I realized I had left my bottle of OFF! behind at the lodge. The mosquitoes couldn't believe their luck. Over the next few hours, they tore into me.

Despite the relentless bugs, the hike was gorgeous. I think part of the reason the mosquitoes were so eager to attack me was that these trails see so few people—it might be hours or even days before any other hikers pulled up to this dock. Wandering through the dense trees, it felt like I was experiencing the landscape much as the voyageurs had. The only difference was, when I came across a beaver dam midway through my hike, I was able to appreciate it for the incredible feat of animal engineering that it was instead of tearing it apart looking for something to wear to the opera.

That night at dinner, I was talking with some southern Minnesotans who had traveled up to Voyageurs for a few days of fishing. Literally everyone else at the lodge was there to fish. I mentioned how I felt like I was giving the park short shrift.

"Well, that just means you'll have to come back," one of them said.

I supposed it did. Sometimes the best trips are reconnaissance missions. I'm sure the voyageurs didn't know what they were doing when they came to Minnesota for the first time, either. Roosevelt didn't "get" Europe on his initial visit. Travel takes some trial and error.

"In fact, you really should come back in the winter," another said.

I laughed. Northern Minnesota in the winter? No thanks.

"No, really," he said. "That's when the park is at its best, although nobody ever talks about it. You know how you said there aren't many trails? Just wait until winter, man. The entire lake freezes. The Park Service grooms a bunch of trails on the ice. *Snowmobile* trails. It's awesome."

That night, unable to sleep after another heart-pounding scare from the lodge's resident bat, I decided to look up videos of people snowmobiling across the lake in the winter. It *did* look awesome. It also looked entirely mosquito-free, which was a plus. More than anything, it looked like an adventure. I vowed to return to Voyageurs some January to snowmobile. It would be freezing cold, no doubt, but I suppose that's just the kind of weather in which a beaver hat might actually be appropriate.

In Alaska, they call snowmobiles "snowmachines." Why, I'm not quite sure—I've traveled to plenty of chilly places, and only in the forty-ninth state do they swap *mobile* for *machine*. The machines are a popular mode of transportation in rural communities, sometimes referred to as "iron dogs" in honor of the *actual* dogs they've replaced.

Leashed to a sled, teams of Alaskan huskies once delivered everything from food to mail across the state. They were how people got around. As Alaskan judge James Wickersham wrote in 1938, "He who gives time to the study of the history of Alaska, learns that the dog, next to man, has been the most important factor in its past and present development."

In the early 1900s, naturalist Charles Sheldon traveled to the base of Mount McKinley on a dogsledding expedition. He was convinced that the mountain, and the wilderness surrounding it, needed to become part of a national park.

An earlier American expedition had come up with the McKinley moniker, but Sheldon suggested that the mountain be called Denali, the name already given it by the local Athabascan people. It meant "the High One," and it seemed fitting for the 20,310-foot mountain. The peak of McKinley was the highest in all of North America. To have such a mighty mountain honor William McKinley, a five-foot-seven Ohioan who had never so much as set foot in Alaska, seemed silly.

McKinley, Theodore Roosevelt's predecessor, served as our twenty-fifth president. It wasn't until late in the second term of our forty-fourth that the mountain's name was officially changed to Denali. When Obama announced the renaming in 2015, some bitter Ohioans took it personally. House Speaker John Boehner said he was "deeply disappointed" by the decision. Candidate Trump tweeted that he would change it back, a promise that, as of this writing, is unfulfilled.

As it turned out, Alaska's senators—both Republicans—surprised Trump by letting him know they *liked* Denali. There was a beauty in the name, one that a surprisingly woke Charles Sheldon had argued for his entire life. In his memoir *The Wilderness of Denali*, Sheldon wrote that "the Indians who have lived for countless generations in the presence of these colossal mountains have given them names that are both euphonious and appropriate . . . Can it be denied that the names they gave to the most imposing features of their country should be preserved?"

Sheldon's guide in Alaska was Harry Karstens, a man who was said to know his way around a dogsled better than anyone. When, thanks to Sheldon's lobbying efforts, Mount McKinley National Park was established in 1917, Sheldon recommended his old guide be considered for the job of superintendent.

Karstens took the job in 1921, and that first winter, he went out and bought seven Alaskan huskies—the park's first-ever dog team. There have been dogs at the park ever since.

While I understood that the sled dogs were an important part of Denali's past, I was surprised to learn that they were still very much a part of its present. When I met ranger Jen Raffaeli at Denali's kennels, I asked her a question I was sure she got asked every day. Basically, "Why on earth are you still traveling around using dogs a hundred years later? Haven't you heard of snowmachines?"

But Jen argued that snowmachines are still machines, and in the snow, they often fail when dogs do not.

"You know, if you're out at fifty below, and you try and start up a snowmachine, it may or may not start," Jen patiently explained.

"At fifty below, I go out and say, 'Good morning.' These guys all jump up."

She gestured to Sylvie, a six-year-old husky, who, as if on cue, jumped right up.

"Plus, if I have to choose one to snuggle with at the end of the day, I'll choose Sylvie over a snowmachine," Jen said, giving Sylvie a reassuring pat on the head.

Each summer, Denali welcomes a new litter of puppies, carefully bred from the dog team's all-star members. For that year's litter of puppies, Jen had selected a dog named Annie to be the mother, a large four-year-old who had impressed her over the past few winters with her stamina and confidence in the "lead dog" position. Jen thought her team could use a few more Annies.

For a Denali dog, Annie has a fairly ordinary name. While all names need to be short and easy to pronounce—you don't want to be speeding toward the edge of a cliff screaming for Supercalifragilisticexpialidocious to turn left—they're generally a little offbeat, bestowed as part of a very specific yearly theme. The dogs of 2010, for example, were named after the Latin terms for Alaskan bumblebees—names like Sitken, Lucor, and Rupee. Sylvie was derived from a species of forest bumblebee, *Bombus sylvicola*.

New mother Annie was part of the 2012 mining-claims-themed litter. Since Alaskan mining claims were often named after people, the 2012 dogs ended up with more "normal" names. Had Annie been born the next year, as part of the climbing-knots litter, she might have ended up a Prusik or a Clove.

For the litter born during the Park Service Centennial, the choice of theme was easy. They were the birthday litter: Cupcake, Party, Piñata, Happy, and Hundo (short for One Hundred). I'd been emailing with Jen for months, tracking Annie's breeding progress. I knew I had to time things just right if I wanted to catch the new puppies at maximum cuteness. When I finally walked into the enclosure to meet the dogs I'd been dreaming about, it was clear I had made the right choice.

As Efrain rolled camera, I sat across from Jen and conducted the most adorable interview of my life. When she placed three of the puppies in my lap, all at once, my heart almost exploded.

Whenever Jen could tell a puppy was starting to tire of my attention, she would swap it out for another one. She had been with them since the night they were born and was already dialed into their budding personalities. One day, that bond might help save Jen and her team from sledding onto a patch of unstable ice or falling off a cliff. An ability to read nonverbal cues is key to successful dog mushing.

Each winter, when she travels out into the backcountry with her sled team, Jen is constantly monitoring the dogs to see if they sense some danger she might not.

"Dogs have brains and hearts and memories better than most rangers," she said. "And dogs' instincts are usually correct."

It's actually easier to get around Denali in the winter. In the summer, swampy tundra and bumpy tussocks of grass make overland travel difficult—and when there's a river crossing, near impossible.

"But in winter, those huge, daunting rivers are frozen into highways of ice," Jen told me. In winter, she and her team become Ice Road Mushers, hauling supplies by dogsled to locations that would have required a helicopter drop in the summer.

Once the snows come, these new puppies will get to follow the team. They won't hook into a sled—not their first year—but they'll run alongside, learning the ropes. Some may turn into all-star lead dogs like their mother. Some might end up being more utility players.

Most important, they'll collectively travel across the park *quietly*. Snowmachines are loud, humming monsters. A dog team can cut through Denali's backcountry—a federal wilderness area—in near silence, their built-in GPS guiding them to locations they've visited in past seasons.

· · ·

Before leaving the kennel, I asked Efrain to snap a few photos of me with the puppies.

"Are these going on your Tinder profile?" he asked.

"Um . . . Maybe . . ."

Efrain was already responsible for five out of six of my profile pictures. It almost felt like cheating. While other guys were struggling to take poorly lit shirtless selfies in their bathroom mirrors, I was traveling to the country's most scenic backdrops with a professional photographer.

Now I was about to add an armful of puppies into the mix. Good luck swiping left, ladies.

"Don't you think the girls are going to be mad when they find out these aren't your dogs?" he asked.

It was a valid point. Cuddling with puppies that aren't actually yours isn't as obviously deceitful as, say, Photoshopping on abs that you do not actually have, but I guess it could be considered a very mild form of catfishing. (Or dogfishing, as it were.)

"I mean, *technically*, they *are* mine," I rationalized. "I pay taxes. These dogs belong to all of us. That's what the parks are all about, right?"

Efrain rolled his eyes and held up the iPhone as I wiggled the puppies into position.

"Hold on, hold on," I said. "I think I should make a sort of pouty *awwww* face."

A few photos later, and I knew we'd wasted enough of Jen's time. She needed to set up for one of the kennel's popular presentations. During the summer, the sled dogs are teaching tools—a way to tell park visitors the story of how this landscape has been traveled since before it was even a park.

In the winter, as Jen trains her new canine recruits, she'll also be saying goodbye to some old friends. After ten years or so, the Denali dogs get to retire.

The rafters of the kennel's tack room look like the ceiling of an NBA arena, the name plates of former Denali superstars hanging down from the beams. There's Tamrak, Skipper, Keta, Widgeon, and Tabu, all retired runners from past litters.

Jen maintains a waiting list full of families eager to adopt a sled dog. She screens first for location; since the dogs don't do well in warmer climates, most end up going to families in Alaska. She said she recently adopted one out to a family in Minnesota—not far from Voyageurs—but that's about as far south as she's generally willing to go.

But just as important as geography is activity. Jen looks for families with highly active lifestyles, families who are willing to commit to running the dogs multiple miles a day. Sled dogs can live for fifteen or more years, and they still have plenty of pep in their step when their Denali days are done. Their desire to run is baked into their doggy DNA—retired or not, they simply *can't* sit back and stay still. They have to keep moving.

Heading back down Denali's main road, I realized I might be wired the same way. This year of perpetual motion was a first for me, but I had been bitten hard by the travel bug long before the mosquitoes of Voyageurs ever got their shot at me. My family's trip out west when I was a teenager had opened my eyes to a world I'd never seen before. From then on, I knew I wanted to make travel a priority in my life, although it took a while for my finances to catch up to my ambitions.

After college, I dove headfirst into the airline miles and hotel points world. Before long, I started planning trips funded almost entirely by credit cards. Not by *credit*—fortunately, I knew enough to not go into debt to subsidize my wanderlust—but by all of the airline miles and hotel points that the credit cards provided. I became a plastic-wielding wizard, learning the ins and outs of all of the various rewards programs, opening and closing accounts just for the sign-up offers. I would scour the internet for deals, buying discounted products with the sole intention of turning around and reselling them on eBay. After the listing fees and shipping charges, it was essentially a wash, but I wasn't doing it to earn money—I was doing it to earn miles.

You've undoubtedly seen a story like this on the news. Some nerd with a spreadsheet who claims to have beat the system and is now flying around the world for pennies. "It can't be that easy," you say. And you're right—it isn't. But I wanted to hike Machu Picchu. I wanted to go to the World Expo in Shanghai. I wanted to ride a bike in Copenhagen and a train in Tokyo, and so all of the work I put into executing my elaborate little schemes was more than worth it to me. Obsessing over travel was my unofficial part-time job long before anyone ever thought of paying me to go somewhere.

This year of *constant* travel felt like something I'd been training for my whole life. All of the annoying logistics? I secretly *loved* them. I was good at them. Sure, I enjoyed the challenge of climbing a mountain, but I also enjoyed the challenge of figuring out how to get to the mountain in the first place.

My favorite part of traveling, though, has always been the way my trips have challenged me to rethink my preconceived notions about other places and people. Roosevelt's boyhood journey to Germany—where he experienced the kindness and generosity of the Germans firsthand—elicited a similar reaction. In his autobiography, he wrote that after his trip, "it would have been quite impossible to make me feel that the Germans were really foreigners."

Hitting the parks, I was visiting places in America that sometimes felt as foreign to me as any foreign country. Lodges full of fishermen with unfamiliar accents, obsessed with how the walleye and trout were biting that day. Wild, rural Alaska, where a pack of dogs still managed to be the most reliable mode of transportation. Dickinson, North Dakota—a city half an hour away from Theodore Roosevelt National Park, where a rapid oil boom and subsequent bust had left it looking like a brand-new ghost town.

From an unfinished road in the Smoky Mountains to a reopened crossing on the Mexican border, I was exposing myself to perspectives and people I wouldn't have come across otherwise. But wherever I traveled, there was no mistaking that I was always a visitor. I was welcomed, but I never really belonged.

I thought of a passage I'd read in Roosevelt's autobiography. Somehow, in the midst of visiting everywhere from Kenya to the Grand Canyon, Roosevelt had stayed in one place long enough to raise six children. Looking back at his life, the man who had been everywhere and done everything—who had held our country's highest office—wrote that "a household of children, if things go reasonably well, certainly makes all other forms of success and achievement lose their importance by comparison."

A household full of children couldn't have felt more foreign and far off to me while I was living out of a suitcase. Plus, that's not the kind of journey you can plan for—it's a path that may or may not appear. But I was open to the idea of it, at least. There's a reason huskies travel in packs. As Roosevelt wrote, "It may be true that he travels farthest who travels alone; but the goal thus reached is not worth reaching."

18

LOVE

(Canyonlands, North Cascades)

In one day of hiking in a park, I say hello to more strangers than I do in a month of walking around a city.

Offer a cheery "hello" to someone on a big city sidewalk, and they just might reach for their pepper spray. An unsolicited "hi" can be seen as an act of aggression, a signifier of mental instability, or, at the very least, the prelude to an annoying sales pitch to donate to the Parrot Rosacea Council or the Flat Jupiter Foundation. Even in West Virginia, a place renowned for its friendliness, it's not like people are greeting every person they pass inside the Piggly Wiggly. But out on the trail, people actually do stuff like that. Every time I walk by someone, there's always a greeting. Maybe not a verbal hello, but there's at least an acknowledgment. A nod, a wave. An "I see you."

Saying hello is also, in a small way, a safety precaution, especially on more remote trails. If you go missing, you want to be remembered by whoever saw you last. If you stopped to chat with that person, even better.

"He said he was heading out to the Moskey Basin campsite" is helpful information for search-and-rescue squads.

"He was the jerk who didn't even bother to say hello" is not. Nor is it the obituary you want on the local news.

Seeing someone on a trail in a park is like seeing someone wearing the T-shirt of your favorite band. You instantly recognize that you have something in common, and you feel that connection. You have both chosen to come to a specific place on a specific day to enjoy your leisure time. The easy choice would have been to stay inside, where there is air-conditioning and Wi-Fi and pizza bagels. Instead you are the people who have opted outside. That at least warrants a nod.

"Hello!"

A man in his late sixties smiled as I moved over to let him pass by me on the trail. We were walking in opposite directions, and while we probably could have fit next to each other, the drop-off on the other side was steep. Better safe than dead.

"Thank you," the woman walking behind him added.

"Hey, I'll take any chance I can to stop and look at this view," I said.

All three of us paused for a moment to take in the red sandstone formations of Utah's Canyonlands National Park, a landscape writer Edward Abbey once described as "the most weird, wonderful, magical place on earth."

Canyonlands is a name that seems more suited to a video game than to a national park, and its four separate districts sound like realms to be conquered: Island in the Sky, The Needles, Rivers, The Maze. I assumed that if you somehow made it through the mysterious challenges of all four, an old knight would appear to offer you a chance to drink from the Holy Grail.

I wouldn't have time to visit all the districts on this trip, so I'd decided to focus on Island in the Sky—high up on a mesa, it's the most accessible and popular district, for good reason. Whereas the view from the rim of the Grand Canyon is basically either straight across or straight down, Island in the Sky offers texture. There are canyons within canyons, drop-offs, and outcroppings as far as the eye can see.

"Where are you from?" the woman asked.

"Well, it's a long story," I said, launching into my usual spiel.

"I grew up in West Virginia, went to college in Connecticut, then lived in California for ten years. But now . . ."

I paused before the big reveal, my guaranteed oh-isn't-he-so-*interesting* showstopper.

"I don't really *have* a home. I just kind of live on the road."

"Oh we've lived on the road for nine years," the woman said with a laugh. "We gave up our home a *long* time ago."

Wait. What? Did I just get out-hobo-ed?

Linda and Tony Oyster had been married for thirty-five years. They met, as many couples do, in a bar. But a bar in Florida was the last place Tony ever thought he'd find romance, or ever find himself.

"I don't drink," Tony told me. "You can count on one hand the number of bars I've been to in my entire life. But for some reason, I decided to walk into that one that night."

Tony had been feeling a little lost. His first marriage had ended just three months earlier. Whether it was loneliness or boredom or fate, something compelled him to walk into O'Hare's in Palm Beach, Florida, that evening. Linda was already inside.

"My apartment was just *too* hot that night," Linda said. She had been married before as well and had been living on her own in an apartment with weak air-conditioning. "I came in because I was trying to find someplace cool."

Inside, she and Tony struck up a conversation.

"We just kept talking and talking. And, well, it turned out we sure liked talking to each other," Tony said.

They got married and began to travel together; Tony's job took them all around the world. As hard as it was to picture Tony as a businessman—he was wearing loose hiking clothes and a brown cowboy hat—he had apparently worked for a big-deal consulting firm back in Florida. For his fiftieth birthday, he was able to convince his bosses to give him several months off so he and Linda could drive from Palm Beach to Alaska and back, camping in their pop-up trailer along the way.

Tony wasn't quite ready to retire, but after that trip, he started to plot his exit. The Oysters sold their home and bought a motor home—a forty-foot Alpine Coach. They moved into an RV park in Florida.

"Wait, so every day, you're coming home from your job . . . What was your title, again?" I asked.

"Treasurer," Tony said.

"Okay, so you're the treasurer of this company, and you're coming home from work and sleeping in an *RV*? Did everyone at the office think you were crazy?"

"Well, they didn't think he was that crazy when the hurricanes came," Linda said.

I had put down my backpack and walked with the Oysters to a wider section of the trail so that other hikers could get by us. Each one shouted a cheery "hello" as they passed. I wasn't going anywhere, though. I had to hear the rest of this story.

"You know Florida," Tony said. "Every once in a while, a hurricane comes through. All my coworkers would be boarding up their houses, and we'd just pop in the RV, drive up to Alabama, play golf for a few weeks, then come back!"

Eventually, after years of saving money and living on wheels, the Oysters decided the time had finally come to hit the road.

"We added up all the nickels and dimes we had, and thought we had enough to do it," Tony said. "And we had our health. That was the most important thing. We didn't know how long we'd have that. So it just made sense to do it then."

On Tony's sixtieth birthday—June 11, 2007—a decade after he and Linda had driven the Dalton Highway in Alaska, he drove his Jeep to his office for the last time. He signed his exit papers, said his goodbyes, and left.

"I walked out the front door of that company, and there was Linda waiting for me in the parking lot, and she was standing at *our* front door," Tony said. "She had driven the mobile home to pick me up. She had gone ahead and hooked the Jeep up to the back of the RV all by herself. So I just walked right inside and we drove away."

I couldn't believe it.

"Wait, you left that night? Like, straight from your desk out onto the open road?"

"Well, why wait?" Linda laughed.

"Were you nervous? Were you worried at all? That this was all finally happening?"

"We felt free!" she said. "At last, we were going to do what we'd *always* wanted to do."

And that's exactly what they've been doing every day since. The Oysters made it as far as Orlando that first night, then eventually headed up to the Northeast. These days, they spend most of their time out west, rarely driving more than four hours a day. They sleep in the RV, but they spend their days outside. Sometimes at national parks—they had just come from Arches and the Grand Canyon—and sometimes near any one of the hundreds of obscure lakes and mountains that only reveal themselves to those who live life on the road. They'll stop for a week, sometimes a month or more, in each destination. Unless it looks like rain.

"We can probably count on *two* hands the days we've seen any kind of rain," Tony said. "We kind of follow the weather."

"No rain in almost *nine* years?" I asked. "Come on."

"We *really* don't like rain," Linda said.

By this point, I had started to worry I had lingered for too long, but the Oysters didn't seem like they were in a hurry, which I guess was the whole point of their lifestyle. They were never in a hurry. I had more of Canyonlands to see, but it was hard to imagine the park contained anything more interesting than the couple in front of me. I felt like they were secret bonus characters I'd somehow unlocked in this Island in the Sky realm. Wise vagabonds who had materialized to teach me their ways.

"So what's it been like spending so much time together?" I asked.

"Well, we *always* spent time together," Tony said. "Back when I was working, Linda would come meet me every day for lunch. We just like being around each other. I'm her best friend and she's my best friend."

"If his buddies were organizing a golf game, they would always invite me too," Linda said. "They knew they had to."

Like or not, the Oysters were a package deal.

"Sure," I said. "But still, doesn't it get difficult? That's a lot of time to spend in a small place."

They looked at each other and shrugged.

"Honestly . . . no," Tony said. "You might not believe that, but it doesn't. We like it."

"Well, so what's the secret? How do you do it?"

Tony paused and considered this.

"I think the key is *respect*. We just respect each other. If one of us doesn't want to do something, it's fine. It's instantly fine. There's no bargaining back and forth."

"And we just let things go," Linda said. "It's always best to just let it go."

The Oysters still managed to find alone time—Tony was a morning person and Linda was a night owl, so they had hours each day to themselves while the other was asleep. Tony would take morning walks, while Linda might stay up late and read or watch a movie. But for the most part, they liked to do things together. Life was better that way, they said.

Our conversation had been the best-case scenario of a hiking hello, a moment of connection that felt like it was only possible in a park. But it was a fleeting moment. I still had miles more to hike, as did they. We exchanged contact information, wished each other well, and headed off in our separate directions. Except they were headed off *together*. Watching them go, I envied the type of connection that they shared. Life seemed better that way.

. . .

Like Tony Oyster, I've never enjoyed meeting people in bars, so after my breakup I turned to the internet. It was a low-key, low-commitment way to just see what was out there.

My friends told me there had been a great leap forward in on-line dating. Now romance was just a swipe away on my phone. You could match at 4 P.M. and be out on a date with someone by 7 P.M. I downloaded Tinder, Bumble, and Happn, and started swiping.

Left, Right, Left, Right, Left, Left, Left, Right. I felt like I was judging my own reality competition show from the comfort of my couch. Her favorite band was System of a Down? *Left.* More than one of her photos involved a puppy face Snapchat filter? *Left.* The countertop in her bathroom selfie was abnormally messy? She used the princess emoji to describe herself? She never takes off her sunglasses? *Left, Left, Left.*

It was disgustingly superficial and insanely addictive. It was like a video game with people as the prize. Whenever someone would match back, the phone would beep, and I'd get an instant ego boost.

I had spent hours agonizing over my pictures, trying to select a mix that projected an image of *regular fun guy.* Here's me standing by a glacier in Iceland! *Brrr!* Smiling by a waterfall in Croatia! *So worldly!* Making paella in a cooking class! *I may not be a good cook, but I'm trying!*

What I knew, and what none of my matches did, was that most of those photos had been taken by my ex-fiancée. One was even taken *with* her, at a group dinner we went to in Pasadena. We were probably holding hands under the table, but the photo had been taken in such a way that it was easy to crop her out. It felt oddly satisfying doing that, like I was somehow removing her from my story. She was now, quite literally, out of the picture, and I was just a regular fun guy who likes eating spaghetti on patios. *Yum!*

I made a few rules for myself. If I came across the profile of someone who specifically stated they were in search of something long-term, or were "marriage-minded," or were "looking for the real deal," I would not bother them. I knew that person they were looking for wasn't me yet, and it didn't seem fair to waste anyone's time. I just wanted to have dinner with a stranger. To see what it felt like to sit across the table from someone again.

I went on a few awkward dates before I left town, but most of my swiping since had been out on the road. Even just opening the apps in a new town offered interesting lessons on the subtle differences between American cities. Not surprisingly, the women in Los Angeles had a disproportionate number of professionally taken headshots, and profiles in Nashville had more mentions of God than the ones in Fresno. According to my unscientific swiping, Spokane, Washington, and Asheville, North Carolina, had more nose rings per capita than any other two cities in America. Every other woman there seemed to have some kind of face jewelry. Had there been some sort of Groupon?

Sometimes I would use Tinder's passport feature to set my location to a city I hadn't even arrived in yet. On days when I was traveling with Efrain, I'd ask him to drive so I could swipe from the passenger seat, talking to matches who were still two hundred miles away. By the time we finally rolled into town, I had already set up dinner plans.

Efrain never minded when I would ditch him for a stranger. He had a girlfriend, so he lived vicariously through my adventures. He never ended up meeting any of my dates, although he claimed to have his favorites. He always asked about the woman I'd gone out with in Tennessee who'd sent me an amazing Spotify playlist afterward for our drive across the South.

"*Every song*, dude. Every song is good. Marry her."

Two months later, we stopped at a taco stand in Provo, Utah, recommended to me by my date back in Salt Lake City. We were shocked to find such delicious Mexican food miles from the BYU campus.

"This girl *nailed it* with the taco recommendation," he said. "These are amazing. Plus, you said she writes children's books. That's what the leads in romantic comedies do. That or, like, cupcake baker or something. I'm telling you, marry her."

"I'm pretty sure I'd have to become a Mormon," I said.

"Worth it, dude," he said, his mouth full of carne asada. "Just make sure to serve these at your wedding."

In between shoots, Efrain would fly home to visit his girlfriend while I stayed out hitting more parks on my own. She joked that she was jealous of me. After all, I got to hang out with her boyfriend in all of the places *she* wanted to visit with him one day.

In turn, I was jealous of what the two of them had. It was still a fairly new relationship—they had just started dating when I'd initially called Efrain about the CBS gig. At the time, it wasn't clear if they were going to *keep* dating. But they decided to give it a go, and it seemed like the occasional stretches apart had brought them closer together. When Efrain and I would link back up, he would tell me stories of their weekend trips and quiet domestic evenings. I got to see their relationship grow and deepen as the year went on.

For me, though, it was one first date after another. And as interesting as it was to hear other people's stories, I quickly got bored of hearing my own. I became very good at telling it, though. I would mention the parks, of course, and then, depending on the audience, I might add or delete little anecdotes as the date went on. *Is this someone who might enjoy hearing about how I once dislocated my knee while '80s dancing? Or would I be better off mentioning that time I fell off the side of Machu Picchu?* My jokes, my segues— I had them down pat. But from my perspective, it felt like I kept giving a series of performances of the same one-man show.

I was learning about different people, but I didn't know how much I was learning about myself. Not that that was the goal, necessarily, but the deeper, more meaningful introspection that can be the best part of a relationship never comes from a first date. I never gave myself a chance to dive deeper. I was always on to the next town, the next restaurant, the next park, the next person.

. . .

"Hello!"

The Cascade Pass Trail had become socked in with a thick fog, adding an extra layer of spooky to Washington's already mystical mountains. Washington is the number one state for Sasquatch spottings, and North Cascades National Park is said to be where many of the beasts prefer to hang out. I thought that by announcing my presence, I might signal to the two young women stopped ahead of me on the trail that it was a friendly hiker, not an angry Bigfoot, clomping down toward them in the mist. I still managed to startle them.

"Oh! Hey!" the shorter one said, jumping up. It was a Wednesday, and there was hardly anyone out on the mountain.

"Were you just up at the top?" she asked. "Is it as foggy as it is here?"

"Oh, if you think *this* is bad, then you haven't seen anything yet," I said. "And . . . if you like *not seeing anything*, then you are going to *love* the top."

The women both groaned. The steep, challenging hike was famous for its views, but the summit, twenty minutes farther up the mountain, was a thick soup of white and gray.

"I'm starting to think there's a reason why nobody else is out here," the taller one said. "Hi. I'm Claire, this is Melissa. And *you* must be the other car in the parking lot."

They were visiting from the East Coast, friends from med school who had decided to go on a whirlwind tour of the Pacific Northwest. Mount Rainier, Crater Lake, and sea kayaking in Anacortes—a place I'd never even heard of—were all on the itinerary. It sounded like a great trip.

"Unfortunately, today was our only shot for North Cascades," Claire said.

"Well, this won't make you feel better, but I camped here last night and it was beautiful," I said, suddenly self-conscious about how sweaty and stinky I must have been after a night in the woods. Claire looked like she smelled like honeysuckle and jasmine. She was beautiful.

"We thought about camping," she said. "Was it cold?"

"No, not bad at all. They had a special program at night, where a ranger set up a projector in an amphitheater. This photographer who shoots North Cascades all the time came to show some of his work. You know what he said his favorite place to photograph in all of the park was?"

"Oh no. *This?*"

"Yup. I mean, the pictures did look pretty amazing. Who knows—maybe it will clear up if we wait?"

We stood and talked for another twenty minutes. I told them about my trip so far. Claire couldn't believe I didn't go kayaking when I was in Florida. She *loved* kayaking. There was just something about being surrounded by water, she said.

Our chat turned into an impromptu lunch break. I teased Claire and Melissa about how healthy and doctorly their snacks were, mostly because I was embarrassed about how awful everything was that I had brought.

"So what's your medical opinion on this thing of Lunchables I got at the gas station?" I asked, pulling out the yellow-wrapped square from my backpack. "It's got smoke flavor, pasteurized 'cheddar cheese product,' sodium ascorbate . . ."

"Stop, stop!" Claire yelled, plugging her ears.

"Hold on, I haven't gotten to the cookie. It comes with a free Oreo!"

"Are you in second grade? Just be glad you're eating that on your way *down* the mountain."

The fog didn't look like it was clearing. There wouldn't be a view at the top, but since Claire and Melissa had already come so far, they figured they might as well make it to the summit anyway.

"We should probably head up if we're going to do it," Melissa said. "We've got a long drive back to Seattle tonight."

"Yeah, me too," I said.

"Oh, you're staying in Seattle?" Claire said. "I thought you were camping?"

"I was, but just for last night. For the next couple of nights I'm at a hotel in Bellevue."

"Well, that's not all that outdoorsy of you," she teased.

"What can I say? I'm a fancy hobo. With a lot of Hilton points. If you like miniature toiletries, I am a very good guy to know."

"I'll keep that in mind," she said.

"You know I'm pretty sure Bellevue is really close to where *we're* staying, Claire," Melissa said.

I could have sworn I saw Melissa smirking, and Claire blushing, but the fog made it hard to tell. We stood awkwardly together for a few seconds in silence.

"Well . . . it was really nice meeting you," I said.

"Yeah, really nice meeting you too," Claire said.

I noticed Melissa seemed to have backed away a bit, giving us as much privacy as you can on a narrow trail.

"So . . ."

Had I met Claire on an app, I would have already invited her to dinner. But somehow, meeting her on the trail, I froze.

"Enjoy the rest of your hike. And have fun kayaking—that sounds awesome. Here's hoping the sky clears up. Bye!"

I turned and continued down the trail. *Damn it, Conor.*

Bigfoot would have totally asked for her number.

That night, back at my hotel, I got an email from Claire.

She had googled me.

I had actually tried to google her as well, as soon as I got home, but I didn't know her last name. "Claire+doctor+carrot sticks+ kayaking" wasn't getting me anywhere.

But she remembered my name and the network I worked for, and with that, it wasn't hard to track me down. I had choked in the real world—thank goodness for technology.

I quickly messaged her back. Perhaps she might like to get dinner with me the next night? No processed cheese product involved, I promised. They don't make Dinnerables. She said yes, and the next evening we went to get soup dumplings together.

It was her last night in Seattle, and we couldn't stay out too late. Her kayak excursion with Melissa was the next morning, and then they were continuing on with the rest of their trip. This time, I was the one being left behind.

But we stayed in touch. When I had to fly east for a meeting in New York, we met for dinner again. A month later, one of her long weekend kayaking adventures coincided with one of my off days in California, so we hung out in Monterey. Three dates in three different states. Walking around Carmel-by-the-Sea together, holding hands, it definitely didn't feel like a relationship, but it felt comfortable.

Efrain started flipping out when I told him.

"Dude, this is serious," he said on the phone. "Well, serious for you, at least. This is like, what, your *third* third date?"

He was right. It wasn't my *first* third date—my crazy routing occasionally had me crossing back through cities I'd already visited—but anytime I had gone out with the same person more than twice, it felt noteworthy. And Kayaking Claire was definitely cool and nice and smart. But so was the office manager in Denver, the biologist in Oregon, and the attorney in Arizona. I had met lots of cool, nice people, and had I actually lived in any of their cities, maybe there would have been five or ten dates. But after three, it felt like I could tell, and I could tell again this time with Claire. I knew I still hadn't found my person.

"So what's wrong?" Efrain asked. "What are you looking for that's not there?"

I *wasn't* really looking, and maybe that was part of the problem. I wasn't in the right frame of mind. But perhaps that also helped me see things more clearly. When you're looking for a relationship, you're dead set on *finding* one, and sometimes a situation that's not the right fit feels like something you can squeeze yourself into.

When I had proposed, it had been to someone I'd met when all I was hoping to find was a friend in the desert. And yet, after three dates, I knew I'd found something more.

So nothing was "wrong." But nothing felt quite right yet, either. I definitely missed companionship, and I knew I wanted it again one day, but I wasn't in a rush.

"It just doesn't feel right," I said. "I don't know how to describe it. I guess it's kind of like the subtle difference between a state park and a national park. State parks are great, right? But once you know places like Yosemite are out there, then it's hard not to want something that feels like that. I want a relationship that feels like a *national park*."

Efrain was quiet for a moment.

"Please tell me you've never said that out loud before," he said. "That is the nerdiest damn thing I've ever heard. I think you've been spending too much time in the woods, dude."

John Muir didn't get married until he was nearly forty-two. It's weird thinking of him being married at all. In almost all the photos I have ever seen of him, he is by himself. Leaning on a walking stick, looking at a sequoia, contemplating the majesty of some massive lake. He was "John of the Mountains," a near-mythical figure with a long, Santa Claus beard. But there was also a Mrs. Claus.

Muir met Louisa Strentzel in 1874 at the Oakland home of Ezra and Jeanne Carr. It was a setup. The Carrs had gotten to know Muir back in Wisconsin, and had stayed friends with him after they all moved westward to California. Ezra was a science professor, but it was Jeanne who ended up becoming Muir's biggest champion and mentor, encouraging his writing, sending it off to magazines, and corresponding with him throughout his adventures. Eventually, Jeanne decided it was time for her wandering friend to settle down.

Louisa lived on an orchard with her parents in nearby Martinez, California, and was well known for her skill on the piano. She was smart and industrious, and after graduating from the Bay Area's Young Ladies Seminary, she went to work helping her father with the family fruit business.

Jeanne later described Louisa as "the only woman that I ever knew, who seemed a mate for John." But getting the couple together, given John's constant traveling, was a frustrating bit of matchmaking. It took years. Jeanne would write to Louisa and John separately, looking for any chance to put them in the same room at the same time. Eventually, her plan began to pan out. On trips back from the Sierras, Muir would call upon the Strentzels. In June 1879, he proposed to Louisa.

Muir of the Mountains became Muir the Family Man. He had two daughters with Louisa and ran the orchard with her after her father passed away. Their Victorian mansion is now the John Muir National Historic Site, managed by the Park Service. Upstairs, visitors can take a tour of Muir's "scribble den," where he wrote some of his most influential works.

Muir's grave site is a mile away. When he died in 1914, nearly a decade after Louisa, he was not interred in any of the land he had fought so hard to protect. Instead, he was brought back to a pleasant but not particularly remarkable acre of pear trees in Martinez so that he could be laid to rest beside the woman he loved.

John and Louisa Muir were not like Tony and Linda Oyster. They did not travel and camp together. Louisa liked the comforts of home, and John never quite cured himself of his wandering ways. With Louisa's encouragement, he would sometimes disappear back to the mountains for months on end. He loved his children and his wife, but there seemed to be a limit to how much he could let himself be loved. As he once wrote to Louisa on a boat bound for Alaska, "I have been alone, as far as the isolation that distance makes, so much of my lifetime that separation seems more natural than absolute contact, which seems too good and indulgent to be true."

I hoped the same thing wasn't happening to me. Ever since I'd started my trip, I had gotten better at being alone than I had ever been before. It had become my new normal. Those connections I would forge on the trail or through an app could be powerful, but they were rare—the bulk of my time was spent hiking, driving, and sleeping by myself.

All the time alone was making me stronger, but it was also making me selfish. When Claire and I spent the day in Monterey, it felt strange collaborating on our itinerary—she wanted to see and do things I had no interest in. I didn't have to compromise when I was alone. Ultimately, though, it reminded me how nice it felt to be part of a team.

I liked wandering alone outside, but I also liked inside jokes. I liked the kind of references and history and intimacy and connection that takes more than three dates to develop. Everyone may be interesting enough to share a dinner with, but it's much harder to find someone to share an RV with. That's what I wanted one day.

Even though I sometimes referred to it as "finding my person," I didn't really believe that. I no longer thought that there was just one person in the world who could make me happy. I *couldn't* think that.

I reminded myself that Tony and Linda Oyster had both been married before. They'd had separate loves and lives long before a hot night in Florida brought them together. To use Efrain's least favorite analogy, there's not just *one* national park. There are dozens. They're rare, but they're out there, spread across the country, equally awesome but totally unique.

All I knew was that, whenever it came time to stop wandering, I wanted a national park kind of love. Something that felt different and special compared with everything else surrounding it. Something that was fun and inspiring. Something that felt like it was worth guarding and protecting forever.

19

FOOD

(Gates of the Arctic, Kobuk Valley, Cuyahoga Valley)

Despite its name, Gates of the Arctic National Park doesn't have any gates. It's not clear where you'd even put an entrance station—the park doesn't have any roads. In its nearly eight and a half million acres of Alaskan wilderness, there isn't even a single marked *trail.*

Gates is seven times larger than the Grand Canyon but receives six hundred times fewer visitors. According to the park's website, the brave souls who do make the journey "must have the knowledge and skills to be truly self-sufficient in the remote location and demanding climate and terrain."

Gates is as wild as parks get.

The entirety of this northernmost national park lies north of the Arctic Circle, nestled in the Brooks Mountain Range. The peaks of two mountains—Boreal and Frigid Crags—are the metaphorical "gates" from which it takes its name. ("Frigid Crag" has since become my new favorite insult.)

On my way into the park, as I flew through the mountains at eye level, they seemed close enough to touch. I started to worry that I might *actually* have a chance to touch one. Occasionally, a surprise gust of wind would push our small plane through the sky, scaring the crap out of me while barely fazing the pilot.

I was sitting in the copilot position, watching the yoke in front of me twist left and right. In front of me stretched a temptingly flippable array of switches and levers, any one of which, if moved to the wrong position, could send us plummeting to our death. Or maybe they just controlled the radio. I didn't know, and I was so scared that I might accidentally bump the controls that I sat on my hands and stared out the window.

All around, bright-green and yellow tundra crept up steep, sharp gray peaks. The granite spine of the mountains looked lunar, as if it existed in an entirely different world than the small clusters of spruce I could see on the slopes seven thousand feet below. In the valleys between the peaks, narrow strands of water made white by rapids twisted like rivulets of spilled milk, draining down from some unseen source miles away.

When we banked left, I could see a few paths in the distance, cutting through the brush. They looked like the kind of trails the park claimed not to have. Perhaps I'd misread the guidebook?

"What are those lines down there?" I asked into my headset microphone. Even though we were sitting shoulder-to-shoulder, the roar of the propellers made normal conversation with the pilot impossible.

"Caribou tracks," his voice crackled back into my earphones.

The Western Arctic caribou herd is the largest in the United States, and Gates of the Arctic is smack dab in the middle of their annual migration path. Every fall, more than two hundred thousand animals march through the tundra, following routes they've carved out over thousands of years. Like people, caribou generally prefer the path of least resistance, so when they head south for the winter, they follow the same trails their ancestors took.

"South," it should be noted, is relative in Alaska. It's not like the caribou end up at some beach sipping margaritas and playing

(above) I visited my first national parks on my family's 1995 trip out west. I fell in love with Utah's Bryce Canyon—it looked so different from the world I knew. While the park received fewer than 1 million visitors in 1995, that number had ballooned to nearly 2.4 million when I returned in 2016. *Courtesy of the author*

(left) Today, there are weekends when Zion's popular Narrows trail is barely wide enough to contain the crowds. *National Park Service*

It's still possible to find solitude at popular parks if you venture just a few miles farther down the trail. This hike to secluded Double O Arch at Arches National Park was one of my favorites. *Courtesy of the author*

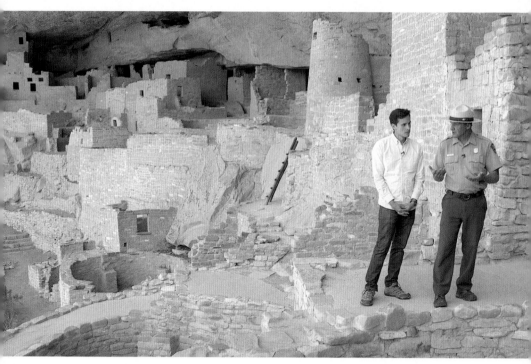

The cliff dwellings of Mesa Verde were constructed in the late twelfth century by the Ancestral Pueblo people. As ranger David Franks explained, they were occupied for only a hundred years—for reasons archaeologists still don't understand, the Ancestral Pueblo people suddenly vacated the homes they had risked their lives to build. *CBS News*

From the original Cherokee inhabitants to rural 1940s farmers, many were forced to leave the land that is now Great Smoky Mountains National Park. The park promised to build a road to connect families to the mountain cemeteries they had left behind. It was never finished— today, locals call it the Road to Nowhere. *Courtesy of the author*

Where the sidewalk bends. Dry Tortugas National Park, seventy miles off the coast of Key West, once served as a prison for the likes of Samuel Mudd—the doctor who set the leg of John Wilkes Booth. *Courtesy of the author*

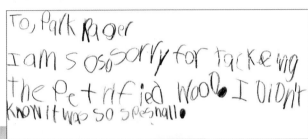

To, Park Rager
I am so so sorry for tackeing
the Petrfied Wood I DiDn't
KNOW it was So speshall.

(above) It's no surprise that some of the wood at Petrified Forest goes missing each year—the shiny silica has tempted would-be wood burglars since the park's inception. But it *is* surprising how many of these stolen souvenirs are mailed back, attached to apology notes from reformed criminals seeking forgiveness. *Courtesy of the author*

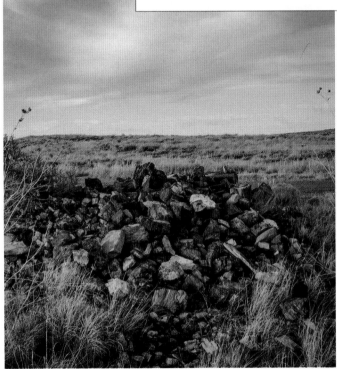

(left) Unfortunately, once a piece has been removed from its original location, it can't be put back. Instead, it ends up here, in what rangers call "the conscience pile." *Courtesy of the author*

At Great Basin, the rangers have a saying: "Half the park is after dark." Just 300 miles from Las Vegas—the brightest spot on earth—Great Basin's famously dark night skies offer an increasingly rare view of the Milky Way. *Courtesy of the author*

A little light is necessary to explore the underground wonders of Mammoth Cave— the first visitors would write their names onto the ceiling with candle smoke. While that's illegal today, this bit of 1800s graffiti is federally protected. *CBS News*

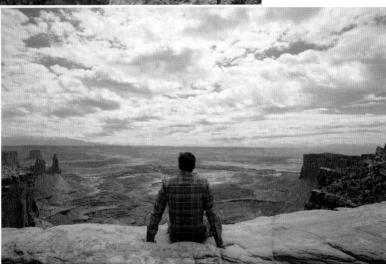

"Here the romance of my life began." Long before he became president, Theodore Roosevelt traveled to the Dakota Territory to heal a broken heart. Today, Theodore Roosevelt National Park honors his legacy as a conservationist. *Courtesy of the author*

After my breakup, my friends told me I needed a change of scenery. I may have taken their advice a little too literally—I doubt a trip to every national park in the country was what they had in mind. But it ended up being just what I needed—it's impossible not to gain some perspective when you keep coming across views like this one at Canyonlands National Park. *Courtesy of the author*

I fell hard for the sled dogs of Denali. The canine rangers have been part of the park since its inception—I arrived just in time to cuddle some of the new recruits. *Courtesy of the author*

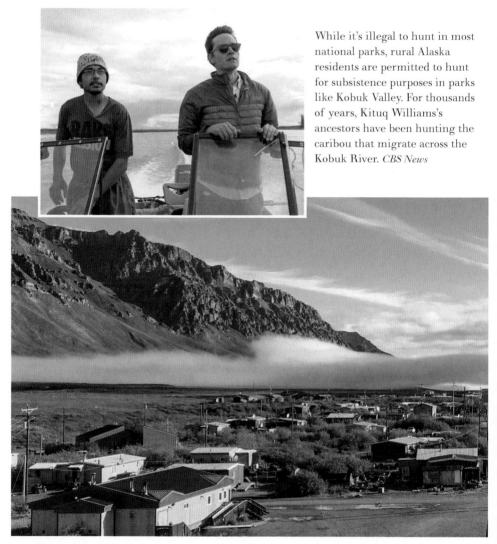

While it's illegal to hunt in most national parks, rural Alaska residents are permitted to hunt for subsistence purposes in parks like Kobuk Valley. For thousands of years, Kituq Williams's ancestors have been hunting the caribou that migrate across the Kobuk River. *CBS News*

The remote village of Anaktuvuk Pass (population ≈ 300) is located inside of Gates of the Arctic National Park, entirely disconnected from the Alaskan road system. While some groceries are flown in, "a box of bullets costs less than a frozen pizza does." *Courtesy of the author*

When chef Ben Bebenroth heard Ohio's Cuyahoga Valley National Park was bringing its old farms back to life, he decided to move out of the city and onto government soil. Today, the vegetables served at his downtown Cleveland restaurant are grown inside of a national park. *CBS News*

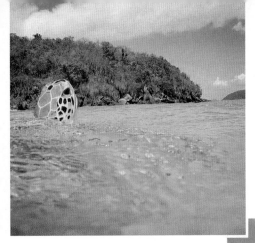

Coming up for air, or for the views? A sea turtle at Virgin Islands National Park. *Courtesy of the author*

"A lot of people want to come here to have a reset of the mind." As ranger Corinne Fenner explained, Virgin Islands National Park has always been about getting away from it all. *CBS News*

Getting away from it all is getting harder as cell service penetrates the wilderness. For now, Washington's Olympic National Park contains plenty of cellular dead zones, but Verizon has filed an application to place a tower near the visitor center. *Courtesy of the author*

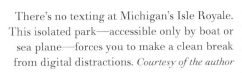

There's no texting at Michigan's Isle Royale. This isolated park—accessible only by boat or sea plane—forces you to make a clean break from digital distractions. *Courtesy of the author*

In the winter, Yellowstone's Old Faithful turns into a snowcano. When the geyser's hot water hits the freezing air, it forms a cloud and starts snowing. *Courtesy of the author*

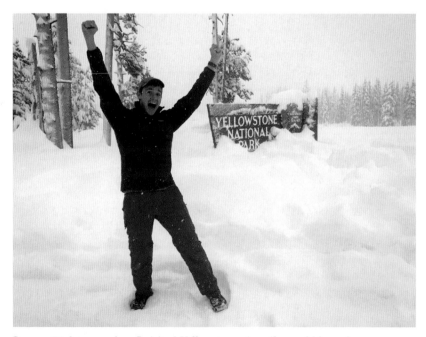

It was −34 degrees when I visited Yellowstone. A smile would have frozen on my face no matter what. The country's first national park was my last stop on the journey of a lifetime. *Courtesy of the author*

paddleball. Even after walking two thousand miles, they still never come close to making it out of the state.

I started spotting caribou tracks everywhere. I still didn't see any caribou, though. The pilot told me the migration hadn't kicked into full swing. As I scanned for any signs of life, I saw something far more shocking up ahead. I saw signs of what looked like . . . *people.*

Out of nowhere, a tiny group of buildings appeared in the distance—the town of Anaktuvuk Pass. I knew it was coming eventually, but it was still startling to see a roadless village pop up so deep in the wilderness. From up above, the haphazard collection of colorful sheds and tiny mobile homes looked like game pieces from some Alaskan edition of Risk.

As we started our descent into the village, I couldn't wrap my head around how on earth the three hundred people who called this place home had ever made it so far out here. But I knew *why* they had. They had followed the caribou.

Park ranger Al Smith met me at the gravel-and-dirt airstrip. For the past several years, Al had volunteered for this remote assignment. He was the one full-time representative of the Park Service in the one town within Gates of the Arctic's massive boundaries. It was a job that required a very specific type of person, one who didn't mind working lonely, impossibly long days in the land of the midnight sun.

Al is constantly on call, and every visitor to the park is advised to check in with him at his small house. There he keeps several detailed maps of the area, along with a few bear-resistant food containers to loan out and a logbook for keeping track of where a visiting hiker might be headed. Since there are no trails, the descriptions are often something like "northwest-ish for six or so days."

Anaktuvuk Pass was settled in the early 1950s by the Nunamiut people, a semi-nomadic group of Native Iñupiat Alaskans. The inland Iñupiat had roamed Alaska for thousands of years, moving camp to follow the caribou until modern life made it easier to stay put. Anaktuvuk, with its proximity to the migration routes, was an especially good stopping point. The word *anaktuvuk* literally translates to "Place of Many Caribou Droppings." In Alaska, living in a shitty village is something to brag about.

My quick tour of the town took all of five minutes. There were no roads, per se, but there was still a general grid, with small homes laid out along wide dirt paths. You could easily walk from one end of Anaktuvuk to the other, but everyone seemed to get around by ATV. For a village of three hundred in the middle of nowhere, it was surprisingly noisy—all day long, I heard the constant growl of four-wheelers, taking residents back and forth to the school, the store, or just doing laps around the neighborhood for fun.

That night, ranger Al invited me to his park-provided housing and made me one of the best pizzas I'd ever had in my life. Over the years, Al has become a fantastic cook. When you live in Anaktuvuk Pass, your culinary cravings can only be satiated by your own cooking, so Al learned how to make all of his favorite dishes. His love of pizza inspired him to specially modify the park oven into something that might churn out pies in Brooklyn.

He had to be smart about planning ahead, and brought as many groceries as possible with him at the beginning of the season. His cupboard was a carefully plotted mix of olives, sauces, crackers, and curries. For everything else, there was a small grocery store in town, but it was shockingly overpriced. (Well, shockingly expensive, at least. When I stopped to consider the journey that the twelve-pack of Dr Pepper had to make in the belly of a bush plane just to get to the shelf, its twenty-two-dollar price tag actually started to seem fair.) Al had been doing this gig long enough to know it was best to avoid buying anything locally, so he had his meals planned down to the last pepperoni.

Still, he knew his kitchen—his entire existence—in Anaktuvuk Pass was an anomaly. The community respected him, and everyone waved as we walked through town together, but this was not his culture or his home. The next morning, to help me understand what life was like for the people who were born here, he put out a call on Facebook. Anyone who wanted to chat could stop by the ranger station. A few minutes later, sixteen-year-old In'uli Toopet-look showed up.

In'uli was wearing a baggy sweatshirt, shorts, and sandals. As we sat on the back of his four-wheeler, he told me pizza is not a dish he's likely to splurge on.

"A box of bullets costs less than a frozen pizza does," he said.

In'uli's family, like most families in Anaktuvuk, still relies heavily on the caribou meat that brought their ancestors to this place. When the government protected the land surrounding the village in the 1980s, the locals were afraid they'd have to stop hunting. After all, if you shoot a deer at Acadia National Park, you could end up in jail. But ANILCA—the Alaska National Interest Lands Conservation Act, which established Gates of the Arctic and a number of other parks—provided an exception for families like the Toopet-looks. In the Alaska national parks, local rural residents are allowed to hunt.

"What we do is subsistence hunting, and that's for food. Everything that's in the animal we catch is used," In'uli emphasized.

Sport hunting—which is very popular in Alaska—remains illegal in the parks. Although killing an animal for fun would never even occur to In'uli.

"That's something that's not good in our tradition," he said. "For us, nothing really is for sport unless it's basketball or something like that."

In'uli took me back to his house to show me the freezer he kept outside. When he threw open the lid of the white icebox, I gasped.

Caribou legs and hooves stuck out at odd angles. The fur was still on the hindquarters. Several larger cuts underneath were loosely covered with trash bags. Everything had clearly been butchered out in the field.

At Trader Joe's, it's easy to forget that the rows of red rectangles on white Styrofoam trays were ever part of an animal. But there was no mystery to any of the meat in In'uli's freezer.

"I definitely know that I was the one who brought it home to the dinner table," In'uli said. "That's important . . . I know it was killed respectfully."

As we spoke, In'uli's uncles were out on a hunt. He would have joined them, but he had school the next day.

"My mom's divorced, so I'm pretty much the man of the house," he said. "So I go out. I hunt. I fish and I trap. It's just what I do to help out the family."

Hunting may not have been sport for In'uli, but he clearly loved the ritual and the responsibility that came along with it. The summer before, he had accidentally stayed out tracking caribou for a few days straight. With the constant daylight, it's easy to lose track of time.

"My mom was pretty worried when I got back," he said, laughing.

Tell a kid to "come home at dark" in Alaska, and they might not show up till September.

Compared with Gates of the Arctic, Alaska's Kobuk Valley National Park is a whole other level of remoteness. At least Gates of the Arctic has "Ranger Al's House of Brick Oven Pizza and Topographic Maps." Kobuk Valley doesn't have anything. There are no park offices of any kind. No roads, no trails, and certainly no visitor center. For that, it would probably need some visitors. Most years, Kobuk Valley is the least visited of all the national parks, although it's tough to know the exact numbers, since some years, nobody bothers counting.

"It's a well-used park. It just isn't a tourist-type park," explained Lois Dalle-Molle, the acting superintendent for the Western Arctic National Parklands. I met her at her office back in Kotzebue, around eighty miles away from the park itself. Inside a long, bow-shaped building, a small NPS staff is tasked with managing over eleven million acres of remote Alaskan monuments, preserves, and parks.

The frequent use Lois was referencing was the subsistence use by the locals, most of whom lived in the tiny town of Ambler (population 260), just outside the park's boundary. That's where Don Williams had built his house in the 1960s, along the banks of the Kobuk River. An ex–Park Service employee, Don was a legend among the current group of park workers. Every ranger I spoke to in Alaska said I had to meet him.

To get to Ambler, I had arranged a seaplane flight departing from Kotzebue. Right before I was scheduled to take off, Lois gave me a blue terry-cloth towel with KOBUK VALLEY printed on it in white.

"You can use it as a sign," she explained.

Kobuk Valley is such a remote park that the few tourists who do visit are often hardcore NPS nerds, the kind of people who geek out over getting their picture taken with a sign. People like me.

So far, I had taken a sign photo at every single park, and I was well on my way to assembling an end-of-the-year album of goofy grins and changing hair lengths. I assumed Kobuk would end up being the one gap in my final slideshow. But to satisfy the super fans like me who might be passing through, the Park Service had printed up special "centennial towels." As soon as the pilot told me we'd officially crossed into Kobuk airspace, I held up my piece of terry cloth and said cheese.

When we touched down on the Kobuk River, Don Williams was waiting to meet me at the dock. I'd spoken to him on the phone, and he had told me how excited he was to have a visitor.

Don was beaming, and, as soon as I'd wiggled out of the back of the seaplane, he gave my hand a hearty shake. He looked like an athletic Ed Asner. Country life seemed to suit him well—I couldn't believe this great-grandfather in a red flannel jacket and blue jeans was eighty years old.

I hopped onto the back of Don's green Arctic Cat ATV, and we careened down a dirt path toward his cabin on the outskirts of Ambler. In one of the most remote towns in the country, Don had picked one of the most remote spots for himself.

"Downtown," he said, "is just too busy."

For years, Don's home didn't even have an address. Then someone tried to ship him something via UPS.

"They said, 'Well, you gotta have a street address . . .'" So I made one up: 127 Caribou Way," he laughed.

As we pulled up to 127 Caribou Way, I was surprised at how simple it was. I'd thought perhaps Don had taken advantage of cheap land in the middle of nowhere to build his dream cabin. But on his lot by the river, there was just a modest work shed, an outhouse, and a tiny, light-purple building Don called home.

Inside, the house was one room, broken up into sections by dividers formed from stacks of Don's possessions. Family photos were everywhere, but the most prominent face was John Wayne's, printed in sepia tone on a five-by-five-foot fleece blanket draped over Don's worn-out easy chair. AMERICAN COWBOY, it said across the top.

Don loved westerns. He had first signed on to work with the Park Service at Grand Teton because he'd heard that's where *Shane* was filmed. The movie came out in 1953, back when Don was in high school in Ohio. After he'd graduated, he'd hopped on a Greyhound bus bound for Wyoming. His dream was to live among the giant mountains he'd seen on the big screen.

Don loved his new gig, but after a few years working in Grand Teton, he heard a story about even grander mountains. A friend of his had just come back from a state that had just been added to the flag, a place just as beautiful as Wyoming, but with far fewer people. *Alaska*, the friend told him, was the *real* "Wild West."

Don was sold. He threw his belongings into his new Ford Econoline van and drove north to take a job at Denali National Park. He later found work at Katmai National Park and then headed north to visit Kobuk Valley.

Kobuk wasn't under NPS control back then. It was just a wild stretch of wetlands that mixed tundra with taiga, a forest of pine and spruce. Don fell in love—with the scenery, just as his friend had predicted, but also . . . with a woman. Nobody had predicted that.

Don met Mary, a young Iñupiat woman who had grown up in Ambler. They hit it off instantly, although it took a while for Don to win her relatives' trust. They thought he might be a Russian spy—white people rarely came to Ambler. When Don wed Mary in 1968, he was the first white man to ever marry in the village.

Don and Mary have "probably ten or eleven grandchildren, and I think ten great-grandchildren."

Don wasn't exactly sure when I asked him. He needed to think.

He'd arranged for one of those grandchildren, Kituq, to take me out hunting. While Don had moved to Ambler to live off the land, most of his days behind a rifle are behind him. Instead he's taken on a side job counting caribou for the Alaska Fish and Game service. He spends hours in his shed, poring over aerial photos of the migration with a jeweler's loupe, clicking away on a tally counter he holds in his left hand. I watched him work, moving the loupe an inch at a time. Click click click, all day long. One image had 15,982 caribou. The next had 7,115.

I was hoping to just see one, in person. Walking down to the river, Kituq proudly showed me the rifle he had just gotten as a graduation present, a Remington 770. He told me he and his new gun had already taken down a couple of black bears and a dozen or so caribou, and he was hoping he might find another today.

As we boarded the steel boat, I picked up the camo-colored life jacket lying on the floor and tried to put it on. I twisted and turned, but I could barely fit my arms into the holes. Kituq cracked up laughing. The vest was clearly meant for a three-year-old. The men in Ambler don't wear life jackets.

Or apparently any sort of jacket, at least not on a sunny day like this one. It was in the mid-fifties—T-shirt weather for Kituq. I, on the other hand, was wearing my fully zipped North Face Thermo-Ball puffer jacket. Looking at us, it wasn't hard to figure out which one had grown up north of the Arctic Circle.

We sped out of Ambler onto the Kobuk River. After a few miles, we officially entered the national park, crossing an invisible dividing line Kituq knew based on a slight bend in the river. He pulled the boat over near a site known as Onion Portage, named after the wild onions that bloom throughout the woods. For more than ten thousand years, the caribou had been crossing the river in this exact place.

As Kituq loaded his rifle, I tensed up. The gun made me nervous, but I knew Kituq knew what he was doing. He had been going on hunts since he was in diapers, brought by his dad and grandfather to this very spot.

Mostly, I was nervous because what we were about to do went against everything I'd ever been taught about national parks. It's illegal to pick a wildflower at Yosemite, and here in Kobuk Valley, Kituq was about to shoot the wildlife.

As we sat together, Kituq told me he generally waits until the caribou reach the water's edge before taking a shot. That way, he doesn't have to drag the carcass as far back to the boat—a male can weigh up to four hundred pounds. That's a lot of meat.

"Do you ever get bored of eating it?" I asked. "What all can you make with it?"

"Man, you can make a lotta things with it," Kituq said, launching into a monologue that felt like Bubba's shrimp speech to Forrest Gump. "You can make some caribou burgers. You can make caribou soup. You can just boil it and have caribou meat just like that. Or you can fry it on a pan or have some caribou steaks . . ."

As he went on, extolling the virtues of caribou jerky, caribou bone marrow, and caribou chili, I thought I heard something rustling in the woods. I froze.

"Is that . . . is that one there?" I whispered.

Kituq got quiet, scanned the forest, and shook his head.

"No," he said. "I think we're too early."

The full caribou migration at Kobuk wouldn't be starting for another couple of weeks. Kituq had been hoping we might catch a premature arrival, but none showed up that afternoon. In a way, I was relieved. I didn't know how I felt about watching a caribou die right in front of me. Afterward would have come the skinning, the cutting, and the preparation. I'm sure it wouldn't have surprised Kituq that the guy who wanted to wear a kiddie life preserver also happened to get a little queasy around blood.

Kituq had grown up hunting. He was eight when he killed his first caribou, but, per the village's tradition, he didn't keep the meat for himself.

"You don't keep what you kill the first time," he told me. "You give it away. To an elder."

Even today, he donates most of the meat he harvests to village elders who can't hunt.

"I don't take their money or gas or nothing," he made sure to clarify. "I just do it out of respect."

Respect was a word I heard a lot in rural Alaska. Back in Anaktuvuk Pass, In'uli had told me he *thanks* every caribou he kills. A respectful kill, he said, was more important than anything else. Living in such a harsh, remote environment, you learn from an early age to respect the earth for the life-sustaining resources it provides.

Ohio's Cuyahoga Valley National Park is the polar opposite of the parks near the North Pole. Within twenty miles of Cuyahoga's visitor center, there are thirty different McDonald's and well over one hundred Starbucks. The park's more than thirty thousand acres lie smack dab in between Cleveland and Akron. Like Gates of the Arctic, Cuyahoga Valley doesn't have any official gates, but for a very different reason: Gates would slow down the traffic on the highways that pass through the park.

Of the fewer than ten "recommended hikes" on the park's website, one is listed simply as the "I-80 Overlook."

"Sure it is noisy," the description reads. "But the view is great. A little cropping in the photo and you might just forget about the highway."

At least the park has a sense of humor about itself. In a family that includes all-stars like Yellowstone and Yosemite, Cuyahoga often feels like the black sheep. There are certainly some scenic spots—plenty of waterfalls and picturesque hillsides—but there are also four golf courses. Its vibe is much more city park than national park. In 1973, the director of the National Park Service said that Cuyahoga "will be a park over my dead body."

Four years earlier, the Cuyahoga River had become so famously polluted it *caught on fire*. In August 1969, *Time* described it as a river that "oozes rather than flows." In part, that disaster is what motivated Clevelanders to lobby so forcefully for federal protection. They wanted to save the little urban oasis they had left. In 1974, President Gerald Ford signed the bill creating Cuyahoga National Recreation Area. In 2000, it became a national park.

Northern Ohio was once pastoral and pristine. Long before Cleveland was a center of industry, it was a center of agriculture. What began as a community of small subsistence farmers grew into a larger industry when the Ohio and Erie Canal was finished in the early 1830s and farmers could float their harvests to other consumers. Settlers came to work the fertile soil.

But when manufacturing jobs in town started offering better wages for less work, farm life began to look less attractive. By the mid-twentieth century, most of the Cuyahoga Valley farms had closed down.

Much of the old farmland falls within the boundaries of the park. When the Park Service first took control in the 1970s, they focused on developing a network of hiking and biking trails. At the time, the vacant farmhouses dotting the land weren't considered a priority.

Eventually, though, park managers started to see the crumbling structures as both a liability—someone could get hurt exploring one—and a missed opportunity. Cuyahoga had become a pretty place for urbanites to come and bike, but the story of the land underneath their tires had been lost.

. . .

"It's part of what we're charged to protect and preserve—not only the natural resources, but that story of the people living and working in the valley," ranger Pamela Barnes told me when I met her at a berry farm in the middle of the park. "That was the story we needed to figure out: how we were going to bring it back to life."

Pam said the Park Service had first considered turning the old barns and houses into museums. Maybe put up a few signs, dress some wax figurines in old-timey clothes, and call it a day. But then they started to wonder . . . what if they could actually get these places up and running again? Wouldn't that be a more effective way to tell the story?

So the park announced that they would start taking applications to *lease* the properties. The farms had closed because they were too small to compete, but by the turn of the millennium, consumers had started to specifically seek out produce that came from small farms. They wanted food with a *story*.

"So, from this farm to that table, how far is it?"

"Twenty point nine miles."

I was sitting with chef Ben Bebenroth in the middle of a field of radishes and kale and giant gourds that would soon be on the menu at his restaurant. The farm-to-table movement is all about knowing where your food comes from, and Ben now had it down to the tenth of a mile.

In 2012, Ben had opened Spice Kitchen + Bar, a hip restaurant in Cleveland's up-and-coming Gordon Square Arts District. His menu focused heavily on farm-to-table cuisine, but he didn't feel a personal connection to any of those farms.

Ben had tried growing some of his own vegetables at home (too many, according to his wife, Jackie—their small yard was absolute chaos), but he still wasn't satisfied. When he heard about Cuyahoga's

leasing program, the former marine with a culinary school background decided to pursue the one career even riskier than restau-
rateur—he became a *farmer*. With his wife and two young children,
Ben moved out of the city, and inside of a national park.

When the Bebenroths first moved into their 1870s farmhouse,
the thirteen acres surrounding it were entirely overgrown. The last
couple of years had been spent slowly bringing the farm back to its
former glory while learning what's hardest to grow, what's easiest,
and what's the most cost-effective. Turns out the margins on lettuce aren't as high as the margin on figs. The family's livelihood
was now linked to their land.

Today the halibut at Spice Kitchen comes served on a base of
couscous "composto," sprinkled with little stems and scraps of vegetables from the farm that would have otherwise gone into a com-
post pile. When you're the one who grew something, you feel an
obligation to use every part.

"It's a shame to see something that you've touched so many
times and spent so much energy and water on end up in a bucket,"
Ben said.

The farming life is still hard in Cuyahoga Valley, although today
it comes with a whole new set of challenges. Since the land is now
owned by the federal government, there are all sorts of restrictions
on what Ben can and can't do on it.

"If we're going to dig a hole deeper than two feet, we need an
archaeological survey done," Ben lamented. Often, approvals for
improvements that seem simple can take weeks. And of course, you
can't kill any of the usual creatures that see farms as smorgasbords.
The groundhogs, the raccoons—they're all federally protected.

"So you just grow a little bit extra," Ben said with a shrug.
Clearly the benefits outweighed the drawbacks for him.

I asked if he was ever frustrated when his diners didn't realize
all the thought and effort required to get a summer squash or a
piece of watermelon to their plates.

"Only . . . daily," he replied, laughing. "But you know, I don't really want people to appreciate the *challenge* that was overcome to get that to the plate. I want them to appreciate the experience and the texture and the flavor and the aroma and all the things that matter, right? Like, no one wants to eat the food from the *sad* chef."

Ben did not seem sad. I don't know anything about cooking *or* farming, but I knew happy when I saw it. I was surprised how envious I was of his life. I think I just admired his guts. He was doing exactly what he wanted on his own terms.

I spent the afternoon unsuccessfully trying to catch chickens with Ben's kids, Sydney and Burke. Moving to the park was just as much a lifestyle decision as it was a business one for Ben and Jackie. Yes, they could raise chickens, but they could also raise their children on the land.

"I think of the life lessons they're gaining from being surrounded in a natural environment," Ben said as he looked out at the Ohio greenery around us. "*This* is the basis for their decision making for the rest of their lives. Everything will emanate from this experience."

The kids were getting ready to head off to a friend's house for a sleepover. That night, Ben and Jackie were hosting one of their "Plated Landscape" dinners in their backyard. Every once in a while, instead of bringing the farm to the table, they bring the tables to the farm, hosting a special multicourse dinner in their onsite barn.

That evening, as guests from downtown started to arrive, they were encouraged to wander the fields. I watched their eyes— curious and excited—as they strolled through the rows of fresh vegetables. Back when the Cuyahoga farms were first built, back when food was fresh because it had to be, every American felt a link to the landscape. Today that link has been largely lost.

Don Williams had left Ohio for the wilderness of Kobuk Valley decades earlier because he wanted to find a place where you could still live off the land. In the wilderness of Alaska, the Iñupiat continue to carry on the subsistence traditions of their ancestors. But on this night in suburban Ohio, a park program was helping a group of well-heeled city folk reestablish their connection to the earth that fed them.

In that way, Cuyahoga's proximity to skyscrapers might be its greatest strength, not its greatest weakness. Living in the wilderness, you can't help but feel connected to the land. But to feel that connection in a city—even if it's just for an evening—seems a far more difficult feat. That was the much-needed nourishment this park had found a way to provide.

20

MOUNTAINS

(Guadalupe Mountains, Rocky Mountain)

Guadalupe Peak is the highest point in the state of Texas. If you live in Texas, I am sure that is very impressive.

At 8,751 feet, Guadalupe is no slouch, but it's not even in the same league as average mountains in states like Washington or Wyoming. There are five mountains in Los Angeles County alone that are taller than Guadalupe. Alaska's Denali is well over two Guadalupes *put together.* Everything, it turns out, is not bigger in Texas.

Guadalupe Mountains National Park is one of the least visited parks in the Lower 48, and the entry in my guidebook said that most visitors come to claim "Top of Texas" bragging rights. They take a picture with the pyramid-shaped monument at the mountain's summit, then sign their name in a logbook that's kept up top, safe inside a plastic box.

Reading that entry, I was surprised by how much I suddenly wanted to write my own name in that book. Now that I knew Guadalupe Peak was the tallest in Texas, it seemed like I'd be wasting my visit if I failed to stand on top of it. I was reminded of climber George Mallory's response when he was asked why he wanted to summit Everest, the tallest mountain in the world: "Because it's there."

"I mean, sure. You should do it. If . . . you're into that sort of thing."

When I announced my ambitious plan for the day to the ranger behind the visitor center desk, I had assumed she would give me a pat on the back and a "yee-haw!" for attempting to conquer the Lone Star State's highest point.

I was surprised when she seemed less than enthusiastic about my choice.

"If I'm *into that sort of thing?*" I asked.

"You know, peak bagging," she said.

I was offended at the implication. Being "into peak bagging" sounds like a weird fetish. In a way, I guess it kind of is.

Peak baggers are hikers who specifically seek out high points exclusively for their highness, without regard to any other attribute. They are people for whom every trip into the wilderness is measured in terms of feet from sea level.

I was most definitely *not* a peak bagger, I assured the ranger. I had only recently learned people like that even existed, thanks to, of all things, online dating. It must be lonely at the top, because peak baggers are all over Tinder.

When first I saw "14er" pop up on a few profiles, I thought the number might be some kind of drug code, something like "420 friendly."

But a search confirmed that "14er" had nothing to do with marijuana. Not officially, at least, although there's some overlap, as legal-weed Colorado is where you are most likely to find a 14er. The Rocky Mountain State is ground zero for peak baggers. Or, as a peak bagger would probably put it, it is ground + 14,000.

There are fewer than one hundred mountain peaks in the United States with elevations of at least fourteen thousand feet, and more than *half* of those 14ers are found in Colorado. A shockingly high number of Tinder profiles in Denver feature photos of women standing on top of a fourteen-thousand-foot summit, smiling and holding a handmade sign. GRAYS PEAK, 14,270. TABEGUACHE PEAK, 14,155.

I could never figure out where those signs actually came from. Did people hike up to the top with a Sharpie and cardboard in their backpacks? Or are there just a bunch of old Domino's boxes at the top, left behind for other hikers to pose with?

It was clear some sort of photo proof was key, as the only thing climbers love more than peak bagging is peak *bragging*. On websites like 14ers.com, hikers track their progress, counting down how many fourteen-thousand-foot summits they've nabbed. Woe be to all of the lovely 13,900-foot mountains of Colorado, which go underappreciated every year just because they're not over some arbitrary cutoff. For peak baggers, it is elevation above everything else.

Surprisingly, Colorado's Rocky Mountain National Park contains only one 14er, but it's a doozy. Longs Peak (14,255 feet) is the highest peak you can see from downtown Denver, its distant, jagged, white outline looming a mile and a half *higher* than the Mile High City. It's a *bucket-list* Rocky Mountain, one that native Coloradans and visitors alike feel compelled to tackle.

The pull of the peak predates the park itself. In fact, Longs Peak is largely responsible for *why* Rocky Mountain became a national park. The mountain caught the interest of one man, and he devoted his life to sharing it with others.

Enos Mills was one of Colorado's original peak baggers. Born in Kansas in 1870, he hitchhiked alone to Colorado when he was just fourteen years old. He'd had some unexplained illnesses, and a doctor had told him the mountain air might do him some good.

Whatever it was that had been plaguing Enos, it disappeared in Colorado. He loved his new Rocky Mountain home, and he went through a dramatic transformation. The kid who had been forced to stay indoors all his life became a wilderness guide.

Enos bought a hotel—the Longs Peak Inn—that became the de facto stop for any adventurer who had Longs on their itinerary. All told, he made it to the top close to three hundred different times, summiting with all types of people in all seasons and in all conditions. To force his guests to contemplate the majesty of their mountain surroundings, Enos outlawed music and dancing at his hotel, like some alpine version of *Footloose*.

On a camping trip to California, Enos met John Muir. He fell hard for the naturalist's philosophy, his way with words, and the work he'd done to protect Yosemite and other wild places. Enos decided he wanted to be just like Muir, and he made it his life's work to advocate for the protection of the Rocky Mountains. Just like Muir, he began writing. His books included *Wild Life on the Rockies, The Spell of the Rockies, Bird Memories of the Rockies*, and *The Rocky Mountain Wonderland.*

Dude really loved the Rockies.

In 1907, Mills visited twenty-seven states and gave over five hundred lectures about Colorado's natural wonders. As his campaign continued, he kept his mentor updated on his progress.

"As you well know," Mills wrote to Muir on a piece of Longs Peak Inn stationery, "it is the work that you have done that has encouraged me in all that I have accomplished and in the big work I am planning to do."

Muir might have provided the encouragement Mills needed to protect the Rockies, but I suspect that Kansas provided the inspiration. Remember William Gladstone Steel, the "father of Crater Lake"? The guy who first read about Oregon's blue waters in the newspaper used to wrap his sandwich? That fateful lunch happened back in Oswego, Kansas, not far from where Enos Mills had grown up.

I do not think it is a coincidence that the two men responsible for two of our earliest and most stunning national parks both came from a state renowned for its scenic sameness. Had they been born in Boulder or Medford, they might have taken their surroundings for granted. They might have assumed *everywhere* looked like that. But since they came to their new homes from a state largely devoid of lakes or mountains, they knew that what they were seeing was special. Had Dorothy grown up in New York City instead of on the prairie, Oz may not have looked as spectacular.

As I traveled from park to park, I noticed that, more times than not, the urge to protect the land from future development has come from an outsider. Mills's idol John Muir grew up in Scotland, where shipbuilding and sheep farming had left the landscape largely treeless. Imagine, then, how impressive the redwoods must have been for a guy who had barely seen a mighty oak. The highest mountain in all of Scotland is just *half* the height of Half Dome. Yosemite shocked Muir.

George Masa, a photographer whose large-format pictures helped convince Congress to protect the Great Smoky Mountains, grew up in Osaka, Japan. Virginia McClurg, the woman most responsible for the protection of Mesa Verde and the author of *Picturesque Colorado* and *Picturesque Utah*, grew up in a somewhat less picturesque part of Virginia. Who else could see the Everglades as a magical *River of Grass* and not a sweltering swamp but Marjory Stoneman Douglas, a woman who moved to muggy Florida after growing up in chilly Minnesota?

With fresh eyes and fresh perspective, these new arrivals were able to remind locals and legislators that they were living next to something that had been there all along, just waiting to be appreciated. Something worth saving.

"In years to come, when I am asleep beneath the pines, thousands of families will find rest and hope in this park," Enos Mills said of his beloved Colorado mountains. In 1915, Rocky Mountain became a national park, and today the yearly visitation is measured in *millions,* not thousands. It's one of the most visited national parks in the country.

. . .

When I visited the park, I had considered ascending Longs Peak, until I discovered the 14er had another number associated with it. Since 1915, more than sixty people have died on the mountain.

In the summer of 2010, three hikers died climbing Longs in a matter of three months. In each case, it sounded like something small had gone wrong. That's all it takes. A slipped step or a broken hold, and you can tumble hundreds of feet to your death. Researching the mountain, I was surprised by how many of the fatalities involved hikers who sounded far more capable and prepared than I was. The stories I read weren't of tourists wearing flip-flops or teenagers playing leapfrog across the boulder field. These were experienced, fit hikers who were dying.

Many of the fatalities over the years have occurred on the way *down* the mountain. An Austrian study of the Alps found that 75 percent of falls on that mountain range came during the descent. Going down is never perceived as being as difficult as going up.

After summiting, hikers are exhausted. They're overconfident. They might feel as if the hardest part is over when, in reality, it's just beginning. When a peak bagger takes a photo at the top of the mountain, he or she is only celebrating the halfway mark of the journey. A photo taken back in the parking lot, safe and sound at the end of the day, actually represents the more remarkable achievement.

With Longs Peak, I think the knowledge that I still had more parks ahead of me made me more risk-averse than I would have been otherwise. I wasn't necessarily worried I'd die—although I'd considered the possibility—but I feared that even a hard fall or a twisted ankle would take me out of commission for a few weeks. That was more time than I had to spare. Longs Peak didn't seem worth the risk.

Instead, I opted for a series of smaller hikes. My meandering, magical walk out to Rocky Mountain's Cub Lake took twice as long as it should have, since I kept pausing to take pictures of all the elk I came across on the trail. If a website devoted to bagging *boulders* existed, I'm sure the large one on which I decided to eat my picnic lunch would have ranked near the top of the list. I still got to look at the Rocky Mountains all day long; I just mostly saw them from the ground up.

Perhaps one day I'll try to climb Longs. For now, though, the only summit of a 14er I've ever set foot on is one you can drive up. It is a mountain named after a man who knew the wisdom of turning back.

Explorer Zebulon Pike was sent westward by Thomas Jefferson. In November 1806, he attempted to climb to the top of a 14,114-foot-high mountain near Colorado Springs. He didn't make it. As he later wrote, his climbing party "had only light overalls on, and no stockings," and was "every way ill provided to endure the inclemency of the region." Pike's men barely had enough food with them and didn't see what they could hunt should they get delayed, so Pike decided to call it. They turned around and headed back to the bottom for safety. The peak was left un-bagged.

The mountain was named by later mapmakers in honor of Pike. By the late 1800s, Pikes Peak, three and a half hours south of Rocky Mountain National Park, had become a popular tourist attraction. While the first visitors used prairie wagons and teams of mules to reach the summit, by the time I visited, the trip was entirely gasoline-powered—a two-lane twisty mountain pass had been paved all the way to the top. At the summit, tourists elbowed one another inside a souvenir shop famous for its donuts, fried using a special recipe designed for cooking at fourteen thousand feet.

"Take them down to the bottom and they won't taste as good," the clerk working the register told me. I told him there was no need to worry about that. Within minutes, I had inhaled the two I'd bought. I'd been feeling a little light-headed thanks to the thin mountain air, but the sugar rush helped me adjust. I walked outside to check out the view.

In every direction, the Rocky Mountains, which appeared to be rocky and mountainous from the ground, looked to be nothing more than a limitless expanse of green and brown hills. Pikes Peak towered over them all. I looked down at Colorado Springs and tried to figure out where my hotel might be, but the few landmarks I thought I knew were in different places than I had remembered. Downtown, the tallest building looked like a shed, and the giant sixteen-wheel trucks chugging along I-25 were impossible to make out. Everything looked so *different* from so far up, and none of it— at least nothing that humans had made—looked even the slightest bit important.

That is one of the reasons we climb mountains. So that we can get a different perspective on what's down below. It's why we pay to stand on the observation deck of the Space Needle and why planes have windows. It's thrilling to be so high up, like an out-of-body experience. For a moment, we are able to pull away from the place we inhabit and look down on it from above, like a bird might. Like a god might.

But the top of a mountain is also an uncomfortable place. The wind whipped my face on the top of Pikes Peak. My eyes hurt, and I blew my runny nose with the paper napkin that had held my donut, now a very unpleasant mix of scratchy and sticky. Mountaintops allow us to visit, but then they do their best to push us away. We are not meant for such great heights.

When Wellesley professor Katharine Lee Bates ascended Pikes more than one hundred years before I did, she didn't stay at the summit long. A couple members of her party developed altitude sickness, so she had to descend quickly to allow them to recover.

However, her brief time on the mountaintop proved to be full of inspiration. As she later recalled, "Our sojourn on the peak remains in memory hardly more than one ecstatic gaze. It was then and there, as I was looking out over the sea-like expanse of fertile country spreading away so far under those ample skies, that the opening lines of the hymn floated into my mind."

Two years later, on July 4, 1895, her poem "America" was published in *The Congregationalist* newspaper. In subsequent years, Bates made small tweaks to the stanzas. Her original "halcyon skies" became "spacious skies." The "enameled plain" morphed into the "fruited plain." And instead of a "music-hearted sea," Bates decided to go with the more all-encompassing "from sea to shining sea."

But even though she removed the word *music*, others found music in Bates's words. By the early 1900s, dozens of different melodies had been paired with her poem. The most enduring match came courtesy of a hymn composed by a choir director in Newark. A tune that was originally written to accompany the words to "O Mother Dear, Jerusalem," was repurposed to sing the praises of "O Beautiful for Spacious Skies."

In one year, I sang it fifty-nine times.

On my way to the summit of Cadillac Mountain back in January, I thought how cool it would be if I could somehow edit together some year-end "super cut" of my journey, a video that would tie together all the parks. For a guy who had yet to successfully visit his *first* park, it was a pretty ambitious idea.

I decided a song might work well. The melody could be the link, but the backdrop would provide constantly changing scenery. I considered singing the national anthem, but that song is mostly about war and full of hard-to-hit high notes. Instead, I opted for our *unofficial* anthem, which also happened to be the name the Park Service had given to its annual pass: "America the Beautiful."

Standing in a field of snow in Maine, crooning into my iPhone, I hadn't considered how potentially embarrassing it would eventually be to have to do the same thing at more crowded parks. From the bustling rim of the Grand Canyon to a Hot Springs bathhouse to echoey Mammoth Cave, I quickly came to dread my ritual public performances. But I kept singing, and by the time I arrived at Guadalupe Mountains in Texas, I had come too far to stop. Once I finally made it to the top of the sixth highest peak in the state, I belted out the lyrics.

"From sea . . . to . . . shi . . . ning . . . sea!"

I finished and turned around, half expecting to see the entire offensive line of the Dallas Cowboys pointing and laughing on the trail below me. But there was no one there. I'd hardly seen a soul all day—from what I could tell, the few cars in the parking lot belonged to hikers who had headed in the other direction, climbing the trail that led to the high peak logbook.

Hunter Peak, where I was standing, was just 381 feet lower than Guadalupe. But the ranger at the visitor center had convinced me it had the best view. She was right—the 360-degree panorama of the Texas desert, broken apart by a network of dry riverbeds, was stunning.

I sang my song once again for good measure, then started my descent toward the parking lot. I reminded myself that the hardest part was yet to come. The walk down was brutal on my knees, and the Texas sun was unrelenting. By the time I made it to the parking lot, I had never been happier to see my car. I drove straight to dinner.

While I may not have made it to the state's high point that day, I unquestionably experienced a new personal low that evening. After a hard sell from my waitress, I finally caved and signed up for the Chili's Rewards Program. I had been hitting so many Chili's on the road that I'd reached the point where setting up an account just made good financial sense.

Out came my skillet queso and chips, then my mix-and-match fajitas, and, before my stomach could communicate to my brain that it was full, my molten chocolate cake. If peaks were measured in calories instead of feet, the meal I ate that night would have been higher than the highest point in nineteen states, and just thirteen calories away from topping Mount Greylock, the highest point in Massachusetts (3,487 feet).

As I ate my mountain of food and looked over the pictures I'd taken, I was grateful the ranger had recommended the trail less traveled. Sure, I may not have summited the most well-known mountain, but I had earned a different, far more legit Texas-bragging right; I had done the cool *locals* mountain. By resisting the popular choice, I had instead found an in-the-know spot that was secretly way better. This, I am aware, was a strange thought to be having inside a Chili's.

I did start to worry, though, that even if I wasn't peak bagging, I might be *park* bagging. Hadn't I based my entire year on a similarly arbitrary distinction? A far *more* arbitrary distinction, actually. Height, at least, is quantifiable. What separates national parks from national forests and seashores and recreation areas is sometimes impossible to discern.

By focusing exclusively on the parks, I had known from the beginning that I'd be leaving out all sorts of beautiful, worthy spots. Viewed through that lens, my park bagging was limiting me. But it was also what had inspired me. Without that list to work off, I never would have conceived of the trip in the first place. The park list had given me a structure. It had given me a mission.

Those hikers trying to summit all of Colorado's 14ers are undoubtedly missing out on amazing 13ers and 12ers. But if they weren't chasing some sort of goal, they might not head up into the mountains at all.

The morning after my Guadalupe Mountains hike, I could barely walk. Climbing eight thousand feet had left my legs so sore that I could only imagine what fourteen thousand feet would have done to them. Fortunately, I had a day of sitting ahead of me. I waddled out to my car, plugged my iPhone into the dash, and started my drive north to Albuquerque.

> Listen, baby . . .
> Ain't no mountain high
> Ain't no valley low
> Ain't no river wide enough, baby.

"America the Beautiful" might have been the song I'd chosen to sing all year long, but the song I listened to the most was the Marvin Gaye and Tammi Terrell duet "Ain't No Mountain High Enough."

When it had played on my very first drive of the year, I was convinced it was an omen. I hadn't pressed anything to cue it up. I mean, *come on.* Of all the possible songs, somehow the one about *mountains* and *rivers* and *valleys*, about how nothing was going to stand in their way, was what began my trip? It was too perfect. I couldn't stop grinning as I'd headed out on the road that first day.

Then my phone played "All That Jazz."

I'd realized what was happening. My iTunes downloads were playing in alphabetical order. All year long, every single time I plugged in my phone, the first few bars of "Ain't No Mountain High Enough" would start playing until I fired up Spotify. I must have heard those opening notes a thousand times.

But the morning after Guadalupe, I let the song play all the way through.

> No wind, no rain
> Or winters cold
> can stop me baby, na na baby
> 'Cause you are my goal . . .

I still had more parks left to bag; there was more of the mountain yet to climb. But I'd come far enough that it had started to feel like I might actually be able to pull it off. If I did, I wondered what the view from the top would look like. And after I finally saw whatever was waiting for me there, I wondered how I'd ever find my way down.

21

DIVERSITY

(Mount Rainier, Shenandoah)

I've been to Mount Rainier National Park four times, and I've only seen Mount Rainier once. It was on my second trip, during a brief two-hour stretch in the middle of the day, when the omnipresent clouds of Washington parted just enough so that I could see the icy 14,411-foot peak towering above me. Mount Rainier's stark beauty is only matched by its potential danger—should the stratovolcano wake up and erupt, it would wreak havoc on nearby communities.

On clear days, Rainier can be seen looming behind the Seattle skyline; Seattleites are obsessed with the mountain's game of hide-and-seek. The Twitter account @IsMtRainierOut does nothing but tweet about whether the mountain is visible each day. It has twice as many followers as I do.

Locals say you can see Rainier less than 25 percent of the time. Fortunately, that's not why people go to the park. Surrounding the mountain, there are more than two hundred thousand acres full of beautiful meadows, gushing waterfalls, ancient forests, and more than 275 miles of maintained trails.

But while a trip to Mount Rainier may or may not yield a view of its glistening white summit, you are guaranteed to see plenty of white people hiking below it—an estimated 94 percent of Mount Rainier's more than one million visitors are white. Just 1 percent are African American. Alicia Highland knows she stands out.

"Oh, people *always* treat me differently when they see me in an outdoor space," Alicia told me as we walked around Mount Rainier's Longmire Campground. "They're like, *Oh look, it's this black unicorn hiking on this trail!*"

She rolled her eyes and laughed. Hers was an infectious, warm laugh, the kind that made you want to say something funny so that you might hear it again. I laughed along with her, even though I knew I was guilty of sometimes having a similar reaction.

It had taken me a few months before I began to realize just how few African Americans I was seeing in the parks. Hot Springs: Zero. Big Bend: Zero. Acadia: Zero. Everglades, just two hours from Miami: Zero. From that moment on, I started noticing *every* African American I saw in a park. I didn't intend for these encounters to register, but they always did.

Alicia was visiting Mount Rainier with the Student Conservation Association (SCA), an organization she'd been involved with since college. Each year, thousands of young SCA volunteers across the country work on all types of public lands, building trails, clearing brush, and doing much of the necessary hard labor that keeps a park running. Alicia first worked on an SCA crew at Everglades National Park in Florida, then led a crew herself at Cumberland Island National Seashore in Georgia. She found she had a knack for teaching and leadership and enrolled at University of Washington to get her master's in environmental education. She was graduating the very next day.

"Congratulations!" I said when she told me. "What's next? Any idea what you want to do?"

"Well, I've got a backpacking trip to Alaska planned. Then . . . who knows!" Alicia said, shrugging and throwing up her hands in mock exasperation. "I kind of need to figure out what I'm going to do with my life. But whatever I do, I'm going to continue working in youth development. I want to get young folks and people of color outdoors."

I told Alicia about my journey through the parks and about what I'd been seeing so far. Or, more accurately, what I hadn't been seeing. The scenery was diverse, but the crowds, well . . . not so much.

She smiled and gave me the kindest *no shit, Sherlock* look you can imagine. While it might have taken *me* months to internalize how unbelievably white the parks were, that had been Alicia's experience her entire life.

Alicia was born in Cincinnati, Ohio. There was a small creek behind her house, and some of her earliest memories are of chasing around salamanders and owls in her backyard. After her father's job briefly took the family to Chicago, the Highlands moved back to Ohio, this time to the much smaller town of Munroe Falls, population 5,012, according to the 2010 Census; 1.5 percent of that population was black.

"Until then, we had always lived in very ethnically and culturally diverse places," Alicia said. "But then, in third grade, I remember someone called me the N-word. And I didn't even really know what it *meant*, but I knew that there was something very different about being in this place, in this space, in this town, than in any other town I'd ever lived in."

Alicia was still a salamander-chasing girl at heart, so she joined the local branch of the Girl Scouts, where she was one of only two people of color in her troop. She found a like-minded group of friends, but she still felt like she didn't quite belong.

"Even though the Girl Scouts was kind of like a safe space for me—because we were all just a bunch of nerdy girls playing in the woods—there were always things that I noticed," she said.

"Like what?" I asked.

"Well, like, when we'd go to camp. I would always have to do my hair a certain way, so that it would look nice all week. All the other girls could just put their hair in ponytails. Or . . . lotion. I'd have to bring *lotion*, you know? And so it was this kind of dawning awareness, that my skin's different, my hair's different, there are different things about me."

Alicia's parents dutifully drove her to all the hikes and retreats and Thin Mint cookie sales, but they struggled to get what she found *fun* about the woods.

"My mom didn't quite understand why I wanted to spend so much time outside," Alicia said. "It was a generational difference, I think. She grew up in rural South Carolina, and they used to spend a *lot* of time outside. For her, it was like, 'We had to be outside because we were *poor*. Why are you trying to spend so much time outside when we have *air-conditioning*?' "

I grew up just a few hours away from Alicia's hometown. My parents would regularly take us hiking for fun on weekends, but those types of trips weren't part of Alicia's childhood. My love of nature just meant following a trail that had already been laid out for me. Alicia had to find her way into the woods on her own.

When she went off to Ohio State for college, she majored in natural resources management. Perhaps her passion could one day become her career, she thought. For many of her white classmates, it was the first time they had ever taken a college class with a black person.

"They would stare at me," Alicia said. "It was very uncomfortable, one of the most uncomfortable experiences I've ever had in my entire life."

"One day, we were out doing a field methods class and one of my classmates came up to me. He was very nice, and he came up to me and was like, 'What are you *doing* here? You're a *black woman*, what are you doing in natural resources? You should be, like, in business or something like that.' "

Up until that point, Alicia might have privately wondered if she belonged, but hearing it put so bluntly from one of her peers was crushing.

"I was just like, *Oh God. What* am *I doing here?* I didn't feel supported, I didn't feel like I belonged in the field of conservation or wildlife management. I was *tired* of being the only person of color out here, doing this work. I was tired of people not understanding what my life is like," she said.

So Alicia dropped out of school and moved back home with her parents. Back to the air-conditioning. For two and a half years, she worked at a local restaurant, trying to figure out her next move. *Should* she study business? It would probably be easier. But no, that couldn't be the answer. She still felt drawn to the outdoors.

Alicia decided to give college another shot. She enrolled at Kent State University, just twenty minutes away from home, and transferred her credits toward a conservation biology degree. At Kent State, she had her first-ever science professor of color.

"It was the first time I had ever looked at my professor and said, 'Oh, this person *looks* like me, this person speaks with an accent,'" Alicia said. "He was great. He didn't let us slide on anything. He was from Costa Rica, and he had done all these amazing projects. And I was just like, 'Oh my goodness, so there *are* people like me out there doing tremendous work, and I can be like them, too.' That was the first time I'd ever felt that. And that was incredibly powerful."

As she told me this, I tried to remember if I had *ever* had a non-white science teacher. I didn't think I had. When I chose not to major in biology or chemistry or forestry, it wasn't because I didn't think it was *possible* for me to go into those fields. It was because I didn't feel like it.

Fortunately, Alicia's college experience ended up being better the second time around. But outside of the classroom, she continued to run into closed minds and closed doors. For a summer internship, she managed to secure a job working with the Forest Service at White River National Forest in Colorado, with an emphasis, it turned out, on the "white."

"Colorado was a total eye-opener for me," Alicia said. "That was the first time I'd been to a wealthy white ski resort. I realized there's so much of the world that's closed off to me. Like, I don't have the wealth or the access to go *heli-skiing*. Who jumps out of a *helicopter* to go *skiing*? How did you even think to put those two things together?"

It wasn't like Alicia's coworkers at the Forest Service were pulling down fancy Vail resort money, but she was surprised at how many of them came from families that did. Everyone else seemed to feel far more comfortable in that world. They knew about things like packrafting and slacklining and all sorts of other outdoor activities she'd never even *heard* of.

On Alicia's third day on the job, one of the permanent staff members approached her.

"It was this white guy, maybe in his thirties," Alicia remembered. "He said 'Oh, look at you. By the end of the summer you're going to be my boss.'"

"And I was just like, 'Oh. What does *that* mean?' And he was of course alluding to the fact that I'm a black woman. That affirmative action was going to make me his supervisor. Like, I literally had *just* gotten there. I didn't know anyone. And I instantly saw that people saw me not as someone who was deserving of being in these positions, but as someone who was a threat to them. Or someone who was there because they had preferential treatment. And it's like, 'Well, *you're* here because you got preferential treatment for your entire life.'"

I laughed the kind of uncomfortable laugh that only a white guy in his mid-thirties who has gotten preferential treatment his whole life can. I knew full well that most rangers, as well as all those heli-skiers and mountain bikers Alicia met in Colorado, looked just like me. I might not have grown up going to fancy Rocky Mountain resorts either, but at least when I saw preppy kids hanging out in the ski lodge in movies, they just looked like versions of me with better haircuts and better clothes.

I know the privilege of my race, gender, class, and sexual orientation has permeated everything in my life, even if it's a topic I don't think about nearly enough. To think that somehow that privilege only applied in the classroom or the workplace and not in the outdoors would be naïve. I *knew* it did, but it took spending more time outside to think about *how* it did.

Because it wasn't just that Alicia's colleagues and classmates treated her like she shouldn't be *working* in nature. She was frequently made to feel as if she shouldn't be *playing* there, either. Hiking, camping, kayaking, climbing—those weren't activities that people of color were traditionally seen participating in.

Whenever the underrepresentation of minorities in the national parks is brought up, it is sometimes discussed as an economic issue. And to some extent, that's true. The average white family is wealthier than the average black family, and that extra money can be spent on plane tickets, fuel, accommodations, snacks, backpacks, and snowshoes. National parks themselves might not be that expensive, but everything else involved with experiencing one can be.

Also, the parks—at least the big, famous ones—are far removed from the urban population centers that contain higher percentages of minorities. Sure, you'll see a lot of white people at Acadia, but Maine is nearly 95 percent white. Yellowstone is in Wyoming, a state that's over 90 percent white. Utah, Montana, North Dakota, Idaho . . . they all have smaller-than-average minority populations. But at Congaree National Park in South Carolina—a state that's only 65 percent or so white—a 2012 survey found that park visitors were *94 percent white.*

Even when you take income and geography into consideration, the parks still aren't as diverse as they could be and should be. That's why ranger Shelton Johnson wrote a letter to Oprah.

In 2010, during the final season of *The Oprah Winfrey Show*, Oprah traveled to Yosemite. She called up her longtime best pal (and current *CBS This Morning* anchor) Gayle King, and the two of them drove into the park together in a giant red Chevy Tahoe, towing a camping trailer behind them.

"Black people reporting in!" Gayle joked when she pulled up to the park entrance gate. The ranger who chuckled and took her entrance fee was white, just like most of Yosemite's rangers. Just like most of Yosemite's visitors.

The summer before Oprah's visit, a study had found that just 1 percent of Yosemite's visitors identified as black.

Shelton Johnson didn't need an official report to confirm what he'd been seeing with his own eyes.

Shelton began his Park Service career in 1987 as a ranger at Yellowstone. He then moved on to Great Basin in Nevada, and eventually made his way to Yosemite, where he had served as a ranger ever since 1994. Shelton was African American, and it troubled him how few visitors to the park were.

"My entire career, I have been bothered by the lack of African Americans visiting national parks," he wrote to Oprah. "It has bothered me when I look out and I meet people from Germany, from Spain, from *Africa*, and yet I can't find an African American family from Chicago, or from Boston, or from Detroit."

So Shelton asked for Oprah's help. Perhaps a visit from her could showcase the park to her audience and inspire more minority visitors to come experience its treasures. Oprah and Gayle hopped into the SUV to come meet Shelton in person.

As soon as they arrived at the park, Shelton took them to see the Grizzly Giant. ("Is that a tree or is that a *bear*?" Gayle joked.) The 209-foot-tall giant sequoia is the most famous tree in all of Yosemite, and Oprah and Gayle oohed and aahed and took pictures underneath it.

But as impressed as they were by the sequoia's giant branches, they seemed even more excited to take a picture with Woody Square, a minister from San Leandro, California, who was visiting the park with his wife.

"Dear God, I see a black person!" Oprah said when she spotted Woody standing by a bench in Yosemite's Mariposa Grove. The three laughed together about what a rare sighting it was in a national park ("I'm the first one here!" Woody joked). They wandered into a clearing so they could take a picture together, something to commemorate "the other black person we saw."

In a 2015 follow-up, Shelton said that he went from seeing African American visitors in the park once every week or so to "essentially on a daily basis." That's the power of having one of the most famous African Americans in the world come visit your park.

If the name Shelton Johnson sounds familiar, it's because he's become a bit of a celebrity himself. He was the breakout star of Ken Burns's 2009 documentary *The National Parks: America's Best Idea.* Shelton Johnson may just be the best park ranger who ever lived.

Before joining the Park Service, Shelton taught kids as a Peace Corps volunteer. He studied poetry at the University of Michigan, and every last line of his in that documentary was delivered with the wisdom and cadence of a poet.

Here's how he describes himself on his LinkedIn page:

"My objective is basically the same as the conservationist, John Muir. He once wrote words to the effect that he 'lived only to encourage people to look at Nature's loveliness,' and that is precisely what I'm trying to do for people of color here in the United States who don't have a connection to their National Parks and Wilderness lands."

Part of Shelton's strategy has been to focus on highlighting overlooked African American contributions to the national parks. At Yosemite, he gives regular presentations on the Buffalo Soldiers, the African American regiments who served as some of Yosemite's first rangers. Before the Park Service was established, the U.S. Army was in charge of Yosemite and Sequoia National Parks, and those approximately five hundred African American soldiers patrolled them, tasked with everything from putting out forest fires to stopping poachers.

In 1903, Captain Charles Young served as the first African American superintendent of a national park, leading the Ninth

Calvary at Sequoia National Park. And yet more than a century later, only a smattering of park units are run by leaders of color. The Park Service doesn't mirror the diversity of the country it seeks to serve.

In 2013, the Park Service created an Office of Relevancy, Diversity, and Inclusion. New initiatives like the Mosaics in Science Diversity Internship Program seek to attract youth "under-represented in natural resource science career fields." But change has been slow in coming. The most recent statistics from the Park Service estimate that its workforce is still 83 percent white.

While the diversity of the staff hasn't changed dramatically, the Park Service *has* increased the diversity of the types of stories it tells. There are still plenty of inspirational quotes from old dead white guys, and no shortage of creeks and mountains and visitor centers named for white geologists, presidents, and philanthropists, but in recent years there's been an effort to broaden the scope of the narrative.

At Mount Rainier, park leaders have invited members of the local Nisqually tribe to share their oral histories with rangers so that aspects of Nisqually history can be better woven into park presentations and museum exhibits. Today, it's not uncommon for an evening ranger program to begin with what's known as a "land acknowledgment," a formal statement that pays tribute to the six associated Washington tribes on whose ancestral land Rainier now sits. Tribal members can visit the park for free—sections off limits to the general public have been set aside to facilitate traditional cultural practices.

While trapped Floyd Collins might be the most famous and dramatic story at Kentucky's Mammoth Cave, tour guides today make a point of mentioning that some of the *original* guides were enslaved African Americans. Several of the passages visitors enjoy in the cave were first discovered by renowned African American guide Stephen Bishop.

During the Obama administration, several new park sites were created that focused specifically on preserving the stories of minority groups. There's now Freedom Riders National Monument in Anniston, Alabama, located in the former Greyhound bus station where civil rights activists were attacked while protesting segregation on interstate buses. In Keene, California, the former headquarters of the United Farm Workers has been protected as part of César E. Chávez National Monument. In the middle of Manhattan, Stonewall National Monument became the first national monument dedicated to LGBT history.

There's Harriet Tubman Underground Railroad National Historical Park in Maryland, Belmont-Paul Women's Equality National Monument in Washington, D.C. (home of the National Woman's Party), and Birmingham Civil Rights National Monument in Alabama.

Preserving our cultural heritage is as much a part of the Park Service mission as preserving our scenic beauty, and each of these new sites serves as a potential gateway to everything else that exists under the Park Service umbrella. But still, touring a bus station in Alabama is not necessarily going to inspire someone to go climb a mountain in Alaska.

To understand why certain groups might be more reluctant to head into the wilderness, it's worth thinking more deeply about the history of the parks themselves.

Well into the 1940s, Virginia's Shenandoah National Park had segregated facilities. When black visitors arrived to check out one of the first national parks in the East, they were forced to use separate campgrounds, dining halls, and restrooms.

Early Shenandoah tourists were handed maps that highlighted several cottages, campgrounds, lunchrooms, and—in an area on the eastern side of the park with slightly less desirable scenery— a lone "picnic ground for colored people." When I stopped into the visitor center museum along the park's famous Skyline Drive, I came across a replica of a sign that had once pointed the way to the LEWIS MOUNTAIN NEGRO AREA.

Next to the sign, a small display chronicled the history of segregation at Shenandoah. The park was at least making an effort to acknowledge its racist past, which unfortunately wasn't that different from the story of Virginia schools and offices during the Jim Crow era. But while people *have to* go to school and to work, they don't have to go to a park. Feel unwelcome at one even once, and you may never want to come back. You may tell your kids not to, either. That Lewis Mountain sign came down a long time ago, but it's hard to overestimate its legacy.

"It's the historical trauma of being a black person in this all-white space," Alicia had told me back at Mount Rainier. "There is something inherently not safe about that. In our past, a black person going into the woods means that you can be lynched, you can be murdered, you could be raped, you can be all these things. If someone doesn't like you, for whatever reason, you can never come back again."

There is obviously no longer a WHITES ONLY sign at Shenandoah's popular campgrounds, but when you walk around, it's easy to wonder if maybe you just didn't *see* it. The most recent study of Shenandoah found that park visitors were 92 percent white.

Outdoor Afro is a group currently working to "change the face of conservation." Started in 2009 as a blog by CEO Rue Mapp, Outdoor Afro has grown into a national nonprofit network devoted to connecting African Americans to the outdoors by first connecting them with one another.

"We can go out with people who look like us, in a big group, and not be the only one out there," Alicia told me. "Feeling safe is a big part of it. It's not that the interest isn't *there*. It's just like, 'I don't feel safe doing that by myself, so I'm not gonna take that risk.'"

Outdoor Afro leaders—who tend to be more experienced guides like Alicia—help ease first-timers into the wilderness. Sometimes feeling safe just means being with someone else who can teach you how to filter water from a stream, strap on a mountain-climbing harness, or light a campfire. Groups have gone kayaking in the

Coosa River in Alabama, camping at Black Rock Park in Texas, and backpacking at Shenandoah.

Outdoor Afro is just one of a number of "affinity groups" that have sprung up to fill in the gaps for communities who are underrepresented in the parks. Latino Outdoors envisions "a world where all Latino families and children have access to nature, celebrate their unique cultural connection to the outdoors, and are supported as the next generation of Latino leadership in the outdoors." The Venture Out Project is "committed to facilitating backpacking and wilderness trips for the queer and trans community in a safe and inclusive environment."

For decades, if you were to flip through the pages of magazines like *Backpacker* or *Outside,* you'd see photo after photo of white guys with big backpacks. Patagonia, North Face, REI, Osprey—they were all monochromatic. Slowly, though, those depictions in advertising are starting to change. Native Womens Wilderness, founded "to inspire and raise the voices of Native Women in the outdoor realm," lists among its many goals: "Promote women of color in the mainstream advertising campaigns of outdoor retailers."

Figuring out how to alter the demographics of a place like Yosemite is a long, complicated process, but changing the demographics of who is represented in commercials, magazine spreads, and in-store displays can happen by the end of the next fiscal quarter. Every time it does, Alicia notices.

"I think representation is just *huge*," she said. "Being outside, hiking, camping, any of that—in order for you to recognize that's an interest that you have, there has to be a gateway to it. If you see this thing that looks like it *might* be cool, but you never see anyone who looks like you doing it, or no one you know talks about it, then it just kinda feels like, 'Oh, this is something outside of my reach.' But if you just put a black person on a Patagonia ad, not *making* the clothes, but *using* the clothes, then it opens up a whole new world of possibility for folks . . . It begins to normalize a behavior that may have seemed out of the ordinary before."

The parks are more popular than ever, and companies like Patagonia have a clear economic incentive to market to minority groups. Anyone who can manage to become the go-to sleeping bag or rain jacket or granola bar brand for millions of potential hikers will be sitting on a mountain of money. In the '90s, Subaru famously went after the lesbian car buying demographic to great success, and has sponsored pride parades and created gay-targeted ads. It turns out you can love whomever you want *and* all-wheel drive.

For the Park Service, though, inclusivity is a moral imperative—America's "best idea" is supposed to be for *all* Americans.

Obama's interior secretary Sally Jewell doesn't just look like someone you might see in an REI ad. She had been the *CEO* of REI.

I met Secretary Jewell at the base of Mount Rainier, although she had seen the view from the mountain's top. She grew up in Washington and had summited Rainier seven times in all, most recently leading an all-female team up the mountain in 2010. Perhaps more than any other interior secretary in history, Jewell walked the walk. And she walked *fast.*

Before I met Jewell, her advance team had warned me the secretary was a speedy hiker. Boy, were they right. Her legs must have been half the length of mine, but I struggled to keep up as she zipped around Rainier's trails.

She didn't have much time. Jewell had come back home to speak at the University of Washington's commencement the next day, the same ceremony Alicia would be attending. She was spending the day before checking in on the staff at Rainier, and I only had a few moments to chat with her before she had to head back to Seattle. We were mostly there to talk about an initiative she was spearheading to connect young people and veterans to the parks, but I asked her what she thought about the need to tackle the park's overall diversity problem.

"It's going to be essential if we're going to have these places," she said. "The future population of our country in a representative democracy is going to make decisions about where money's spent in the future. If they've never felt welcome on their public lands, how could we expect them to prioritize preserving places like this?"

In short, nothing less than the future of the national parks is on the line. By 2045, the United States is expected to have a majority nonwhite population, and if the majority of the voting public does not feel a strong connection to the parks, which cost billions of dollars to run and sit on eighty-five million acres of land, then they may cease to *be* parks. The "National Park Idea" is an idea, not a guarantee, and if it's an idea that's going to survive, then it's about time we get some new ideas about how to make the parks more inclusive.

"*Everyone* should have the opportunity to experience the transformation that comes with being in these magnificent outdoor spaces," Alicia said when I asked why she was determined to get more people of color outdoors. Not everyone is going to want to free-climb Half Dome, and not everyone is going to enjoy hiking or kayaking or bird-watching in the wilderness. There will always be people who give camping a try and decide they never want to do it again because sleeping on the ground *sucks*. It's not about making everyone fall in love with the parks. It's about making sure everyone has a *chance* to.

There's a tall stone arch at Yellowstone's North Entrance, its cornerstone laid by Teddy Roosevelt in the early 1900s. YELLOWSTONE NATIONAL PARK is written on the lower left-hand side, but by far the most prominent words stretch across the top, impossible to miss.

In large, capital letters carved into stone, the sign atop the arch reads: FOR THE BENEFIT AND ENJOYMENT OF THE PEOPLE. They were the first words Shelton Johnson saw on his first trip to the park. As he told Ken Burns, "It doesn't say for the benefit and enjoyment of *some* of the people, or a *few* of the people—it says *all* of the people. And for me, that meant democracy, and for me, that meant I was welcome."

22

DISCONNECTING

(Isle Royale, Olympic, Virgin Islands)

While the average visit to a national park typically lasts a few hours, the average visit to Isle Royale lasts a few *days*. The remote group of islands off the coast of Michigan's Upper Peninsula is only accessible by seaplane or boat, and so, once travelers put Isle Royale on their itinerary, they tend to go all-in. They also tend to come back—the park is known for its high level of repeat visitation.

But unless you grew up in Minnesota or Michigan, you've likely never heard of it. It's where people from Duluth and Detroit go to trade the hustle and bustle of city life for the solitude of the wilderness. My friend Robin grew up in Michigan. Here's how he responded when I emailed to ask him about the park:

"Michiganders—which is to say, residents of the Lower Peninsula, because that is what we mostly are—regard the Upper Peninsula with a mixture of awe and wariness. It is just a much wilder place. And then Isle Royale . . . I mean, it is to the Upper Peninsula what the Upper Peninsula is to the Lower Peninsula."

To access Isle Royale, I first had to travel to the small UP town

of Houghton, Michigan, where I spent the night at the Holiday Inn and set up an auto-response for my email. For the next four days, I was going to be entirely unreachable. Early the next morning, I took a cab to the county airport, boarded a Cessna 206 seaplane, and flew out over Lake Superior.

There were only two other passengers on my flight—surveyors who were doing work for the U.S. Geological Survey. After forty minutes or so, nearly into Canadian airspace, we finally came upon Isle Royale—the largest island in the largest of the Great Lakes. Covered with white spruce and balsam fir trees, the forty-five-mile-long island has an area nearly ten times that of Manhattan and exactly zero permanent residents. For five and a half months, the park shuts down entirely—harsh winter conditions make it too dangerous to reach. National parks in *Alaska* don't even close for the winter.

Ninety-nine percent of Isle Royale is federally designated wilderness, as defined by the Wilderness Act of 1964. According to the law, which regulates how everything from power tools to helicopters can be used in parks, wilderness is "undeveloped Federal land, retaining its primeval character and influence, without permanent improvements or human habitation." That means no buildings, no roads. Perhaps most important, from a visitor perspective, the land must have "outstanding opportunities for solitude or a primitive and unconfined type of recreation."

As wild as many parks might seem, more than half of the national parks do not contain any legal "wilderness" at all, which may come as a surprise to anyone who's gotten lost in the spires of Canyonlands or come face-to-face with a grizzly deep in the backcountry of Glacier. Even Yellowstone, as impossible as it is to believe, contains no designated wilderness.

That's what I was looking forward to at Isle Royale: 132,018 acres of wilderness confined only by the chilly water lapping at its shores. Once the seaplane let me off at Windigo dock, I headed straight up the hill to the visitor center, part of the 1 percent of the island that's *not* wild. On the opposite end of the island, there's a similarly developed section that's home to a hotel with air-conditioning and hot meals. The pictures of the lodge looked nice, but staying there seemed like a cheat, especially for my first time on the island. I wanted the full experience.

I was planning on hiking more than thirty miles and had plotted a loop around the southeast corner of Isle Royale. But after walking just a few yards to the visitor center, I was already starting to rethink my decision. My fully loaded backpack felt impossibly heavy on my shoulders. In retrospect, the look the pilot had given me when he'd hefted the pack onto the plane should have warned me that I'd overdone it.

In the past, most of my hiking had been *day* hiking. Trudging around with everything I might need for multiple days and nights on my back was a whole different skill set, and I didn't have enough experience to purge all of the unnecessary items I'd brought. At least the pack would only get lighter, I told myself—I'd be eating all of the meals inside as I went along.

I picked up my camping permit and told the ranger where I was planning on heading. She approved of my route and double-checked to make sure I had a water purification filter. There are no water fountains in the wilderness, so everything I was going to drink would have to come from streams in the park or from Lake Superior itself. I assured her I'd brought one, although I neglected to mention it was brand new and so far only tested in my hotel sink. She wished me well and I was on my way. It was the last conversation I would have for more than three days.

Without anyone to talk to, I was left alone with my thoughts, which, for the first few miles, were a near-constant loop of *I. Hate. This. Stupid. Backpack.* But eventually, I either destroyed the nerve endings in my shoulders or settled into a groove—I'm not sure which—and started to enjoy myself.

The trails at Isle Royale are narrow and surrounded by trees, so there's not much in the way of distractions, and not much to do except put one foot in front of the other. After so much planning and plotting, I found it to be a relief. For once, I didn't have to think about what to say or do next. I just followed the trail.

An early, unexpected benefit of the island's solitude was that I could hike in my new formfitting synthetic shirt. I knew synthetic fabrics were supposed to do a much better job of wicking away moisture, but after I received mine in the mail, I realized that they were equally adept at highlighting all of my insecurities. One of my favorite comedians, Nate Bargatze, has a line about Under Armour shirts—"I look better *without* a shirt on than with that shirt on."

But after two hours and zero humans, I decided it was safe to change into my synthetic sausage casing. It felt much better than the heavy, sweat-drenched cotton shirt I'd worn on the plane, and somehow the new sensation against my skin gave me an extra boost of energy to push through the last few miles.

After eight and a half miles, I finally made it to my campsite at Feldtmann Lake, one of Isle Royale's numerous interior lakes. Some of those lakes have their own islands, and some of those islands have their own small ponds, and some of those ponds have their own boulders or rocks in the middle. The park is like a matryoshka doll of land and water.

My hydration pack was nearly empty, and when I dipped the thin rubber hose of my purifier into the lake's water, I felt like I could drink it dry. With the last bit of energy I had left, I started pumping the liquid through the filter's chambers and into my pack.

The pump supposedly removes the dangerous bacteria and protozoans lurking in the water, although I would have felt more confident taking a gulp if I'd had an indicator that something was actually *happening*. Maybe the water could change color? Or taste lemony once it had been treated?

I remembered toothpaste companies had once done something similar with toothpaste. The cooling sensation you get while brushing doesn't actually *do* anything and was only added to convince people that good things were happening in their mouths. Or . . .

was I confusing that with the shampoo tingle? I reached for my phone to look up the answer, and then I remembered—I didn't have service.

Had there been a few bars, I knew my hunt for toothpaste facts would have just been the beginning of what could have been an hour of scrolling. Checking emails, responding to texts, liking my friends' Instagram posts. I felt a bit of anxiety set in—what might be happening out there in the world? What if someone needed to reach me? I had come to Isle Royale to get away from it all, and before the sun had even set, I was more than ready to invite "it" back in.

Fortunately, the island saved me from myself. The park is more than just geographically disconnected—it's one of a shrinking number of places that's technologically disconnected as well. As long as I was there, the rest of the world would have to wait. For the next few days, the island *was* my world.

With my hydration pack full, I wandered to the nearby campsite and set up my tent, then ate a dinner of packaged salmon and buffalo jerky, enjoying the views and the quiet until the sun went down.

My muscles were tired, but I still wasn't. Amped up from the day's adventure, I thought of how I might spend the rest of my evening. Anywhere else, I might have swiped until sleep finally set in, or perhaps have watched an episode or two of a show I barely cared about. Instead, I cuddled up in my sleeping bag and read a book.

In 2012, Cheryl Strayed published *Wild*, an account of her three-month-long hike on the Pacific Crest Trail. Propelled by strong reviews and Oprah's endorsement, the book became one of the year's bestsellers. I had seen the film when it came out in 2014, but I hadn't tackled the book until the year I headed out into the parks. It was one of several outdoor narratives I'd been jumping in and out of whenever I had downtime. That night, seeking a sympathetic voice after a day spent carrying around a too-big backpack, I picked *Wild* back up. By the end of my time on the island, I had nearly finished it.

While Strayed's book came out in 2012, the journey it documents happened in 1995. Reading through her account two decades later, I couldn't believe how much the world had changed since then.

The scenery, for the most part, had not. When Strayed arrives at Crater Lake near the end of her trip and describes it as "the most unspeakably pure ultramarine blue I'd ever seen," I knew exactly what she meant—I'd had an identical reaction. But there was so much else in the book I couldn't relate to. Not just the parts about shooting up black tar heroin. Everything that had to do with the *logistics* of her journey felt so foreign.

The story begins at a gas station in Mojave, California, where Strayed nervously sizes up customers entering and exiting the store, trying to discern who might be a murderer or rapist before requesting a ride to the trailhead. Finally, she approaches a pair of strangers, who agree to take her to the PCT. It's the first of several anxiety-inducing hitchhiking episodes.

From the book, it's pretty easy to tell which gas station Strayed is referring to. Today it's a sixteen-dollar Uber ride from there to the trail. If Strayed stood in that parking lot now, she would know that Tim has a 4.93 rating, has been driving for three years, and has been given forty-seven compliments for "Great Conversation" and four for "Awesome Music," all before she ever stepped into his Camry.

Throughout her hike, Strayed gets disoriented, wanders off the trail, and finds herself on an unknown road. Maybe it's Highway 89, maybe it's not—she has no way of knowing. She doesn't have GPS, and Google Maps didn't exist in 1995. She has a paper map, a compass, and a guidebook—a large volume whose pages she periodically burns to lighten her pack.

While I was reading Strayed's book on a device that could hold a thousand more—an entire library's worth of knowledge—the

Amazon Kindle didn't exist when Strayed walked the PCT. Books were her prized possessions on the trail, and she couldn't wait until a new one arrived in one of her "re-supply" boxes—shipments of gear and freeze-dried food she had packed in advance. Her friend Lisa periodically mailed the boxes to small-town post offices, coordinating the drop-off locations with Strayed on *pay phone* calls.

The pay phone is Strayed's lifeline. When she finds one near a restaurant she calls her ex-husband. When she finds one near a state park, she calls REI to order new boots to replace a pair she'd lost, and then calls again to see if they've arrived. Nobody ever calls *her*. They can't—she's impossible to reach.

There are those today who resent the success of *Wild* for what it did to the PCT. It made the trail popular; it made it "crowded." Thanks to Strayed, the old-timers say, the experience just isn't what it used to be.

But the PCT experience changed long before that book came out. It changed as soon as technology arrived on the trail. *Wild* might have inspired thousands of people to retrace Strayed's steps, but every hiker who steps out today does so with bundles of electronics in their backpacks. Plenty of modern PCT hikers take *two* phones on the trail—a primary device and a cheap backup—each running on a different carrier to increase their chances of remaining connected. Hikers comparing notes online estimate that more than 70 percent of the PCT has cellphone service, and the other 30 percent can't be far behind.

Today, PCTers walk with GPS units and solar chargers and Fitbits and e-readers and emergency locator beacons and power bricks. Anything they might have forgotten, they can order via Amazon Prime from a mountaintop. Thanks to technology, the world described in *Wild* just isn't as wild anymore.

But it *is* safer. Today, not bringing a cellphone on a journey like Strayed's would seem downright irresponsible. How could you possibly leave it behind, when adding just six extra ounces to your backpack could provide you with a literal—and potentially lifesaving—call for help?

. . .

"Excuse me! Do you happen to have a cellphone?"

I was just about to start down the Sol Duc Falls Trail at Olympic National Park when a worried-looking hiker flagged me down from across the lot. Something was clearly wrong.

Sol Duc is located in Olympic's remote northwest corner, an hour's drive from the town of Port Angeles, Washington. More than 95 percent of the park is designated wilderness. From its bright-green rain forests to its primitive rocky coast, Olympic is one of the least developed parks in the Lower 48. I hadn't had cell service for most of the day.

"I do, but I don't think it's going to do you any good," I said. "What's the matter?"

His name was Chris, he said, and he quickly explained that he'd been leading a group of high schoolers on a backcountry excursion. One of them had gotten ill. At first, they'd thought it was a garden-variety stomachache, but it hadn't passed, and now Chris was worried that perhaps it might be appendicitis. The kid was in pain, and he needed to go home.

Chris had brought a satellite phone, but it was malfunctioning. His own cellphone had zero bars. Three miles deeper into the forest, the rest of the campers were waiting with the sick kid. Chris had hiked alone back to the lot hoping he might have better luck here.

"Well, we can try," I said, pulling my iPhone out of my pocket. But just as I'd feared . . . "No service."

Chris and I started walking around the parking lot together, waiting to see if anything might pop up. And then, all of a sudden, near a picnic table, something did. Just one bar, but it might be enough.

"You don't mind?" Chris asked. "I might have to make a few calls."

"Oh my gosh, of course not," I said. "Please, take as much time as you need." The falls could wait.

I waited until I heard Chris make a connection, then walked away to give him some privacy. Across the lot, I could hear him explaining the situation and coordinating with someone on the other end to get a car to transport the kid. He was calm and collected—the kind of leader you'd want taking care of your sick son on a trip into the backcountry.

I walked back over and pantomimed that they could use *my* car if they wanted, but Chris waved me off. As he later explained, the group had hiked so far in that it would take hours to get the kid out. Making the trek at night seemed too risky, and the illness hadn't reached emergency level yet. He'd asked for the transportation to be there at first light the next day—he would bring the kid back then. He hung up, thanked me, and hurried back to rejoin his campers.

Advocates of greater connectivity in parks point to these types of situations as the primary reason the parks should expand coverage. There are countless examples of injured or lost hikers receiving assistance thanks to a strong signal. Cellphones can save lives.

As I later learned, Verizon had recently filed an application to build a new tower at Olympic's Hurricane Ridge Visitor Center— less than twelve miles from where Chris's group was camped out in the woods. The Telecommunications Act of 1996 requires parks to review such proposals, and there is no shortage of requests—the major U.S. companies all want to expand their footprint in the wild. Slowly but surely, that's been happening.

Washington's Mount Rainier National Park has allowed Verizon and T-Mobile to install cellular equipment in the attic of its Paradise visitor center. At Sequoia in California, they approved a Verizon tower disguised as a pine tree. High-speed connections have already been installed around the main visitor areas of parks from Grand Canyon to Yosemite to Yellowstone.

Each park is tasked with determining the environmental impact of a proposal. At Olympic, Verizon emphasized that there will be no negative effects on air quality, ground water, soil, or vegetation. Disguised properly, the visual impact of the tower would be minimal.

But it's much harder to quantify the impact of the signal a tower can put out. Surely some service from that Verizon tower would spill over into Olympic's wilderness. The Wilderness Act promises land for solitude and primitive recreation—how primitive can it be if it's blanketed with a 4G signal? Does the same cellular service that could potentially save a life also kill off what's been a key draw of the parks since their inception—their inherent ability to force us to disconnect from the chaos of our lives?

Frederick Kappel, onetime chairman of AT&T, was a frequent visitor to Virgin Islands National Park. While there, he would stay at Caneel Bay, a resort inside park boundaries with a famous no-phones policy. According to a 1965 *Sports Illustrated* article, when Kappel offered to personally pay to have a phone installed in his room, "management told him, politely, that he might own a few million phones in America, but he was not going to have even one at Caneel Bay. Kappel was aggrieved, but not enough to keep him from coming back to the ringless peace of Caneel every year."

That "ringless peace" came at the insistence of a man with even more money than Kappel. Caneel Bay was owned by Laurance Rockefeller, the billionaire venture capitalist and grandson of John D. Rockefeller. In 1952, when Laurance sailed to the island of St. John, in the U.S. Virgin Islands, he thought it was one of the most beautiful, serene places he'd ever seen. So he bought it. It's good to be a Rockefeller.

Laurence started acquiring land across the island with the intention of donating it to the federal government, much as his father had done at parks from Grand Teton to Acadia to Shenandoah. In December 1956, Rockefeller officially handed over his acquisitions to the Department of the Interior, establishing U.S. Virgin

Islands National Park. His park gift came with just one condition: He wanted to run a luxury hotel inside it.

Rockefeller designed Caneel Bay to be one of the first-ever eco-resorts, blending the façade into the landscape as seamlessly as possible. All the buildings are just two stories tall and set back from the beach among the trees. In addition to the lack of phones, none of the 166 guest rooms have a television. The lack of interior amenities was intentional—Rockefeller wanted his guests to appreciate the nature he'd worked so hard to acquire.

I'm sure I would have appreciated Caneel Bay even more if I'd visited it immediately after a park like Isle Royale. The comfortable king beds, fresh sushi dinners, and open-air massage suites of Caneel would have been especially welcome after a few nights of sleeping on the ground. Instead, I had hit Virgin Islands National Park early in the year, when Efrain and I traveled there to shoot a story on the hotel's history.

As we sat together with our complimentary drinks on the private Caneel Bay ferry over to St. John, it occurred to me that the other passengers must have assumed we were a couple. After all, everyone *else* was paired up. Our camera equipment—which would have given away our true purpose—had been whisked away by the porters, so for the moment we appeared to be well-heeled vacationers like everyone else, headed off to recharge and rekindle our romance in the tropics.

"A lot of people want to come here to have a reset of the mind," ranger Corinne Fenner told me after I arrived on the island. "That was the reason that Rockefeller came here originally. He wanted to have a soul-restoring retreat."

I'd met up with Corinne at Maho Bay, her favorite beach in the park. (There's far more to Virgin Islands National Park than just the grounds of Caneel.) Maho looks like a photo you'd see taped up on a cubicle wall in Vermont in the middle of winter. Its mix of white sand, green palms, and glistening turquoise water is exactly what you think of when you think *paradise:* a far-off place you might daydream about but never visit. But now here I was. With my work husband.

Around the bend at Cinnamon Bay, tourists can pitch a tent in the park campground for less than forty dollars a night. But when Rockefeller built his resort, he knew that not everyone would want to rough it. Lugging a forty-pound pack around the woods is one way to disconnect in a national park. Caneel Bay offered another.

"He wanted an experience where visitors can have the luxury of sleeping in a bed, but still experience the benefits of being in a natural setting," Corinne said.

Way back in 1984, a *New York Times* profile mentioned how, at sunny, phone-less Caneel, "normally active, restless people who never get more than six hours sleep in the pressurized North find themselves unable to keep their eyes open after 10:30 P.M." The hotel's focus on nature—and its abhorrence of technology— became its selling point. A 1989 profile in Canada's *Globe and Mail* called the resort "heaven, too, for traveling companions of worka- holics."

But it's no longer just "workaholics" who feel the need to check in with the office on a regular basis. As soon as constant connection became the new normal, Caneel realized it was losing the business of businesspeople who might have *liked* to stay longer and spend more money, but just couldn't deal with all that time away from email. So the resort did the unthinkable—it installed Wi-Fi in the rooms.

Managing director Nikolay Hotze shrugged when I asked him about this. What else could they do?

"It's what people want," he said.

Tell teenagers they can't text at Yosemite, and they might not want to go at all. Part of the reason the national parks are expanding connectivity is so they can stay *relevant*. When you drill down on those record-breaking visitation statistics, you'll find that the majority of park-goers are closer to retirement age. Younger visitors, who have more demands than ever on their attention spans, can sometimes find leaving their screens behind to head out into nature to be a tougher sell.

In a Senate subcommittee on "Encouraging the Next Generation to Visit National Parks," Park Service deputy director Lena McDowall testified in favor of increased cellular connectivity. "Visitors want to be able to use their mobile devices to share photos and experiences with their friends and family," she emphasized.

At nearly every park I visited, I saw signage heavily promoting the Park Service's social media campaign: #FindYourPark. Finding the strength to push back against the pull of our devices is only going to get more difficult as our parks inevitably become more wired. John Muir once said we should all "break clear away, once in a while, and climb a mountain or spend a week in the woods. Wash your spirit clean." That's much easier to do when you're *forced* to make a clean break.

My few days on Isle Royale were the equivalent of a hard reset. After spending so long without touching my phone, I was reminded of how easy—and how beneficial—it can be to go even just a few hours without it. Really, the idea that I would look away—even for a moment—from surroundings so awe inspiring seemed insane. I'd be missing the forest for the tweets.

After thirty miles of walking, I found myself back where I'd started, waiting for my plane to arrive at Windigo dock. It's very common for weather to impact the flights to Isle Royale, and if mine was delayed, I'd have no way of knowing. No flight notifications would be popping up on TripIt.

I'd brought extra food in case I ended up needing to spend an unplanned night. But the skies were crystal clear that morning, so it seemed safe to bust out my "emergency jerky." I sat on the dock and enjoyed the cool air.

As I ate, two men walked out of the woods and joined me down on the dock to wait for the plane. They'd been coming to Isle Royale for years, they said, and had just spent the last week hiking the long spine of the island.

"You've gotta come back and do that," one of them told me. "*That's* the hike you want to do."

"I guess that's what they say about this place," I said. "That people come back. I think I will."

The men, who had only had each other to talk to for the past week, seemed thrilled to have a new conversation partner. They were nice enough, but I was short in my replies, and mostly tuned them out. I wanted to savor these last few minutes.

I could already hear the buzz of the seaplane in the distance. Soon I'd be carried back to the mainland, back to the land of 4G LTE and the flood of missed calls and messages I knew would be waiting for me. Somehow knowing that they were just around the corner made me anxious again. I could feel the solitude of Isle Royale slipping away before I'd even left.

"I tell you what," one of them said. "I'm glad I haven't thought about politics for a week. Who even knows what crazy crap is happening now. It's pretty great being cut off from the outside world."

I looked out at the lake, its clear water softly splashing against the dock. To our left, thousands and thousands of thick trees hugged the coast, a spectacular green wall of wilderness marking the edge of the island.

"I think we're *in* the outside world," I said. "Everyone else is just cut off from this."

23

SUNSET

(Grand Teton, Yellowstone)

It had been close to ten months since I'd seen snow. Fresh snow, anyway. I had been passing by leftover snow all year. The Rocky Mountains still had mounds in May; the rim of Crater Lake still had streaks in July. Even on the sunniest days, I would come across slowly melting souvenirs in the high elevations. It was a Jon Snow kind of snow, constantly, annoyingly reminding you: *Winter Is Coming*.

I just needed it to hold off for a few more hours.

It started to drizzle as I walked out of the Salt Lake City REI. I knew this wasn't good. Drops down here meant flurries in the mountains. I needed to get moving.

I hurried toward my rented Chevy Malibu, wondering if perhaps I should have just flown straight to Jackson Hole instead. It would have been more expensive, but it certainly would have been more convenient. The airport there is the only commercial airport in the country located *inside* a national park, a single runway that cuts through the lower section of Grand Teton. Fifty miles farther north is the south entrance of Yellowstone.

I fell in love with both parks on a summer trip ten years ago, and this year I had made a point of saving them until December so they could be my final two stops. It was like how I used to hold back the butter creams in my Easter box of Russell Stover chocolates. I wanted my last bites of this crazy adventure to be delicious.

I had just blown all of the money I had saved by flying into Salt Lake City on a pair of far-too-fancy orange-and-black snowshoes. Snowshoe shopping, it turns out, is a very slippery slope. I'd never even *been* snowshoeing before, but I justified the purchase by telling myself that it would be my victory present. I typed my hotel—my last Hampton Inn of the year—into Google Maps. Four and a half hours, it said. I dumped my snacks on the passenger seat, and off I went.

Two hours later, the rain had turned to snow, and it was sticking. I realized now that Google had taken me the back way. The scenic route. Technically, it must be faster, and on a sunny day, I'm sure it is. But while the slightly longer interstate route was undoubtedly being salted and scraped, I knew these winding country lanes would be low on the snowplow priority list.

The wind was gusting at twenty-five miles an hour, frequently blocking my visibility with clouds of white. I could feel it pushing the Malibu around, and I'd already skidded on slick patches twice. Who would have guessed that a car named after a sunny celebrity enclave would perform so miserably in the snow?

Just after I crossed the Utah/Wyoming border, I approached a stop sign at the T-junction of Wyoming 89 and U.S. Route 30. Left, the map said. At this point, I had no other choice but to keep trusting it.

As I slowly drove out into the intersection, I turned the Malibu left, but the car's forward momentum continued to pull it straight ahead.

Go left, damn it, left! The *nose* was pointing left, but the Malibu moved in the same direction as before, sliding sideways across the road. I missed my lane entirely and drifted onto the right shoulder, then continued down a gradual embankment. The car finally came to rest in a pile of snow.

My heart was pounding twice as fast as the windshield wipers, quick eighth notes punctuating their steady 4/4 metronome. But I wasn't hurt, the car wasn't damaged, and all I'd hit was a hill of soft snow. I'd been lucky. The embankment wasn't steep—if I could back up, then I could be on my way. I waited another minute or two to calm myself down, then put the car in reverse.

The tires whirred and spun, but the car didn't budge an inch. I tried to go forward—to see if I could maybe drive up and out of the embankment—but I ended up just digging myself farther into the wet, white powder. I tried to reverse again. I got out and tried to dig. To push. Nothing worked.

It was totally dark now. Without the wheels hemming and hawing, it was eerily quiet. I looked around. I really was in the middle of *nowhere*. I started to get worried.

I could already see the headline: "Man Goes to *Almost* Every National Park, Freezes to Death En Route to His Last One." I assumed my bosses would be sad, but I also knew that would be an *amazing* story. I wondered which correspondent they'd fly out here to do a stand-up in front of the highway tribute sign.

I'd get a tribute sign, right? I better.

I checked my phone. Shockingly, this little ditch in the middle of nowhere was right in the middle of a patch of cell service. I had a AAA membership I hadn't used all year, although I hadn't the foggiest idea where AAA might send a truck from. In this weather, it could be hours, if they were even able to get here tonight. But I had warm clothes in my suitcase, there was still gas in the car, and I had snacks. I reminded myself that this could have been *much* worse.

As I began to dial, a Mazda SUV pulled up to the intersection and made the same turn, far more successfully than I had. It was a little discouraging to know the maneuver was definitely *possible*, and that I was just an idiot. The car's window rolled down.

Through the flurries, I could see two women inside. A mother and daughter, perhaps? The younger one seemed to be about my age. The older one called out to me.

"Hey, you need any help?"

"I'm fine," I assured her. "I'm just going to call AAA."

"Yeah? Because you don't look fine . . ."

She was right. I definitely did not look fine. My clothes were soaked and dirty from my failed digging and my face was flushed. But what was the point in dragging two strangers into my misery? I was sure if I waited long enough, AAA would eventually send someone for me.

But the strangers weren't having any of it. They were already out of the vehicle before I could finish my feeble protest.

The older one went straight for the driver's seat of the Malibu and started instructing the younger one to push with me on the hood while she tried to back up. They were locals. They knew what they were doing. I was the doofus who had taken a rental sedan with summer tires into the mountains in mid-December. I needed to trust them.

The pushing wasn't working, but it was definitely more progress than I'd made on my own. The older one—Lisa—ran back to the SUV to get a towrope and a shovel. When you live in the mountains, you keep useful stuff like that in your trunk, not a brand-new pair of expensive snowshoes with the tags still on them.

The younger one—Jessica—told me they worked for a women's boutique back in Jackson. They were returning from a clothing fair in Salt Lake City, where they had spent the day looking at samples. As she spoke, my headlights reflected off the snow and onto her face, giving her an ethereal glow. *Wow.* She was beautiful.

A pickup truck drove by. It slowed, and the window went down.

"Need any help?" the man inside shouted.

Oh, come on. Was I in a hidden-camera commercial for the good people of Wyoming?

Once again, before I could say anything, the man—John—jumped out and joined our team. He had a magnetic flashlight and

290 LEAVE ONLY FOOTPRINTS

a tow hook with him, and he hopped under my car to find a place to attach Lisa's rope. I felt terrible he was getting wet, but he didn't seem to care.

Everyone had a surprising sense of humor about our unexpected pit stop on a lonely mountain road, Jessica in particular. She was teasing me for how little I knew about driving in the snow, even though she had recently moved here herself. As crazy as it sounded, we were all actually having *fun*.

John's truck was the strongest, so I walked with him to affix the line to the back. "I'll tow," he said, "and you and your girlfriend can push."

"Oh, no no," I said. "She's not my girlfriend."

John seemed surprised. He was so quick to help when he pulled over, he hadn't even asked for the full story. He assumed Jessica and Lisa and I were all caravanning together.

"Nope! I just met both of them, like, five minutes ago," I told him. "They pulled off to help right before you did."

He nodded an approving Wyomingite nod. *Damn right they did.* That's what people are *supposed* to do around here.

As I plodded back to the car and placed my hands next to Jessica's on the hood, I glanced over at her and smiled.

The silent night was shattered by our victory screams. We did it! The car was up and out and back on the road. I was dancing around in the snow, giving out hugs. I could tell John didn't want one, but too bad. I squeezed him anyway.

We all said our goodbyes and drove out into the night, my Malibu bringing up the rear.

I drove behind Lisa and Jessica for a while, but I soon lost sight of them. The roads had gotten worse. Way worse. I had learned my lesson, and I was taking it extra slow as I crawled along, passing through small towns with funny names—Smoot, Afton, Grover, and Thayne. I considered finding a gas station parking lot somewhere and waiting out the storm, but the forecast predicted it would get worse before it got better and I hadn't come all this way just to get snowed in in Etna, Wyoming. I decided to press on in silence, my radio off so I could study the sound of my tires on the snow, listening for a warning.

The final leg of my drive, up and over the Snake River Mountain Range, has been redacted. My mom will read this book, and that trip over the mountain was, hands down, the scariest, stupidest driving I have ever done. As I inched along past terrifying drop-offs, made even more terrifying by the fact that *I could not see them at all*, I thought of how mad she would be that I was doing this. So I won't torment her any further by including the slippery turn-by-turn account here (sorry, Mom!). The good news is, I eventually made it to Jackson alive, more than four hours later than I'd intended. Still not inside a park, but finally within striking distance.

The key to making a Hampton Inn breakfast taste amazing is to have a near-death experience the night before. The next morning, I was savoring every last bite. I kept thinking about how lucky I had been. If those people hadn't stopped, I don't know *what* I would have done.

I realized I should have taken down their information so I could send them something later. A thank-you card, a Christmas present, *something*. But I had no way of finding them.

Wait a second. *Maybe I did.* How many women's clothing boutiques could there possibly be in Jackson? Unfortunately, John didn't say where he was from, but I bet if I went downtown I'd at least have a shot at finding Lisa and Jessica.

I first went to the Kmart down the street, bought a couple of Christmas cards, and filled them with gift cards from the gift card rack. Inside, I wrote, "Thanks for being my snow angels." They probably wouldn't even be working, but I was hoping I could at least find their store and give the cards to someone who knew them.

Actually . . . I was hoping Jessica would be there. I'd been thinking about her a lot since last night. I still had a couple of evenings in Jackson before I moved on to Yellowstone, and another on my way back. Maybe we could get dinner?

I realized I was getting ahead of myself. I mean, we pushed a car together in the snow. I barely knew her. But the romantic in me had already fallen for the idea of it all. I spent a year visiting every national park, driving around the country, healing a broken heart, and then finally, on my way to my very last one, I was rescued from the road by . . . my Snow Angel? That's one heck of a love story. The kind of story you might write a book about.

It took three tries before I found the right store. The women of Wyoming are not short on clothing options. But finally, there she was, working the counter. Jessica lit up when she saw me.

"Oh my gosh! We were so worried about you!"

The night before, as we were all getting back on the road, I had told Jessica and Lisa that there was no need to go slow to watch out for me; it was still 120 more miles to Jackson, and I knew I was going to creep along. "Please," I'd said. "Drive ahead. You've already been kind enough."

But now, Jessica told me that as they wound their way up that scary mountain, they started getting concerned about how their new friend might be faring, the guy driving the sedan with summer tires. How was he going to make it across *this*?

"I'm so glad you're okay!" she said. "That road was terrible!"

I smiled. "Well, I guess that makes me a pretty amazing snow driver, huh?"

As we talked and laughed, I realized my snap judgment under the stars wasn't wrong. She was great—funny, smart, and kind.

I'm going to do this. I'm going to ask her out.

I needed a second to work up the confidence, so first I asked her about what brought her to Wyoming. I remembered her saying she was new.

"Oh, my fiancé got a job here," she said. "I came here with him."

And that, my friends . . . *that* is the sound of summer tires skidding to a halt on a road they never should have gone down in the first place.

Of *course* Jessica was engaged. She had been wearing gloves as we tried to liberate my car the night before, and I'd been so happy to see her when I'd walked in the shop that I hadn't bothered to look for a ring. Her fiancé sounded like a great guy, although I was barely listening anymore, mad at myself for getting caught up in some dumb idea of a happy ending. I was embarrassed. It had been too convenient, too tempting to believe for a second that, as my park journey was drawing to a close, perhaps my romantic one was as well. That wasn't how it was going to work for me.

I thanked Jessica again, handed her the other card to give to Lisa, and I headed out into the cold morning air. It snapped me back to reality and reminded me why I had come to Wyoming in the first place.

I had a date with some national parks.

Wyoming, just like Minnesota, was once a key stop on French fur-trading routes. The group of voyageurs who came here named the mountain peaks they found Les Trois Tetons, or "The Three Breasts." It must have been a while since the men had seen actual breasts, because I assure you the peaks do not look any more buxom than any other mountains. *Three* also seems like a very weird quantity to imagine mammaries in. I suppose when you've been in the woods as long as they had, everything starts to look sexy.

The storm had scared off most visitors, so it appeared as if I had most of Grand Teton National Park to myself. Aside from a pair of parallel lines heading off in the opposite direction from where I'd left the Malibu—the telltale marks of a cross-country skier—the snow was totally undisturbed. As I snowshoed along, I was "breaking trail," although I don't know if anyone would call the chaos I was leaving in my wake a "trail." When I glanced back behind me, it looked like the Tasmanian Devil had been drunkenly running through the forest. My wide, uneven gait zigged and zagged haphazardly, dotted with occasional torso-sized indentations where I had toppled over.

I started thinking how nice it would be to have the dogs of Denali here to pull me along. Somewhere in the Alaskan wilderness, the puppies I had met over the summer were getting their first taste of winter, running alongside the team as ranger Jen showed them the ropes.

The bear cubs I'd run into at Katmai would be fast asleep by now, their bellies full of salmon. In October, I saw the park had posted a "Fat Bear Week" bracket on its Facebook page. Every year, Katmai stages a "competition," posting side-by-side pictures of bears taken at the beginning of the season and at the end. Fans vote on which bear got the plumpest. It's a heated battle—the bears can gain up to four pounds a *day* as they prepare for hibernation. After a series of neck-and-neck rounds, bear #480, Otis, had been voted the fattest bear of 2016.

I pushed extra hard through the snow, determined not to end up like Otis. It was almost time for New Year's resolutions, and mine was to take better care of myself.

Efrain told me he had hired a personal trainer when he got back to Phoenix. I hadn't seen him in a couple of months—he had returned home while I stayed out on the road to hit the rest of the parks—but we still talked regularly.

"Do you know where you're going to live yet?" he had asked on our most recent call. That was the big question, and one I still didn't have an answer to. All I knew was that this life of motels and campsites had an expiration date. I would eventually want to stay in one place, and for the last decade, I had always assumed that place *had* to be Los Angeles or New York if I wanted to work in television. But now it looked like it didn't, necessarily. As long as I was willing to get on a plane or get behind the wheel, I could work from almost anywhere.

After seeing so much of the country, it started to seem crazy to me that so many people choose to cluster together in so little of it. I had started to reconsider the benefits of big cities—the unlimited offerings of restaurants and culture that once drew me in seemed like overkill. Large crowds had become harder for me to deal with—weaving my way through overflowing sidewalks and sub- way stations and airport terminals came with a stress I didn't used to feel. That worried me a bit; I knew wherever I finally landed would have more people than a park.

"You must be so proud," Jessica had said when I told her I was down to my final two parks. But I wasn't so much proud as I was *humbled.* In the face of all the conservationists and explorers and scientists and storytellers who had come before, my "achieve- ment," if you could even call it that, seemed so small. All year long, I had just been unwrapping a series of presents others had left out for me.

I still had one more left to open. America's first national park would be my last.

For as popular a park as Yellowstone is, it's surprisingly difficult to access for almost half the year. Starting in early November, most of Yellowstone completely shuts down for a month and a half, bracing for the winter snowfall. Once there's finally enough snow accumu- lation on the roads (parts of Yellowstone get twenty feet a year), rangers start carving paths through the drifts. It's more like groom- ing a ski slope than plowing a street—the actual pavement won't reappear until March at the earliest, when the park shuts down once again to reopen for the summer season.

Winter at Yellowstone is everything summer is not. The crowds and the chaos completely slip away. A winter trip requires ad- vanced planning and dedication, as even the most experienced Wyoming drivers can't handle Yellowstone's snow. Instead, visitors to Old Faithful must arrive either on specialized snow coaches— souped-up vans that look like monster trucks, driven by professional guides—or on snowmachines. (Ever since Alaska, I had developed an annoying affect of calling all snowmobiles *snowmachines*, like a guy who goes to London once and then starts calling bathrooms *loos*.)

My snow coach ride into the heart of the park took hours—the snow was unrelenting, and the driver was being extra careful. It was his very first van load of tourists that winter, and whatever work the park had done on the roads had been wiped out by the storm. When we passed the wooden park sign, it was almost entirely covered in white.

"Do you mind if I hop out to take a quick picture?" I asked the driver.

"Are you sure?" he asked. "It's *freezing* out there."

"I'll only be a second."

I ran outside and dusted off just enough of the sign to make it readable. The driver got out as well, to stretch his legs for a moment before continuing the long, slippery drive up John D. Rockefeller, Jr., Memorial Parkway. I took a quick selfie, then asked if he wouldn't mind taking a picture for me. As he snapped the shutter, I threw my hands—bare and cold from the snow—triumphantly up into the air.

I guess I was a *little* proud after all. I had finally made it. I jumped back into the warmth of the van and crossed into Yellowstone.

When I arrived at the Old Faithful Snow Lodge, there was a Christmas tree in the lobby, decorated with lights and stars and bright gold and red ornaments. The staff was buzzing. It was opening day.

It was strange to feel as if I knew the whereabouts of every person within Yellowstone's 1.2 million acres, but I was pretty sure I did. Every tourist, at least. The Snow Lodge was the only hotel open in the entire park, which meant that, after the day-tripping snowmachiners had all buzzed back home at sunset, those of us in the lodge were the only ones left.

It became clear at dinner that I was the only solo traveler. Everyone else had arrived in pairs or with their families. I received a few pity looks from the waiters, as if the rest of my party must have frozen to death on the way—the only logical explanation for why a single guy was spending the last few days before Christmas alone in a park.

Yellowstone in the winter is not cheap, and it was a trip I'd been budgeting for all year long. Since all the roads are closed, experiencing much of the park requires paying for additional organized tours. After a year of rolling my eyes every time a bus would dump out a group of tourists at an overlook, I had booked a few tours myself. Yellowstone is massive, and my snowshoes could only get me so far.

For my first evening, I'd reserved a spot on the "Steam, Stars and Winter Soundscapes" excursion. All the rest of the Yellowstone tours were scheduled during daylight hours, but this sightseeing trip was less about the sights. When our group boarded the snow coach in front of the lodge, it was pitch dark. We drove out onto a road paralleling the Firehole River and headed north.

Eventually, our driver pulled the van over and let us out. There was a brief commotion as everyone bundled up and tumbled out into the cold, but when we finally settled down, it was stunning how *silent* it was. The occasional squeak of a boot against the snow was magnified tenfold. The entire park was quiet and still.

If you listened closely, though, in the distance you could hear a faint gurgling. Our guide walked us over to the Midway Geyser Basin thermal area, where bubbling pots churned. His flashlight would occasionally illuminate the water as he walked, giving us glimpses of the turmoil inside, until he finally turned the light off altogether and told us to listen.

People come to Yellowstone to *see* the pools and the geysers, but standing there in the dark, we could only hear them. It was eerie and magical—a steady, slow rumbling backbeat broken up by sudden plops and squishes. It sounded like we were listening to a pot of boiling spaghetti from the perspective of the noodles.

My video camera couldn't see anything, but I pressed record anyway. I remembered what Kurt Fristrup, the scientist back at Great Sand Dunes, had said. How surprised he was that nobody ever made audio recordings of a park, because sound evokes memory more powerfully than photos do. I knew this was something I wanted to remember.

The snowstorm had stopped, and the clouds were slowly breaking. Behind them was a deep-black sky, a bright full moon, and a canvas of twinkling stars.

The lodgepole pines all around me, with their snow-draped branches, looked like a thousand giant Christmas trees. After a few more moments in the cold, we wandered back to the van, where thermoses of hot chocolate were waiting for us.

When we returned to the lodge, I wasn't quite ready to call it a night. I still had all my snow gear on, so I walked out the back door on my own, out onto the trails behind the building. I didn't know where I was going—I didn't have a map, and since I hadn't really seen the park in bright daylight yet, I didn't have my bearings.

I decided to wander to a clearing and take a few pictures of the stars. The long exposures meant I had to stay perfectly still.

As stood there, I remembered how Kurt Fristrup had also told me that one of the only places that had ever been measured to be as quiet as Great Sand Dunes was Yellowstone during the winter. The thick blanket of snow absorbed all the extra sound, and now that the rest of the tour group wasn't fidgeting near me, I let that blanket fully envelop me. I couldn't hear a thing.

Then again, I wasn't sure my ears were still working. I couldn't feel them, or my fingers, or the tip of my nose. The temperature was dropping quickly—my eyelashes kept freezing together. I needed to get inside.

As I prepared to wander back, I heard a low rumble. Then a sudden sizzle and a crack, and then a sound like an airplane taking off. Just up the trail, Old Faithful was erupting.

I ran as fast as my frozen toes would let me, toward the thousands of gallons of water shooting straight up into the sky. The benches meant for the hundreds of tourists who watch the summertime eruptions were covered in snow, totally invisible and totally unnecessary. I was the only one out there, watching and shivering in the moonlight.

It was so cold, Old Faithful was erupting *snow*. At least that's what it looked like. As soon as the boiling water hit the air, it formed a *cloud* and then that *cloud* started pouring down snow. The freeze happened so quickly that it all looked like one magical snowcano.

Just a few minutes later, the show was over. The geyser had hit the snooze button, ready to wake again in another hour and a half.

It was time for me to go to sleep. The burst of steam had reminded me how nice a hot shower might feel, so I clomped back to my room, ready to warm up. Through the windows of the lodge, I could see a few families inside, talking and laughing, wearing sweaters patterned in snowflakes and reindeer. Before I walked back into that world, I spent one last frozen moment in this one, enjoying the quiet of a silent night.

Yellowstone was my last park, but it was not my finale. Before my year even began, I knew how I wanted it to finish.

Way back when I was preparing to see Acadia's first sunrise, I had also googled "last sunset USA." Up came Cape Alava, the westernmost point in the contiguous United States. When I zoomed in on the map, I noticed that section of Washington State was outlined in green. *Cape Alava is part of Olympic National Park.* As soon as I saw that, I let out a little cheer. How perfect, I thought. Here comes the answer to the jackpot question in advance: I knew what I'd be doing New Year's Eve.

From that moment on, I didn't really think much about the year's end. It seemed so far off, and the present quickly became all-consuming. It was only when the end was nearly in sight, as I was finalizing my Yellowstone reservations, that I finally turned my attention back to Cape Alava. It seemed odd that, given how much debate over the first-sunrise bragging rights there had been in Maine, I hadn't seen anything similar about the last sunset. Had I not looked hard enough?

I knew for a fact Cape Alava was the westernmost point in the Lower 48. But Cadillac Mountain was not the *easternmost* point and yet, thanks to the curvature of the earth, it still had the first sunrise on January 1. That meant the last sunset location probably moved around as well, right? Why hadn't I thought of that before? What if, on New Year's Eve, the final viewing location was actually some guy's backyard in Oregon?

I decided to email the Naval Observatory for confirmation, explaining what I was up to. A few days later, they wrote back. Unfortunately, they said, the last sunset of the year was *not* at Cape Alava. It wasn't even close.

The sun would set at Cape Alava at 4:35 P.M. on New Year's Eve. But the *final* sunset in the Lower 48 would occur twenty-eight minutes later at a location seven hundred miles south: Point Reyes National Seashore.

I immediately canceled my Seattle hotel and used my points to reserve a room in San Francisco. It looked like I would be heading back to California, back to the state I called home when I still had a home.

I was disappointed to have been wrong about Olympic but felt lucky that I'd still be able to watch the sunset from Park Service land. It was proof of how expansive the park system really is—it stretches from sea to shining sea.

After a quick trip home to West Virginia for Christmas, I flew west. On December 31, I headed north out of San Francisco on State Route 1. Leaving the city, I drove through Golden Gate National Recreation Area, the second most popular Park Service unit in the country. I passed Muir Woods National Monument, created by Teddy Roosevelt in honor of John Muir. I passed Mount Tamalpais, a California state park just as stunning as any federal land. The drive to my first-ever national seashore was a reminder that, while I may have been to all the *parks,* there was so much more beauty out there to explore.

When I finally made it to Point Reyes—71,028 acres of rocky ledges, sandy beaches, coastal grasslands, and coniferous forests—it was clear it was much more than *just* a seashore. Point Reyes is an ecological wonderland, part of a UNESCO International Biosphere Reserve. I could have easily spent many happy days wandering through its wonders, exploring every nook and cranny, but daylight was fading fast, and I needed to get in position.

I drove to the western edge of the park, got out of my car, and started walking toward the cliff's edge. On my way I passed a herd of tourists heading in the opposite direction. The day's last tour of the Point Reyes Lighthouse had just finished, and everyone was heading back home to prepare for their New Year's Eve parties.

Thanks to my friends at the Naval Observatory, I knew that Point Reyes was going to be the last place in the country to watch the sunset that night, but it didn't seem like anyone at *Point Reyes* knew that. While I had initially wondered if I might encounter a crowd similar to Acadia's dedicated group of bundled-up hikers, when I got to the lighthouse overlook, it was obvious that I was going to be the only one out there.

Efrain had asked if I wanted him to come with me, to film together one last time. The next morning, *Sunday Morning* was planning on airing a look back at my year, and if all went according to plan I was hoping to include some footage of this final sunset in the piece. Once darkness fell, there would be just enough time to hustle back to San Francisco, upload the video, and have an editor in New York cut it in early the next morning.

But I felt bad asking Efrain to work on New Year's Eve. He should be with his girlfriend—not with me. I thanked him for his offer—for everything—but told him I could handle this last bit of shooting on my own.

It felt right, going it alone. I would end the year how I began it—just me and a tiny camera, waiting and watching the sun.

The Point Reyes Lighthouse was built in 1870 by the U.S. Lighthouse Service to protect sailors venturing toward the windiest and foggiest place on the Pacific Coast, where an estimated fifty ships have wrecked into its rocks. I thought back to the shipwrecks I had explored at Biscayne National Park. It would have been fifty-one years ago this very evening that the passengers on board the *Mandalay* were happily celebrating New Year's Eve off the coast of Florida.

As the sun dropped lower in the sky, I wondered how all of the people I'd been fortunate enough to meet along the way were winding down their years. I'd seen online that the Bebenroths of Cuyahoga Valley were throwing a New Year's Eve party at their restaurant in Cleveland. It was dark there already—they were probably just now serving the dessert course of their national-parks-inspired tasting menu.

Five hours from now, this same sun would set over Pua and Fanuatanu and everyone else who had welcomed me in American Samoa. Three weeks *earlier*, In'uli Toopetlook and his family would have already witnessed their year's last sunset up in Anaktuvuk Pass. The sun wouldn't rise again in that part of Alaska until sometime in the middle of the day on January 4, popping up for just forty minutes after weeks of darkness. I wondered how the fall hunt had gone for In'uli and hoped that he was ringing in the New Year with a warm pot of caribou stew.

The sun would have already set by now at Great Basin, but that meant the real show there was just beginning. Ever since my visit, I had gotten into the habit of tracking the lunar phases. It looked like New Year's Eve was going to be nearly a new moon, which meant the stars were going to be stunning across the parks tonight.

I wondered where Tony and Linda Oyster had chosen to take their RV tonight. Someplace that wasn't rainy, I knew that much. I thought of them often, wandering the country together. When you can go anywhere, where do you choose to go?

Soon, I knew I would have to answer that same question for myself. All year long, I had always been moving forward, chasing the next step, the next park, and now, this last sunset. It was only as I walked out to the tip of the platform that I felt like I'd finally finished.

The next morning, I was flying to New York for some meetings, but I'd booked a one-way ticket. Where to after that? I had no idea. I didn't even know if CBS had any interest in me beyond the end of this assignment. Seven hours from now, the one-year contract I'd signed would officially expire. I would start the next year just as I'd started this one—unemployed, unattached, full of hope that things were going to work out okay.

I thought about what had first set me adrift, the sea change in my life that had improbably gotten me to this point. Once again, I would be ending a year without a midnight kiss. The year before, my wounds were still so fresh they stung, and as I'd traveled to my first several parks, I'd refused to think of my trip as some sort of a silver lining. I'd wanted my old life back.

Now I couldn't imagine my life having gone any other way. Just as it was impossible for me to picture what the hills of Badlands might have looked like *before* the forces of erosion sculpted them into their current forms, I could no longer imagine a life that hadn't been shaped by my year in the parks.

Visit any national park, and you'll see signs warning you to LEAVE NO TRACE. Starting back in the 1960s, Leave No Trace was developed and promoted as a set of outdoor ethics meant to minimize our impact on the land.

But Leave No Trace doesn't leave a lot of room for acknowledging the impact the land can have on *us*. That's why I've always preferred another popular version of the same slogan: "Take only memories, leave only footprints."

I knew I would be taking the memories and lessons learned from my year spent in the national parks with me for the rest of my life. They would influence how I *lived* that life, and how I saw myself in relation to this vast, wide world.

And at every park, I *always* saw traces of past visitors. Every path I walked, from the forest of Isle Royale to the peaks of Pinnacles, had been forged by someone else. I explored entire communities—from the ruins of Mesa Verde to the cemeteries of the Smoky Mountains—where others once lived. From the old petroglyphs of Capitol Reef to the new fence protecting the pupfish, our imprint is all over the parks. Visiting them all, I was constantly confronted with the consequences of decisions made before my time, and I thought about how decisions being made in my *own* time might play out. It was always possible to trace my experience in a park to the experiences of those who had walked the land long before I ever set foot on it.

That's why I liked the idea of footprints. Their light touch leaves behind a path for others to follow—a sense of the way forward and, perhaps more important, a means to find our way back. One day, I might retrace my own steps in the parks, revisit the places I briefly called home. Maybe I'll have a chance to share their power with someone else.

Teddy Roosevelt found his comfort and inspiration in one landscape—the grim, solitary Badlands. I felt lucky to have found a piece of mine in landscapes all across the country. It meant I would never be too far away should I ever need to call upon the healing powers of the land again. From here on out, I could look back at every single one of the parks I visited and confidently say, "It was *here* that the romance of my life began."

It occurred to me that part of the reason I'd seen so much debate about the year's *first* sunrise, and not its last sunset, was that our beginnings always seem more important than our endings. In life, we can often control how things start. Endings are elusive and amorphous and uncertain.

I had only come to stand at the edge of Point Reyes because, at the last minute, an email from a naval astronomer had convinced me it was where I needed to end up. But now that I was here, it felt like this place had been waiting for me to arrive ever since I started up that mountain in Maine. On this night, the foggiest place in the Pacific didn't have a cloud in the sky. As the sun slipped away into the sea, it reflected off the windows of the lighthouse, shining its bright light back toward me.

I watched as the top of the sun disappeared down into the water. The wind picked up a bit, blowing in from the north. The tiniest sliver of a fingernail moon appeared up above the lighthouse, followed minutes later by the first stars. Along the horizon, a band of pink hugged the ocean, darkening and deepening into a bright orange line that narrowed as night crept in. I waited out on that platform until the final ray had disappeared from the sky, trying to make the evening last as long as possible.

A lighthouse is a beacon, a way finder for those who are lost. But, as I reminded myself, it is not a finish line. I had reached the end of the year—the longest and most spectacular of my life—but I knew this wasn't the end of my journey.

The Point Reyes Lighthouse was constructed to warn sailors that this was *not* a place to stop. Keep going, it says. Your safe harbor is still out there, somewhere else, waiting for you to arrive.

EPILOGUE

(Gateway Arch, Indiana Dunes, White Sands)

For the past forty years, every episode of *Sunday Morning* has ended with a "Moment of Nature." It's the show's signature bit—a final, minute-long scene from a picturesque place. There's never any narration, just the sights and sounds of the great outdoors. It's a rare opportunity on television for the audience to pause and reflect, to look at something beautiful, and to be inspired by it.

Quite often, the featured footage—sent in by a network of freelance videographers across the country—comes from our national parks: wildflowers at Mount Rainier, waterfalls at Yosemite, the wind whipping through Canyonlands. Each week, we receive the same feedback from our viewers—could you please make the moment last just a bit longer?

For any on-camera reporter, it's more than a little humbling to know that the most beloved part of our broadcast is the part that doesn't feature a single person. But we learned long ago that there's no better ending to our show than what John Muir once described as the *grand* show.

"This grand show is eternal," he wrote. "It is always sunrise somewhere; the dew is never all dried at once; a shower is forever falling; vapor is ever rising. Eternal sunrise, eternal sunset, eternal dawn and gloaming, on sea and continents and islands, each in its turn, as the round earth rolls."

In the years since I watched the sun set at Point Reyes, I've been fortunate enough to see it shine on a number of national parks in other nations. From Praslin National Park in Seychelles to Patagonia National Park in Chile, I've witnessed firsthand how America's pioneering concept of preservation has been replicated to great success all across the world.

Unbelievably, these have been *work* trips. CBS eventually offered me a long-term contract—the higher-ups decided that keeping a chief cargo pants correspondent on staff might be good for the show. After spending so many years trying to figure out how to join the team, I'd finally found my niche: nature.

But for as many beautiful places as I've been, there's no place like home. America's parks keep pulling me back. I've returned to over a dozen of them—from Mount Rainier to Mammoth Cave—enjoying sections I may have missed the first time around. Whenever I'm in a park, I know that I'm seeing *our* lakes and mountains and deserts—there's a sense of pride that comes from being a co-owner of such prime real estate.

I've also been to our three "new" national parks. In 2018, what was once known as Jefferson Expansion National Memorial in St. Louis, Missouri, was redesignated Gateway Arch National Park. A year later, an hour southeast of Chicago, a fifteen-thousand-acre stretch of sand dunes and trails formerly known as Indiana Dunes National Lakeshore became Indiana Dunes National Park. And in December of 2019, New Mexico's White Sands, a stunning dunefield first protected as a national monument, became our newest national park. Exploring each one, I was reminded of how the Park Service is constantly expanding and evolving. The adventure continues.

. . .

The battle to ensure the parks *stay* protected continues as well. Recently, there have been some heartbreaking headlines—stories of irreparable damage done during the government shutdown, of drastic budget cuts, and of the rollback of endangered species protections. To enumerate all of them here would miss the point— by the time you read this, there will undoubtedly be some new struggle.

Whenever I see one of these articles, I'm reminded of an article a young Teddy Roosevelt published in *The Outlook* magazine in 1895. He argued that concerned citizens cannot just sit back and hope things will work out for the best. "To sit home, read one's favorite paper, and scoff at the misdeeds of the men who do things is easy, but it is markedly ineffective," he wrote. "It is what evil men count upon the good men's doing."

That is our charge. To not just visit the parks, but *fight* for them. To prioritize and protect them, so that future generations may enjoy their treasures.

Nearly a century ago, journalist Robert Sterling Yard saw our fledging network of parks as a way to unify a fractured country. Their "magic," he argued, came from their ability "to redemocratize in a period which needs it." We may need that magic now more than ever.

The parks are our literal common ground. Crisscrossing the country in the midst of one of the most divisive election years in American politics, I was surprised by how the distinctions between red states and blue states seemed to slip away whenever I was hiking through a forest, scrambling up a sand dune, or sharing a patch of shade. As Yard wrote, "In the national parks, all are just Americans." Visit a park, he says, and "Perhaps for the first time, one realizes the common America—and loves it."

I loved it so much I haven't left. After my year wrapped up, I found I wasn't quite ready to stop wandering. Then somehow another year went by, and I still wasn't done. I've been living on the road, "trying on" new potential home bases, bouncing back and forth between campsites, hotels, and Airbnbs across the country. I'm sure one day I'll pay a utility bill again, but for now the nomadic life has been tough to shake.

When I meet people out on the road, I'm often asked if I have a favorite national park. The best way I know how to answer such an impossible question is with a line from John Muir's *Travels in Alaska*, a book I read during my own travels in Alaska.

"So abundant and novel are the objects of interest in a pure wilderness that unless you are pursuing special studies it matters little where you go, or how often to the same place," he wrote. "Wherever you chance to be always seems at the moment of all places the best."

At the moment, that's a cabin porch in Utah, looking out at the mountains of Zion. Next week—who knows? The scenery changes, but each week ends the same way: I always want the moment of nature to last just a little bit longer.

ACKNOWLEDGMENTS

You know those collapsible Leatherman multi-tools hikers carry that contain every possible instrument—from pliers to screwdrivers to bottle openers—to help out with every imaginable scenario? That's what a good editor is like.

At varying points, my editor, Matt Inman, has served as a cheerleader, critic, therapist, idea machine, architect, and advocate. He always had just the right tweak to fix a problematic passage, and he expertly identified which parts of this manuscript needed a fine-tooth comb and which parts needed a hacksaw. I'm immensely grateful to have had him in my back pocket throughout this process.

(Matt, I think I may have just inadvertently described you as a giant tool? Feel free to edit this.)

My superstar agent, Daniel Greenberg, is like a seasoned ranger who, despite knowing every nook and cranny of a park, still gets excited about showing newcomers the way. This first-time author couldn't have asked for a better guide through the publishing world.

Julie Cepler, Eleanor Thacher, and Gwyneth Stansfield at Crown and Tim Wojcik at LGR have also been key allies in getting these stories out of my computer and into your hands.

Longtime friends Carter Liotta and Katie Cole were some of the very first readers of this book, and I benefited tremendously from the detailed, thoughtful feedback they provided. I also received helpful critiques from Dan Crissman, Rachel Small, and Lee Oglesby, and big-picture advice from Jeff Plunkett, Robin Sloan, Eric Ledgin, and Anna Sale.

Some of the parks and people mentioned in these pages first appeared in segments I produced for *CBS Sunday Morning*. I'm indebted to the entire *Sunday Morning* team, but especially to executive producer Rand Morrison—I still can't believe he agreed to such an outlandish idea. Rand has provided tremendous encouragement and guidance over the years, and I'm eternally grateful to him for giving me the life-changing opportunity to be a part of my favorite show. Thanks for having faith in me.

I'd also like to thank *Sunday Morning*'s Gavin Boyle, Jason Sacca, Amy Rosner, and Cat Lewis for their support and patience when dealing with a correspondent whose beat seems to always be "places with terrible cellphone service." Mike Hernandez, Max Stacy, and Michael Comfort are consummate professionals who were very tolerant of my rookie mistakes.

CBS editors are the best in the business, and I've had the privilege to work with several of them. A special shout-out is in order for George Pozderec ("Hi, George!"), who edited the bulk of my park stories and kept track of the footage sent in from the road. Richard Huff, David Morgan, and Lauren Trieffart all provided assistance in getting the word out about what I was up to. Thanks to David Rhodes for suggesting back in 2011 that my specific brand of weird might fit in well on the sixth floor.

I have received a tremendous amount of assistance—both in my travels and in writing this book—from employees of the National Park Service and the United States Department of the Interior. In addition to the names that have already appeared in these pages, I'd like to thank Nichole Andler, Emma Brown, Scott Burch, Vickie Carson, Emily Davis, Greg Dudgeon, Jennifer Evans, Kathy Faz, Jessica Ferracane, Andy Fisher, Linda Friar, Sally Hurlbert, Sintia Kawasaki-Yee, John Kelly, Jessica Kershaw, Michael Larson, Bret Meldrum, Yvonne Menard, Bradley Mills, Steven Moore, Bruce Noble, Jeffrey Olson, Mark Parry, Kevin Percival, John Quinley, Elizabeth Stern, Dan Stevenson, and Brian Winter. I'm sure there are just as many more I've accidentally omitted.

Whether I was dealing with a lost driver's license in Washington or needing a home-cooked meal in Colorado, I couldn't have survived a life of constant travel without a little help from my friends. Thanks to all of my pals—old and new—who showed me kindness along the way. (You know who you are.) Extra special thanks to Ammar, Shameem, Asiya, and Safiyya for making me an honorary member of your wonderful family.

I'm indebted to all of the strangers who were kind enough to share a story, a meal, or a patch of shade with me while I was in a park. Thanks to Robbie Doman, Jim Fisher, Alicia Highland, and Tony and Linda Oyster for allowing me to pester them long after they'd headed home from their trips. (Last I heard from the Oysters, "home" was an RV park in Oregon.)

Writing this book while living full time on the road meant that I was frequently writing about some of America's most stunning places while sitting in some of its most depressing airports, hotel lobbies, and crowded coffee shops. To transport myself back to the right state of mind, I often cued up the instrumental piano music of composer Ben Cosgrove. I've never met Ben, but his albums inspired by North American landscapes set just the right tone. Check him out.

Before my park-hopping had even wrapped up, I recommended Efrain Robles for a full-time *Sunday Morning* position. These days, I have to fight with other producers and correspondents to schedule him for shoots—everyone wants to work with him. It's not hard to understand why. In addition to being extremely talented, Efrain is just a genuinely good human being. He remains a close friend and confidant, and I feel so lucky to have had him riding shotgun for part of my journey. Thanks for everything.

Finally, if I were to carve a Mount Rushmore of my life, it would feature the faces of the four greatest people I know: my brother, Patrick; my sister, Kathleen; and my parents, Michael and Betty. Thank you for always being my rock.

NOTES

For lessons on everything from canyon geology to pupfish biology, our parks serve as fantastic classrooms. Much of the information found in this book was first found via trailside displays, visitor center exhibits, government brochures, and countless ranger-led campground programs. NPS.gov is far more than a trip-planning resource—it's a repository of fascinating facts and figures on everything from ancient archeology to modern volcanic activity.

In cases where I've quoted a specific study or document directly, I've included the notes below for further reading.

PROLOGUE

3   **more than two million people a year:** All park visitation statistics in this book come from the National Park Service Public Use Statistics Office. Their online portal (https://irma.nps.gov/Stats) offers a fascinating look into everything from the amount of automobile traffic at Everglades to the number of tent campers at Zion.

4   **"nowhere, not even at sea":** Theodore Roosevelt, *Hunting Trips of a Ranchman* (New York: G. P. Putnam's Sons, 1885).

9   **"The mountains are calling and I must go":** John Muir to Sarah Muir Galloway, September 3, 1873, University of the Pacific Library Holt-Atherton Special Collections, http://ark.cdlib.org/ark:/13030/kt9s2039gs.

9   **"She is so marvelously sweet":** Personal diary of Theodore Roosevelt, February 13, 1880, Theodore Roosevelt Papers, Library of Congress Manuscript Division, https://www.theodorerooseveltcenter.org/Research/Digital-Library/Record?libID=o288504. Theodore Roosevelt Digital Library. Dickinson State University.

10   **"cursed":** Henry F. Pringle, *Theodore Roosevelt: A Biography* (New York: Harcourt, Brace, 1931).

10   **"The light has gone out of my life":** Personal diary of Theodore Roosevelt, February 14, 1884, Theodore Roosevelt Papers, Library of Congress Manuscript Division, https://www.theodorerooseveltcenter.org/Research/Digital-Library/Record?libID=o284449. Theodore Roosevelt Digital Library. Dickinson State University.

10   **"perfect freedom":** Charles F. Redmond, *Selections from the Correspondence of Theodore Roosevelt and Henry Cabot Lodge, 1884–1918* (New York: Charles Scribner's Sons, 1925).

11   **"here the romance of my life":** "His Old Friends," *Bismarck (N.D.) Weekly Tribune*, September 21, 1900.

11   **"so fantastically broken in form":** Roosevelt, *Hunting Trips of a Ranchman.*

1: SUNRISE

18   **"Antoine Laumet de la Mothe, sieur de Cadillac":** Much of Laumet's origin story remains unknown. A good jumping-off point for more is Yves F. Zoltvany, "LAUMET, de Lamothe Cadillac, ANTOINE," in *Dictionary of Canadian Biography*, vol. 2 (University of Toronto/Université Laval, 2003–), http://www.biographi.ca/en/bio/laumet_antoine_2E.html.

2: WATER

24   **"Valley of the Vapors":** Lee Standing Bear Moore and Takatoka, *The Story of Manaraka*, https://manataka.org/page2.html.

25   **"four sections of land including said springs":** *An Act Authorizing the Governor of the Territory of Arkansas to Lease the Salt Springs, in Said Territory, and for Other Purposes*, 22nd Congress, 1st sess., April 20, 1832, *Public Statutes at Large* 4 (1832): 505.

28   **"fair sex, who fancy that it improves their complexions":** A. Van Cleef, "The Hot Springs of Arkansas," *Harper's New Monthly Magazine* 56, no. 332 (January 1878): 193–211.

37   **As Wallace J. Nichols chronicles:** Wallace J. Nichols, *Blue Mind: The Surprising Science That Shows How Being Near, In, On, or Under Water Can Make You Happier, Healthier, More Connected, and Better at What You Do* (New York: Little, Brown, 2014).

3: ANIMALS

38   **Sci Fi Channel original movie:** *Mega Python vs. Gatoroid*, directed by Mary Lambert (The Asylum), first aired on Sci Fi on January 29, 2011.

39　**"River of Grass"**: Marjory Stoneman Douglas, *The Everglades: River of Grass* (New York: Rinehart, 1947).

39　**"in this park we shall preserve tarpon and trout"**: This and all additional Truman quotes in this chapter are sourced from Harry S. Truman, "Address on Conservation at the Dedication of Everglades National Park," December 6, 1947, https://www.presidency.ucsb.edu/node/232569.

42　**"wanton destruction of these noble birds"**: This and all additional Dawson quotes in this chapter come from William Leon Dawson, *The Birds of California* (Los Angeles: South Moulton, 1923).

46　KILL THE PUPFISH **bumper stickers**: An old bumper sticker from the fight is part of the Death Valley National Park Archives and is viewable at https://www.nps.gov/museum/exhibits/death_valley/exb/science/DEVA53686_sticker.html.

49　**"When we try to pick out anything by itself"**: John Muir, *My First Summer in the Sierra* (Boston: Houghton Mifflin, 1911). (Interestingly, there's a misquoting of this line that's so popular that the Sierra Club has put up a page debunking it. Muir never wrote, "When one *tugs* at a single thing in nature": https://vault.sierraclub.org/john_muir_exhibit/writings/misquotes.aspx.)

4: GOD

53　**"Here I Am, Lord"**: Dan Schutte, "Here I Am, Lord" (Portland: Oregon Catholic Press, 1981).

54　**"I could recite the New Testament"**: John Muir, *The Story of My Boyhood and Youth* (Boston: Houghton Mifflin, 1913).

54　**"study the inventions of God"**: John Muir, *A Thousand-Mile Walk to the Gulf* (Boston: Houghton Mifflin, 1916).

54　**"to store my mind"**: Muir, *A Thousand-Mile Walk to the Gulf.*

54　**"little shanty made of sugar pine shingles"**: John Muir to David Muir, March 20, 1870, in *The Life and Letters of John Muir*, ed. William Frederic Badè (Boston: Houghton Mifflin, 1924).

55　**"The Colorado River made it"**: J. B. Priestley, *Midnight on the Desert* (London: Heinemann, 1937).

56　**"The hills and groves were God's first temples"**: John Muir, *My First Summer in the Sierra* (Boston: Houghton Mifflin, 1911).

61　**"baptized in the irised foam"**: John Muir to Jeanne C. Smith Carr, July 29, 1870, in *The Life and Letters of John Muir.*

61　**"in balmy sunshine that penetrated to my very soul"**: John Muir to David Gilrye Muir, April 10, 1870, in *The Life and Letters of John Muir.*

61　**"it seems to me almost like a sacrilege to build a church"**: Galen Clark, *California Farmer and Journal of Useful Sciences* 49, no. 10 (May 29, 1879).

62　**"in whose light everything seems equally divine"**: Muir, *My First Summer in the Sierra.*

62　**"The clearest way into the Universe is through a forest wilderness"**: John Muir, *John of the Mountains: The Unpublished Journals of John Muir*, ed. Linnie Marsh Wolfe (Boston: Houghton, Mifflin, 1938).

5: SOUND

69 **"These useful, progressive, blunt-nosed mechanical beetles":** John Muir to Howard Palmer, December 12, 1912, University of the Pacific Library Holt-Atherton Special Collections, http://www.oac.cdlib.org/findaid/ark:/13030/kt0w1031nc.

72 **Werner Herzog's documentary *Grizzly Man:*** *Grizzly Man*, directed by Warner Herzog (Lionsgate Films), September 2, 2005.

75 **"They're both screaming":** "Mauling Sounds Captured on Tape," CBS News/AP, October 8, 2003, https://www.cbsnews.com/news/mauling-sounds-captured-on-tape.

6: TREES

77 **"Their stiff and ungraceful form":** John C. Frémont, *Report of the Exploring Expedition to the Rocky Mountains in the Year 1842, and to Oregon and California in the Years 1843–44*, 28th Congress, 2nd sess., Senate Executive Document 174 (Washington, D.C.: Gales and Seaton, Printers, 1845).

80 **"Any fool can destroy trees":** John Muir, *Our National Parks* (Boston: Houghton Mifflin, 1901).

80 **"The English who saw it declared it to be a Yankee invention":** 38th Congress, 1st sess., *Congressional Globe*, May 17, 1864.

81 **"the rapid destruction of timber":** *An Act to Set Apart a Certain Tract of Land in the State of California as a Public Park*, 51st Congress, 1st sess., September 25, 1980.

82 **"You know, a tree is a tree":** Lou Cannon, *Governor Reagan: His Rise to Power* (New York: PublicAffairs, 2003).

84 **"wood wide web":** Peter Wohlleben, *The Hidden Life of Trees: What They Feel, How They Communicate—Discoveries from a Secret World* (Vancouver: Greystone Books, 2016).

84 **"It is a great victory for every American":** Lyndon B. Johnson, "Remarks upon Signing Four Bills Relating to Conservation and Outdoor Recreation," October 2, 1968, *Public Papers of the Presidents of the United States: Lyndon B. Johnson*, book 2 (1968), https://www.govinfo.gov/app/details/PPP-1968-book2.

85 **"God has cared for these trees":** John Muir, "Save the Redwoods," *Sierra Club Bulletin*, 11, no. 1 (January, 1920).

7: MYSTERY

88 **"conical protuberances":** F. André Michaux, *The North America Sylva*, vol. 3 (Philadelphia: T. Dobson, 1918).

90 **"a game of hide and seek":** This and all additional Hillman quotes sourced from J. W. Hillman, "Discovery of Crater Lake," *Portland Oregonian*, June 7, 1903, https://www.nps.gov/parkhistory/online_books/crla/hrs/hrsaa.htm.

91 **"It was said to be 5,000 feet below":** William Steel's remarks printed in *Proceedings of the National Park Conference* (Washington, D.C.: Government Printing Office, 1917).

92 **"erect position":** Joseph Diller and Horace Patton, *The Geology and Petrog-*

raphy of Crater Lake National Park (Washington, D.C.: Government Printing Office, 1902).

93 **"During the period of observation":** Wayne E. Kartchner and John E. Doerr, Jr., "Wind Currents in Crater Lake as Revealed by the Old Man of the Lake," *Nature Notes from Crater Lake* 11, no. 3 (September 1938): http://npshistory .com/nature_notes/crla/vol11-3c.htm#3.

8: BORDERS

109 **"those possessions are inhabited by alien races":** "Opinions Delivered in the Insular Tariff Cases in the Supreme Court of the United States," May 27, 1901 (Washington, D.C.: Government Printing Office, 1901).

9: VOLCANOES

117 **"a colossal railroad map":** Mark Twain, *Roughing It* (Hartford, Conn.: American Publishing Co., 1872).

10: ICE

131 **"fundamentally the greatest threat":** Jon Jarvis, "Letter from the Director," National Park Service Climate Change Response Strategy, September 2010.

134 **"the size of a Costco":** Jim Acosta, "Glacier, Alaska Bay Boat Tour Frame Obama's Climate Change Message," September 2, 2015, https://www.cnn .com/2015/09/02/politics/obama-alaska-glacier-boat-tour/index.html.

134 **"Now imagine seventy-five of those ice blocks":** This and all subsequent Obama quotes from "Remarks by the President at the GLACIER Conference," White House Office of the Press Secretary, https://obamawhitehouse.archives .gov/the-press-office/2015/09/01/remarks-president-glacier-conference -anchorage-ak.

135 **"legacy building mode":** Julie Hirschfeld Davis, "Paring His Bucket List, Obama Relishes Hiking at an Alaskan Glacier," *New York Times*, September 1, 2015.

11: PEOPLE

139 **In 2016, visitors spent:** Jennifer Leaver, *The State of Utah's Travel and Tourism Industry* (Salt Lake City: Kem C. Gardner Policy Institute, University of Utah, 2018), https://gardner.utah.edu/wp-content/uploads/2018Tourism Report.pdf.

139 **"unprecedented decision":** Lisa J. Church, "Heavy Traffic Forces Shutdown at Entrance to Arches NP," *Times-Independent* (Moab, Utah), May 28, 2015.

145 **"We felt glad to have looked":** David E. Folsom, *The Folsom-Cook Exploration of the Upper Yellowstone in the Year 1869* (St. Paul, Minn.: H. L. Collins, Printers, 1894) (first appeared in the July 1870 issue of *Western Monthly*).

145 **"Let's Close the National Parks":** Bernard DeVoto, "Let's Close the National Parks," *Harper's Magazine,* October 1953.

147 **"national restlessness":** *Report of the Director of the National Park Service* (Washington, D.C.: Government Printing Office, 1920).

147 **"We can pick up the cans":** Ronald A. Foresta, *America's National Parks and Their Keepers* (Washington, D.C.: Resources for the Future, 1985).

13: CANYONS

159 **"In the Grand Canyon":** Theodore Roosevelt, *Presidential Addresses and State Papers of Theodore Roosevelt* (New York: P. F. Collier & Son, 1905[?]).

160 **"combining the proportions of a Swiss chalet":** Harvey H. Kaiser, *The National Park Architecture Sourcebook* (New York: Princeton Architectural Press, 2008).

164 **books about Colter for sale:** Two of those books (which have informed this chapter) are Arnold Berke and Alexander Vertikoff, *Mary Colter: Architect of the Southwest* (New York: Princeton Architectural Press, 2002); and Virginia L. Grattan, *Mary Colter: Builder upon the Red Earth* (Grand Canyon, Ariz.: Grand Canyon Natural History Association, 1992).

164 **"Any number above a couple of thousand years":** John McPhee, *Basin and Range* (New York: Farrar, Straus and Giroux, 1981).

165 **U.S. Geological Survey bulletin:** Wallace R. Hansen, *The Black Canyon of the Gunnison: Today and Yesterday*, bulletin 1191 (Washington, D.C.: Government Printing Office, 1965).

14: FORGIVENESS

169 **"The setting of a leg":** Mudd's correspondence is reprinted in Samuel Alexander Mudd and Nettie Mudd, *The Life of Dr. Samuel A. Mudd: Containing His Letters from Fort Jefferson, Dry Tortugas Island, Where He Was Imprisoned Four Years for Alleged Complicity in the Assassination of Abraham Lincoln* (New York: Neale, 1906).

15: CAVES

182 **"The more I thought of it":** James Larkin White, *Jim White's Own Story: The Discovery and History of Carlsbad Caverns* (Chicago: Curt Teich Co., 1932).

184 **"Kentucky Cave Wars":** David Kem also wrote a very informative book on the cave wars: *The Kentucky Cave Wars* (Lulu.com, 2014).

185 **He eventually received a Pulitzer Prize:** Miller was a reporter for the *Louisville Courier Journal*. In 2018, the paper published a look back at his historic articles. Andrew Wolfson, "Tiny Reporter Couldn't Free Trapped Caver in 1925, but Became Big Hero," *Louisville Courier Journal*, November 18, 2018.

186 **It was a three-column front-page headline:** "Find Floyd Collins Dead in Cave Trap on 18th Day; Lifeless at Least 24 Hours; Foot Must Be Amputated to Get Body Out," *New York Times*, February 17, 1925.

188 **"as though a million tons of black wool":** White, *Jim White's Own Story*.

16: LIGHT

189 **"Loneliest Road in America":** "America, the Most," *Life*, July 1986.

192 **"as close as you can get":** Henry Brean, "Skies Above Great Basin National Park Aren't Just Dark—They're Certifiable," *Las Vegas Review-Journal*, May 5, 2016.

194 **"astronomy capital of the world":** James C. Cornell, Jr., "Light Pollution from a Growing Tucson Threatens 'Astronomy Capital of the World,'" *New York Times*, June 20, 1971.

17: TRAVELERS

198 **"Our one desire was to get back to America":** Roosevelt's description of his travels comes from Theodore Roosevelt, *An Autobiography* (New York: Macmillan, 1913).

199 **"I would not have been president":** *Maltese Cross Cabin*, National Park Service, https://www.nps.gov/thro/learn/historyculture/maltese-cross-cabin .htm.

200 **"few indeed are the men":** Theodore Roosevelt, *The Wilderness Hunter* (New York: G. P. Putnam's Sons, 1893).

200 **"savage desolation":** Roosevelt, *Hunting Trips of a Ranchman*.

200 **"This broken country":** Roosevelt, *Hunting Trips of a Ranchman*.

205 **"He who gives time":** James Wickersham, *Old Yukon: Tales—Trails—Trials* (Washington, D.C.: Washington Law Book, 1938).

206 **"deeply disappointed":** Jennifer Steinhauer, "3,000 Miles from Denali, Ohio Fumes," *New York Times*, September 1, 2015.

206 **tweeted that he would change it back:** Donald J. Trump, Twitter post, August 31, 2015, 8:38 P.M.

206 **they *liked* Denali:** Becky Bohrer, "Alaska Senators Tell Trump They Want Mountain's Name to Stay," Associated Press, October 24, 2017, https://www .apnews.com/6015f6b8dcd846289fe9ce3e9a6804be.

206 **"the Indians who have lived":** Charles Sheldon, *The Wilderness of Denali* (New York: Charles Scribner's Sons, 1930).

18: LOVE

214 **"the most weird, wonderful, magical place on earth":** Edward Abbey and David Petersen, *Postcards from Ed: Dispatches and Salvos from an American Iconoclast* (Minneapolis: Milkweed Editions, 2006).

227 **"the only woman that I ever knew":** Jeanne C. Carr to John Muir and Louie Muir, June 3, 1880, University of the Pacific Library Holt-Atherton Special Collections.

227 **"I have been alone, as far as the isolation that distance makes":** John Muir to Louie Muir, August 2, 1880, in *The Life and Letters of John Muir*.

19: FOOD

240 **"over my dead body":** Carolyn V. Platt, *Cuyahoga Valley National Park Handbook* (Kent, Ohio: Kent State University Press, 2006).

240 **"oozes rather than flows":** "America's Sewage System and the Price of Optimism," *Time*, August 1, 1969.

20: MOUNTAINS

248 **"As you well know":** Enos A. Mills to John Muir, November 24, 1914, University of the Pacific Library Holt-Atherton Special Collections, https:// calisphere.org/item/ark:/13030/kt4779r83p.

249 **"In years to come":** *Rocky Mountain National Park: Brief Park History,* National Park Service, https://www.nps.gov/romo/learn/historyculture/brief.htm.

250 **An Austrian study of the Alps:** M. Faulhaber, E. Pocecco, M. Niedermeier, et al., "Fall-Related Accidents Among Hikers in the Austrian Alps: A 9-Year Retrospective Study," *BMJ Open Sport & Exercise Medicine* 3, no. 1 (2017), 3e:000304. doi: 10.1136/bmjsem-2017-000304.

251 **"had only light overalls on, and no stockings":** Zebulon Montgomery Pike, *The Southwestern Journals of Zebulon Pike, 1806–1807,* ed. Stephen Harding Hart and Archer Butler Hulbert (Albuquerque: University of New Mexico Press, 2006).

21: DIVERSITY

258 **an estimated 94 percent:** The demographic statistics in this chapter come from Park Service reports collected at https://sesrc.wsu.edu/nps. These types of studies—if they're done at all—are done infrequently, meaning most stats are at least a few years out of date. Think of these numbers as you would the Census—general guides for getting a sense of a place.

263 **Oprah traveled to Yosemite:** *The Oprah Winfrey Show,* Harpo Studios, October 29, 2010. The section involving Shelton Johnson is viewable online at http://www.oprah.com/own-oprahshow/oprah-and-gayle-arrive-at-yosemite-national-park-video.

265 **"essentially on a daily basis":** *Ranger Shelton Looks Back at Oprah and Gayle's Camping Adventure,* September 29, 2015, https://www.youtube.com/watch?v=ajGoM5W_JuY.

266 **its workforce is still 83 percent white:** This statistic, from Fiscal Year 2017, was obtained via a request to the NPS Public Affairs Office.

271 **"It doesn't say for the benefit":** Ken Burns, *The National Parks: America's Best Idea* (PBS Distribution, 2009).

22: DISCONNECTING

276 **In 2012, Cheryl Strayed published:** Cheryl Strayed, *Wild: From Lost to Found on the Pacific Crest Trail* (New York: Alfred A. Knopf, 2012).

281 **According to a 1965 *Sports Illustrated* article:** Gwilym S. Brown, "Pioneers in Every Sense," *Sports Illustrated,* June 27, 1965.

283 **a *New York Times* profile:** Charlotte Curtis, "Caneel Bay and Its Allure," *New York Times,* March 25, 1984.

284 **"Visitors want to be able to use their mobile devices":** Senate Energy and Natural Resources Subcommittee on National Parks, September 27, 2017.

284 **"break clear away":** S. Hall Young, *Alaska Days with John Muir* (Chicago: Fleming H. Revell, 1915).

EPILOGUE

308 **"This grand show is eternal":** Muir, *John of the Mountains: The Unpublished Journals of John Muir.*

309 **a young Teddy Roosevelt published:** Theodore Roosevelt, "The Higher Life of American Cities," *Outlook,* December 21, 1895.

309 **"In the national parks, all are just Americans":** Robert S. Yard, "Economic Aspects of Our National Parks Policy," *Scientific Monthly* 16, no. 4 (1923).

310 **"So abundant and novel":** John Muir and Marion Randall Parsons, *Travels in Alaska* (Boston: Houghton Mifflin, 1915).

ABOUT THE AUTHOR

CONOR KNIGHTON is an Emmy Award–winning correspondent for *CBS Sunday Morning,* America's #1 Sunday
morning news program. Depending on your cable package, you may have also seen him hosting shows on Current
TV, AMC, and The Biography Channel or providing com-
mentary for the likes of MTV, E!, and CNN. He has been
to all of America's national parks and what feels like 40
percent of its Hampton Inns.